William J. Frost, MLS, MA
Editor

The Reference Collection:
From the Shelf to the Web

The Reference Collection: From the Shelf to the Web has been co-published simultaneously as *The Reference Librarian*, Numbers 91/92 2005.

*Pre-publication
REVIEWS,
COMMENTARIES,
EVALUATIONS . . .*

"USEFUL, ENTERTAINING, AND INSIGHTFUL. Every reference librarian and reference staff person will want to read this. Reading this book has renewed my enthusiasm for my own special reference topic area. This book distills the essence of current reference technology and practice."

Diane K. Kovacs, MEd
*President
Kovacs Consulting Internet
& Web Training
Co-Author of* The Kovacs Guide
to Electronic Library Collection
Development: Essential Core Subject
Collections, Selection Criteria,
and Guidelines

The Haworth Information Press®
An Imprint of The Haworth Press, Inc.

The Reference Collection: From the Shelf to the Web

The Reference Collection: From the Shelf to the Web has been co-published simultaneously as *The Reference Librarian*, Numbers 91/92 2005.

Monographic Separates from *The Reference Librarian*™

For additional information on these and other Haworth Press titles, including descriptions, tables of contents, reviews, and prices, use the QuickSearch catalog at http://www.HaworthPress.com.

Doing the Work of Reference: Practical Tips for Excelling as a Reference Librarian, edited by
Celia Hales Mabry, PhD (No. 72 and 73, 2001). *"An excellent handbook for reference librarians
who wish to move from novice to expert. Topical coverage is extensive and is presented by the
best guides possible: practicing reference librarians." (Rebecca Watson-Boone, PhD, President,
Center for the Study of Information Professionals, Inc.)*

New Technologies and Reference Services, edited by Bill Katz, PhD (No. 71, 2000). *This important
book explores developing trends in publishing, information literacy in the reference environment,
reference provision in adult basic and community education, searching sessions, outreach
programs, locating moving image materials for multimedia development, and much more.*

***Reference Services for the Adult Learner: Challenging Issues for the Traditional and
Technological Era,*** edited by Kwasi Sarkodie-Mensah, PhD (No. 69/70, 2000). *Containing
research from librarians and adult learners from the United States, Canada, and Australia, this
comprehensive guide offers you strategies for teaching adult patrons that will enable them to
properly use and easily locate all of the materials in your library.*

Library Outreach, Partnerships, and Distance Education: Reference Librarians at the Gateway,
edited by Wendi Arant and Pixey Anne Mosley (No. 67/68, 1999). *Focuses on community outreach
in libraries toward a broader public by extending services based on recent developments in
information technology.*

***From Past-Present to Future-Perfect: A Tribute to Charles A. Bunge and the Challenges of
Contemporary Reference Service,*** edited by Chris D. Ferguson, PhD (No. 66, 1999). *Explore
reprints of selected articles by Charles Bunge, bibliographies of his published work, and original
articles that draw on Bunge's values and ideas in assessing the present and shaping the future of
reference service.*

Reference Services and Media, edited by Martha Merrill, PhD (No. 65, 1999). *Gives you valuable
information about various aspects of reference services and media, including changes, planning
issues, and the use and impact of new technologies.*

***Coming of Age in Reference Services: A Case History of the Washington State University
Libraries,*** edited by Christy Zlatos, MSLS (No. 64, 1999). *A celebration of the perseverance,
ingenuity, and talent of the librarians who have served, past and present, at the Holland Library
reference desk.*

Document Delivery Services: Contrasting Views, edited by Robin Kinder, MLS (No. 63, 1999).
*Reviews the planning and process of implementing document delivery in four university
libraries–Miami University, University of Colorado at Denver, University of Montana at
Missoula, and Purdue University Libraries.*

The Holocaust: Memories, Research, Reference, edited by Robert Hauptman, PhD, and Susan
Hubbs Motin (No. 61/62, 1998). *"A wonderful resource for reference librarians, students, and
teachers . . . on how to present this painful, historical event." (Ephraim Kaye, PhD, The
International School for Holocaust Studies, Yad Vashem, Jerusalem)*

Electronic Resources: Use and User Behavior, edited by Hemalata Iyer, PhD (No. 60, 1998).
*Covers electronic resources and their use in libraries, with emphasis on the Internet and the
Geographic Information Systems (GIS).*

Philosophies of Reference Service, edited by Celia Hales Mabry (No. 59, 1997). *"Recommended
reading for any manager responsible for managing reference services and hiring reference
librarians in any type of library." (Charles R. Anderson, MLS, Associate Director for Public
Services, King County Library System, Bellevue, Washington)*

Business Reference Services and Sources: How End Users and Librarians Work Together, edited
by Katherine M. Shelfer (No. 58, 1997). *"This is an important collection of papers suitable for
all business librarians. . . . Highly recommended!" (Lucy Heckman, MLS, MBA, Business and
Economics Reference Librarian, St. John's University, Jamaica, New York)*

Reference Sources on the Internet: Off the Shelf and onto the Web, edited by Karen R. Diaz
(No. 57, 1997). *Surf off the library shelves and onto the Internet and cut your research time
in half!*

Reference Services for Archives and Manuscripts, edited by Laura B. Cohen (No. 56, 1997).
*"Features stimulating and interesting essays on security in archives, ethics in the archival
profession, and electronic records." ("The Year's Best Professional Reading" (1998), Library
Journal)*

The Reference Collection:
From the Shelf to the Web

William J. Frost, MLS, MA
Editor

The Reference Collection: From the Shelf to the Web has been co-published simultaneously as *The Reference Librarian*, Numbers 91/92 2005.

The Haworth Information Press®
An Imprint of The Haworth Press, Inc.

New York • London • Victoria (AU)
www.HaworthPress.com

Published by

The Haworth Information Press®, 10 Alice Street, Binghamton, NY 13904-1580 USA

The Haworth Information Press® is an imprint of The Haworth Press, Inc., 10 Alice Street, Binghamton, NY 13904-1580 USA.

The Reference Collection: From the Shelf to the Web has been co-published simultaneously as *The Reference Librarian*™, Numbers 91/92 2005.

The development, preparation, and publication of this work has been undertaken with great care. However, the publisher, employees, editors, and agents of The Haworth Press and all imprints of The Haworth Press, Inc., including The Haworth Medical Press® and Pharmaceutical Products Press®, are not responsible for any errors contained herein or for consequences that may ensue from use of materials or information contained in this work. Opinions expressed by the author(s) are not necessarily those of The Haworth Press, Inc. With regard to case studies, identities and circumstances of individuals discussed herein have been changed to protect confidentiality. Any resemblance to actual persons, living or dead, is entirely coincidental.

Cover design by Jennifer M. Gaska.

Library of Congress Cataloging-in-Publication Data

The reference collection : from the shelf to the Web / William J. Frost, editor.
    p. cm.
    "Co-published simultaneously as The reference librarian, numbers 91/92, 2005."
    Includes bibliographical references and index.
    ISBN-13: 978-0-7890-2839-6 (hc. : alk. paper)
    ISBN-10: 0-7890-2839-5 (hc. : alk. paper)
    ISBN-13: 978-0-7890-2840-2 (pbk. : alk. paper)
    ISBN-10: 0-7890-2840-9 (pbk. : alk. paper)
    1. Internet in library reference services. 2. Electronic reference sources. 3. Electronic reference sources–Directories. I. Frost, William J. II. Reference librarian.
  Z711.47 .R44 2005
  025.5'24–dc22
                                         2004022799

Indexing, Abstracting & Website/Internet Coverage

This section provides you with a list of major indexing & abstracting services and other tools for bibliographic access. That is to say, each service began covering this periodical during the year noted in the right column. Most Websites which are listed below have indicated that they will either post, disseminate, compile, archive, cite or alert their own Website users with research-based content from this work. (This list is as current as the copyright date of this publication.)

Abstracting, Website/Indexing Coverage . . . . Year When Coverage Began

- *Academic Abstracts/CD-ROM* 1994

- *Academic Search: database of 2,000 selected academic serials,*
  updated monthly: EBSCO Publishing 1996

- *Academic Search Elite (EBSCO)* 1995

- *Academic Search Premier (EBSCO)*
  <http://www.epnet.com/academic/acasearchprem.asp> 1995

- *Business Source Corporate: coverage of nearly 3,350 quality magazines*
  and journals; designed to meet the diverse information needs of corporations;
  EBSCO Publishing <http://www.epnet.com/corporate/bsourcecorp.asp> 1995

- *Computer and Information Systems Abstracts <http://www.csa.com>* 2004

- *Current Cites [Digital Libraries] [Electronic Publishing] [Multimedia*
  & Hypermedia] [Networks & Networking] [General]
  <http://sunsite.berkeley.edu/CurrentCites/> 2000

- *EBSCOhost Electronic Journals Service (EJS)*
  <http://ejournals.ebsco.com> 2001

- *Educational Administration Abstracts (EAA)* 1991

- *ERIC Database (Education Resource Information Center)*
  <http://www.eric.ed.gov> 2004

- *FRANCIS. INIST/CNRS <http://www.inist.fr>* 1983

- *Google <http://www.google.com>.* 2004

- *Google Scholar <http://scholar.google.com>.* 2004

- *Handbook of Latin American Studies* 1999

(continued)

(continued)

*Special bibliographic notes related to special journal issues
(separates) and indexing/abstracting:*

- indexing/abstracting services in this list will also cover material in any "separate" that is co-published simultaneously with Haworth's special thematic journal issue or DocuSerial. Indexing/abstracting usually covers material at the article/chapter level.
- monographic co-editions are intended for either non-subscribers or libraries which intend to purchase a second copy for their circulating collections.
- monographic co-editions are reported to all jobbers/wholesalers/approval plans. The source journal is listed as the "series" to assist the prevention of duplicate purchasing in the same manner utilized for books-in-series.
- to facilitate user/access services all indexing/abstracting services are encouraged to utilize the co-indexing entry note indicated at the bottom of the first page of each article/chapter/contribution.
- this is intended to assist a library user of any reference tool (whether print, electronic, online, or CD-ROM) to locate the monographic version if the library has purchased this version but not a subscription to the source journal.
- individual articles/chapters in any Haworth publication are also available through the Haworth Document Delivery Service (HDDS).

The Reference Collection:
From the Shelf to the Web

CONTENTS

ABOUT THE EDITOR

William J. Frost received his MLS from the Rutgers Graduate School of Library & Information Science in 1970. Following a brief stint at Rutgers University Libraries, he joined the faculty of Bloomsburg University of Pennsylvania in 1972 as a reference librarian and retired with the rank of Associate Professor as Reference Librarian/Web Manager/Electronic Resources Librarian.

Mr. Frost's interest in instructional technology has led him from slide/tape to HyperCard to video disc to HTML, and to PHP. He is the creator of the Internet Collegiate Reference Collection (icrc.bloomu.edu), described in his article in *Internet Reference Services Quarterly* 7 (1/2), 2002.

IN MEMORIAM

Dr. William (Bill) Katz passed away on September 12, 2004. Dr. Katz was Editor of the Haworth journals *The Acquisitions Librarian* and *The Reference Librarian* as well as *Magazines for Libraries*, *RQ* (the journal of the Reference and Adult Services Division of the American Library Association), and the "Magazines" column in *Library Journal*. In addition to his contributions to library science as an author and editor, he was a much-beloved professor in the School of Information Science and Policy at the State University of New York at Albany and a mentor to many of his former students in their professional lives. His association with The Haworth Press began in 1980 and lasted more than two decades. His steady hand, friendly guidance, and steadfast leadership will be missed by all of us at *The Acquisitions Librarian*, *The Reference Librarian*, and The Haworth Press.

Introduction

William J. Frost

Karen Diaz's former column in *Reference & User Services Quarterly* called "Off the Shelf & Onto the Web" inspired me to compile this volume around the same theme: the migration of reference materials in print to an electronic format accessible on the World Wide Web. This process has achieved tremendous gains since the beginning of the new millennium, with major publishers offering nearly all their reference titles in digital form.

While we reference librarians still refer to print sources, we find ourselves spending an increasing amount of time referring clients to electronic sources and an increasing amount of our materials budget is being transferred as well from books to electronic reference materials. Library schools now offer classes on collection development for electronic materials.

The Internet is the preferred medium for these materials for at least four reasons: Web resources (1) can be licensed for users both within and without the library building, a boon for distance education, (2) need less library technical work and equipment since the information is typically stored on the providers' servers, (3) information is usually updated more frequently than print or CD-ROM, (4) are accessed from a browser, already a familiar tool to most users. And, more recently, citations may link to full text–both from free Web sites and to products of third party vendors.

Internet providers dominate the indexing and abstracting of periodical articles; they will soon be the chief means of accessing periodicals

---

[Haworth co-indexing entry note]: "Introduction." Frost, William J. Co-published simultaneously in *The Reference Librarian* (The Haworth Information Press, an imprint of The Haworth Press, Inc.) No. 91/92, 2005, pp. 1-3; and: *The Reference Collection: From the Shelf to the Web* (ed: William J. Frost) The Haworth Information Press, an imprint of The Haworth Press, Inc., 2005, pp. 1-3. Single or multiple copies of this article are available for a fee from The Haworth Document Delivery Service [1-800-HAWORTH, 9:00 a.m. - 5:00 p.m. (EST). E-mail address: docdelivery@haworthpress.com].

1

for all libraries. Public Web sites are a source of information for students at all levels. The Web is so great a tool for information retrieval and communication that we have seen students exit from libraries en mass when Internet service is lost. The Internet is the first place people look when seeking information.[1]

It seems inconceivable that, in less than a decade of common use, the Internet would become such a popular means of accessing information, not only for the general public, but for reference librarians as well. Recognizing the significance of electronic reference materials, several library periodicals, e.g., *Choice*, regularly include notices and reviews of reference titles in electronic format. The venerable *Guide to Reference Books* will become the *Guide to Reference Sources* and will include Web resources.[2]

The articles in this issue attest to the amount of reference material now accessible via the Internet. Margaret Landesman's history relates how reference collections have evolved over time and how there might be no such thing as a reference collection *per se* in the future. Jeanne Holba Puacz and Jackson Maxwell tell us how public and school libraries, respectively, have faired, while Gaynor Austen and Carolyn Young cover the topic for academic libraries in most of the English-speaking world.

A publisher's perspective on electronic references is presented by John Morse, who assures us that some titles will probably always be available in print. Necia Parker-Gibson explains why library research assignments are more difficult both for teachers to make and students to comprehend in this electronic age. Jennifer Sharkey and Bartow Culp discuss how plagiarizing these assignments and detecting such plagiarism has changed in recent times.

The structure of ready reference Web pages is studied by Steven Sowards. Steve Boss and Michael Nelson relate their experiences with a more recent way of organizing reference sources–federated search tools.

A survey of the most important Web-accessible reference tools–both free and subscription sources–is presented by Dennis Dillon (humanities), Lori Bronars (Sciences), Gary McMillan (medicine), Brian Quinn (social sciences), Gail Golderman and Bruce Connolly (business), and Linda Weber (education). Lori Morse, from her vantage as a member of the Machine-Assisted Reference Section (MARS) of RUSA, produces an annotated list of her top 100 free reference Web sites.

· REFERENCES

1. Roy Tenant, "Determining Our Digital Destiny," *American Libraries*, January, 2000, 54-8.

2. Robert H. Kief, "When Reference Books Are Not Books: The New Edition of the Guide to Reference Books," *Reference & User Services Quarterly* 41 (2002) 330-4.

Getting It Right–
The Evolution of Reference Collections

Margaret Landesman

SUMMARY. Reference works were present in the earliest libraries; and their numbers have grown inexorably ever since. They consume an increasing share of library acquisitions budgets. This article traces the evolution of reference collections, drawing on experiences at the author's library. The author concludes that while reference questions will always be with us; it is perhaps less certain that they will always be answered from "reference works" in collections labeled "reference." *[Article copies available for a fee from The Haworth Document Delivery Service: 1-800-HAWORTH. E-mail address: <docdelivery@haworthpress.com> Website: <http://www.HaworthPress.com> © 2005 by The Haworth Press, Inc. All rights reserved.]*

KEYWORDS. Reference collections, history of reference works, reference media

INTRODUCTION

Libraries build their collections to represent all points of view. Libraries collect good books. Bad books. Biased books. Unbiased books. We don't tell users which poetry books hold good poems and which

Margaret Landesman is Head of Collection Development, Marriott Library, University of Utah, Salt Lake City, UT (E-mail: margaret.landesman@library.utah.edu).

[Haworth co-indexing entry note]: "Getting It Right–The Evolution of Reference Collections." Landesman, Margaret. Co-published simultaneously in *The Reference Librarian* (The Haworth Information Press, an imprint of The Haworth Press, Inc.) No. 91/92, 2005, pp. 5-22; and: *The Reference Collection: From the Shelf to the Web* (ed: William J. Frost) The Haworth Information Press, an imprint of The Haworth Press, Inc., 2005, pp. 5-22. Single or multiple copies of this article are available for a fee from The Haworth Document Delivery Service [1-800-HAWORTH, 9:00 a.m. - 5:00 p.m. (EST). E-mail address: docdelivery@haworthpress.com].

doi:10.1300/J120v44n91_02

bad; and we know that comprehensive research collections need to include the nasty, inaccurate, and biased books as well as the good stuff.

Reference collections, though, are different. We do tell users which sources are the best; and we strive to achieve collections unsullied by marginal, biased, outdated, or poorly organized works.

According to the *Oxford English Dictionary* reference is "the act or expedient of referring or submitting a matter, esp. a dispute or controversy, to some person or authority for consideration, decision, or settlement."[1] Reference books, in short, are supposed to get it right.

Reference books over time change their shape. They change their format. They change in content. But they don't change their core purpose–to connect the user to the information they need.

USERS AND THEIR REFERENCE NEEDS

Users often don't know that what they need is a reference book. Most user requests are for books or journals. It frequently requires a reference librarian to connect a user to a reference book–which works well for users who come to the library–and less well when they visit electronically.[2]

The initial reference tactic favored by users (even perhaps by librarians) is to run through a mental list of people who might know, so as to avoid looking it up. If this tactic fails, users look around to see what they can find. They may find nothing, or they may find, especially online, information ranging from the obviously nutty to the possibly authoritative.

At this point, people do various things (mostly at the last moment). Many go to Barnes & Noble. We hope that users will think of the library; and we would like to increase the number who do. Users have choices–can we get them to choose us?

By looking at what libraries have offered in the way of reference in earlier eras, perhaps we can glean ideas as to directions for the future.

REFERENCE WORKS IN EARLY LIBRARIES

Reference as a place with a sign saying "Reference" is a 19th century innovation. Reference sources, though, are part of the written record as far back as it goes.

King-lists, genealogies, lists of place names, and dictionaries of foreign words were found in the libraries of Assyria, Egypt, Greece, and Rome. In what clearly constitutes a reference collection in every sense of the word, Athens in the fifth century BC placed copies of the authoritative texts of Sophocles' and Euripides' plays in public collections for consultation. Egypt protected the accuracy of religious texts in the same way, as did early Hebrews the Ark of the Covenant.

Libraries today struggle with concerns which have always been issues. The library at Nineva, developed by Assurbanipal into one of the greatest of the ancient world, held over 30,000 tablets in a series of rooms, each containing works on a particular subject. The cuneiform tablets were kept in jars arranged on shelves, with a shelf list inscribed on the wall near the door. Each tablet was tagged as to the jar, shelf, and room it belonged in; and the library offered the reference tool most characteristic of libraries–a catalog. Well-worn tablets, evidently heavily-used, contained lists enumerating the title, the number of tablets, the number of lines, opening words, and a location symbol for each work.[3]

The division of collections into books that circulate and those that don't (both librarians and users tend to equate "non-circulating"·with "reference") has long-standing precedent. The librarians at an Athenian library c. AD 100 swore an oath "No book shall be taken out, since we have sworn an oath to that effect." And Marcus Aurelius wrote to a friend in search of a title suggesting that though the library holding the book in question didn't allow circulation, one might be able to bribe the librarian.

FORMAT CHANGE

Books began to be housed in bound codices made of paper rather than on papyrus rolls around AD 200; but new formats, even improved ones, can be slow to replace older ones. It took around 300 years for the new form to establish itself. And as it did, sadly, access to books became more limited than it had been earlier. Literacy levels were low and written materials scarce. The typical European library contained fifty to a hundred books housed in a couple of chests in a monastery chapel. In what, again, certainly feels like a reference collection, some books were chained in order to curb the temptation towards unauthorized circulation. And just as libraries today keep key works behind the desk, medieval libraries invented the 'book wheel.'[4]

A few libraries, towards the end of the middle ages, had built larger collections. The Sorbonne, established in 1289, left a catalog showing 1,722 volumes split between circulating copies (300 volumes, some listed as lost), chained (300 volumes), and closed stacks (1,086 volumes).[5]

Some books had a reference element added in the form of comments, or 'glosses,' written in the margins and in the spaces between the lines. These interlinear bits of helpful information and assistance with unusual or foreign words were common in scholarly books.[6] And there did exist books conceived solely as reference works, Cassiodorus' *Institutiones Divinarum et Saecularium Litterarum* being the most famous. After establishing a monastery at Vivarium in southern Italy around AD 540, Cassiodorus built a library and authored a guide to daily monastic life containing instructions on how to correct, copy, and repair manuscripts. Of most interest in our context, it contained a clear reference source, an annotated bibliography of the best literature of the time.[7]

For scholars, the core issue was identifying and locating the handful of books which existed on a given topic. Once those books were absorbed, the reader could expect to have a comprehensive knowledge. Though it's difficult now to comprehend such an ambition, the notion that one person could know everything lasted into the early 18th century.

PRINT MEANS MORE COPIES OF MORE TITLES

Printing spread at a pace hard to imagine. Gutenberg's 42-line Bible was printed c. 1455. Remainders were invented less than fifty years later. Tens of thousands of titles and at least ten million volumes had been printed by 1500; and there was already a supply of unpurchased books which on eBay would create scores of instantly famous libraries.[8]

There's not a lot of difference for the user between reading a text as a manuscript volume and reading it as a printed one. But the switch does have a marked effect on book prices, which in turn affects who learns to read and how much reading material they are able to obtain. Reference books, like other titles, became less expensive and easier to come by, so that small libraries and individuals who weren't wealthy might own a few titles.

REFERENCE BECOMES OFFICIAL

In 1876, at a conference of librarians in Boston, Samuel Swett Green of the Worcester Free Public Library offered a proposal titled: "The Desirableness of Establishing Personal Intercourse and Relations between Librarians and Readers in Popular Libraries."

Green's words have not dated (nor have Samuel Rothstein's essays on Reference).

> The more freely a librarian mingles with readers, and the greater the amount of assistance he renders them, the more intense does the conviction of citizens, also, become, that the library is a useful institution, and the more willing do they grow to grant money in larger and larger sums to be used in buying books and employing additional assistants.[9]

Gradually, libraries began to offer reference help. Academic libraries were slower to do so. They were small (students relied on textbooks) and it was assumed they had no great need for a library. Faculty were thought better prepared to help students than were librarians. Nor was it believed that faculty themselves needed assistance in using a library.

However, in an 1882 report of the Harvard College Library, Harvey Ware wrote:

> A new life and spirit seem to pervade the place; and it is safe to say that a public library does not exist in which readers are more cordially welcomed, or more intelligently and courteously aided in the researches, than the library of Harvard college under its present enlightened and modern management.[10]

The term "reference work" appeared in the index to Library Journal for the first time in 1891. And "reference" grew rapidly in popularity to become the archetypal thing-that-librarians-do.

GROWING PRINT REFERENCE COLLECTIONS

The number of print reference titles published has over the years increased at a rate that shows no particular signs of abating. Bill Katz, in *Reference Books from Cuneiform to Computer*, counted entries in OCLC whose titles include the word "reference." He found 230 such works dated between 1400 and 1700, 330 dated 1700-1800, 13,402 from 1800-1900 and 100,974 from 1900-1996.[11] *WorldCat* has since, as one would expect, added a few titles for each of the earlier periods; and it shows 15,506 titles for 1997-2003. How many of these works do libraries add to their collections?

In a 1985 study by Mary Biggs and Victor Biggs, libraries were queried as to reference collection development polices and about the size of their reference collection. College libraries reported a median of 5,000 titles, while master's and non-ARL doctoral institutions reported 12,000. ARL libraries reported a mean of 28,000. The authors concluded: "Although use of the reference collection is usually believed to be rather low, most collections appear to be unmanageably large." They questioned whether collections had grown too big for librarians to know them well enough for maximum effectiveness.[12] The size of reference collections reported might arguably be related more to the size of the acquisitions budget than to any other consideration.

Print reference collections might or might not have continued to grow. We will never know, because even as collections grew, usage shifted to electronic sources.

The effects of "automation" on reference, though, substantially predated reference sources in electronic format. Telephone reference made it possible for users to get answers from outside the library; and public libraries developed ready-reference collections on revolving stacks which sat (and sit?) next to staff desks. Copying technology (photocopying, fax) meant users in search of personal copies were no longer technologically constrained. And as libraries could more easily obtain copies of articles from other libraries, users gained access to a wider range of journals. Transmission from library to library to user, though, remained print-based, or reasons that were as much economic as technical.

INTIMATIONS OF CHANGE

By the late '60s, it became obvious that computers would impact libraries in a major, but somewhat mysterious, fashion. Automation hadn't reached widespread visibility, and working librarians were not yet devoting significant thought to the issues soon to preoccupy the profession.

A handful of librarians and faculty experimented with automated searching, mailing off search requests and receiving (two to four weeks later) a stack of key-punched cards, each carrying a citation.

The first publicly-available system was *MEDLARS* (Medical Literature Analysis and Retrieval System). The National Library of Medicine repurposed the machine-readable tapes that it created to print *Index Medicus* and used them to run *MEDLARS* searches. A medical library could mail searches to NLM. One reel of tape held a month's worth of *Index Medicus*, so that to search for information published over four years, you ran 48 tapes. At $250 an hour, batch processing–gathering together enough searches to make a run feasible–was a necessity. Demand peaked in 1971, when 18,000 searches were performed in the United States,[13] a number that looks ridiculously tiny today. Other publishers (mostly scientific) followed suit. Studies differ on how many databases were available; but the number seems to have gone from under 25 in the mid-60s to 50-100 in 1970.[14]

The University of Utah Medical Library saw itself as an early adapter and in 1973 sent a librarian to UCLA for *MEDLARS* training. She trained all day every day for three weeks.[15]

In retrospect, much of what we do today is obviously descended from those searches. At the time, it simply seemed a new and quite wonderful thing.

AUTOMATION IMPROVES THE CURRENCY OF PRINTED REFERENCE WORKS

Automation's initial impact was gradual and not immediately visible to users. The time line from author to published product shortened, as did time elapsed from publication to library shelf.

In 1976, Tobin wrote: "In the late 60s and early 70s, it took two years to produce a 600-page *Encyclopedia of Associations*. Today it takes less than half that time to produce a 3,000 page, three-book set." The 1975 issue was the first to mention photo-composition and it was then that *EA* began to be issued annually.[16]

Books had always moved from publisher to library at a stately pace–under a year from publication was reasonably prompt. Cataloging was also time-consuming, and large backlogs in acquisitions and cataloging were the norm. As computers became (just barely) affordable in the '70s at larger libraries, and as OCLC arrived on the scene, titles reached the shelf faster.

Owning computers also allowed libraries to themselves become reference publishers, albeit in a somewhat primitive way. Printed lists of journal subscriptions became popular. We called ours the P.S.L. (Public Serials List). And new books lists became easier to generate. The on-order file itself, now often on microfiche, became a useful tool at reference desks.

All of these applications, though, employed batch processing–gathering together a batch of orders, reports, searches, etc., and sending them to the computer, usually once a week. This worked fine for ordering books and printing lists of book or journal titles. But it wasn't compelling as a reference technology–print indexes remained a quicker and cheaper way to search the periodical literature.

LIBRARIES AND COMMERCIAL SEARCH SERVICES

In the early '70s, commercial search services became available and libraries were among their earliest users. DIALOG and SDC's ORBIT both launched in 1972. A librarian stationed at a terminal connected by a dedicated phone line to a search service could enter the search; and the results could be printed out on the spot.

These services were made possible by improvements in storage technology–hard discs meant that the computer could move directly to information stored anywhere on the disc. Batching searches was now a thing of the past. A searcher could now experiment and try different search strategies–though given that the user was paying a search charge based on how many minutes the search took, there were real limits to this. It also made it possible to search every word in a database, so that full-text searching first became a possibility. At the same time, network infrastructures improved and networks became faster and more reliable.

These systems were, though, as far from user-friendly as it comes; and neither end users nor most librarians chose to learn to use them. To keep costs down, much preliminary work had to be done before "dialing up." Users desiring a search couldn't just walk in–they needed to make an appointment; and they left with a stack of printout and a bill.

In the mid-70s, search requests were growing fast and holding long searcher/patron conversations at a busy desk already prone to queuing was proving to be awkward. Academic libraries concluded that they needed a new electronic reference department.

LIBRARIES ADD
"COMPUTER AIDED REFERENCE" DEPARTMENTS

By 1980 the reference desk and the automated searching area were two separate entities. A new job description emerged, "Online Searcher." Searching was viewed as a major research tool; but it would be a mistake to envision it as a pervasive technology. A 1984 survey of 376 higher education institutions found that less than half the libraries (though all the large ones) offered online searching. Among those offering online searching, only 5.8% reported more than 1,000 searches a year.[17,18,19]

As an example of these new departments, the University of Utah established the "Computer Aided Reference Service" (CARS). It was a smallish room with a terminal and a couple of desks. Users made appointments and often had to wait a couple of days, as CARS could handle only one user at a time.[20]

Computer-aided reference had almost no impact on the purchase of print collections, on undergraduate library use, or on the organization and staffing patterns of libraries. Automated searching appealed to some faculty, the occasional graduate student, and to community users—geologists and lawyers—who did not find the idea of paying a charge for a search new and distasteful.

Libraries continued with the purchase of voluminous print and microfilm sets; and there were a lot of them. One of the most eagerly anticipated was the *National Union Catalog, Pre-1956 Imprints*, begun in 1967. In 1981, the Library of Congress published the last of 754 volumes. Well before it was completed, LC had realized that it would be dwarfed by OCLC. In fact, of course, it was pretty well forgotten by then and not much note was taken of its completion.[21]

LIBRARIES TAPE LOAD DATABASES LOCALLY

There was a fairly brief period during which it looked as if libraries were headed towards widespread local tape loading of databases on library computers. This required that the vendor mail bulky reels of machine-readable computer tapes to the library, and that the systems staff then mount each tape to be read into the computer's memory. It was from the start a problem that library computers simply were not big enough to house many databases in this fashion. But there were advantages.

Users kept asking for campus-wide access; and this looked like a way to provide it. Many librarians and technical staff worried that the Internet would never be able to provide the capacity needed to search a growing body of remotely housed databases with acceptable response times. Databases were slow and were down for substantial periods. Stuff worked, but not always.

For some consortia and for larger academic libraries, this was (and is) a sometimes attractive option. Smaller libraries lacked the hardware and technical staff to make it feasible.

In Utah, tape loading was the first statewide initiative. The Wilson Indexes were mounted at Utah State University. The first couple of years were rocky and complaints were loud and frequent. Later, as the technology stabilized, complaints dwindled and, for the most part, librarians seemed no longer to even be aware that the Wilsons were off two hours away in Logan rather than locally loaded. And as it became possible to send the files from publisher to library via FTP, the process became less onerous for the hosting library.

REFERENCE AND STAND-ALONE CD-ROMS

The University of Utah was in a particularly austere budget stretch as CD-ROMs began to appear in the mid-80s. We read about them. We couldn't afford them.

Our introduction stemmed from an item in a technical magazine belonging to one of the (two) systems people, referencing *About Cows*. It cost $15. It described the various breeds of cattle; and had pictures (in color) which would even, in theory, moo. I do not remember why, but they would not moo for us.

CD-ROM databases reversed the direction towards separate electronic and print reference areas. Librarians liked CD-ROMs and wanted them at reference desks. At first, only staff could use them, but users were soon invited. Not so many were initially interested. Interfaces were clunky, and many users had little background familiarity with computers to draw on. Besides, there were queues. A 1989 memo from Marriott Library's Head of General Reference noted: "Please remember that we only have one machine with a CD-ROM drive, and limit your searching time to 15 minutes."

There were problems–new databases started with current information and went forward, lacking the back run depth to be really interesting. Non-Roman fonts did not exist, nor did anyone seem sanguine about the possibility that they might. Many CD-ROMs required software which had to be loaded on each user's machine, and most users did not yet know how to do this on their own.[22]

On the other hand, CD-ROMs offered a much wider title selection. There began to be dictionaries and encyclopedias, software manuals, atlases, and directories. Academic libraries didn't quite know what to do with these, but public libraries did. They bundled them up in bright attractive packages and started circulating them.

Automation had not yet much affected daily life at the Marriott Library. The reference collection kept growing. Desirable titles continued to far exceed budgets. The *Guide to Reference Books*, a highly selective source, in its ninth edition in 1986 grew to 14,000 titles. Psychology titles listed went from three, in 1908 with Kroeger as editor, to 8 in Mudge's 1936 edition, 43 in Winchell's 1951 and 157 in Sheehy's 1986 edition.[23]

MULTIPLE CD-ROM DRIVES
AND THE IMPACT OF EARLY NETWORKS

As libraries figured out how to network CD-ROMs, more users tried them. Undergraduates discovered periodical indexes–and though they offered little full text, the abstract often seemed to suffice. Faculty, as more indexes became available and backruns grew, demanded their purchase with an urgency libraries had not seen before and weren't quite used to. And the libraries themselves began to internalize the idea that electronic reference would pretty much supercede print.

The ability to wire drives together meant that a stack of CD-ROM drives could be connected to each other and then to a terminal and a printer. Each reference desk had its own little system, with a set of its most important databases.

Shortly after, it became possible to create a CD-ROM LAN. The stacks of drives moved to Back of the House and their contents could now be used from several locations throughout the building, with the added advantage that more than one user at a time could search a disc.

Quoting the Marriott Library CD-ROM Database Network Report, May of 1990:

> Students and faculty have been quick to embrace this new tool. Several classes now have assignments requiring students to use CD databases. Many students specifically ask to use CD-ROM da-

tabases and are offended if they must use a printed index. Several students have remarked that they were able to complete days or weeks of research in less than an hour![24]

There were not nearly enough drives to mount all the desirable databases; and committees evolved to "rank" databases. The highest-ranked got slots in the "tower." New discs arrived quarterly or monthly and were checked in like journals and mounted by the systems people–a process that was supposed to be routine, but wasn't always so.

Libraries developed concepts such as "Infogate" and "MarrioNet" (the Marriott Library Network), a single location online where users could see a listing of all available databases. Connecting from outside the building to some databases was both possible and allowed by the publisher, but it was tricky; and the problem of PCs versus Mac and UNIX access dominated many decisions.

Like many libraries, we tried to help users cope and published the University of Utah Information Systems Handbook[25] in 1995. It held descriptions of 150 or so databases, with charts showing the "means of access," which search software was used, and which reference desk to call for help. The "means of access" included:

> Remote access via IBM-Compatible
> Remote Access via Macintosh
> Accessing the Marriott Library Gopher
> Telnet
> Accessing Eccles PC Local Area Network
> Accessing Eccles Health Science Library Gopher

These systems required a pretty determined user.

THE KRISPY KREME ERA

In a final glorious burst of too-many-CD-ROMs, there was the "Krispy Kreme" era: 240 CD-ROMs, arrayed in a doughnut shape, and housed in a metal box. Systems staff wired three or four jukeboxes together and linked them to PC networks.

They were great when they worked; but they were finicky and often didn't; and Systems offered user support from 8-5 Monday to Friday. The big general databases–IAC's InfoTrac, UMI, and a nascent EBSCO product–provided an increasing amount of full text and were instantly beloved by students. Faculty weren't very interested yet as the title and full-text selection were so limited.

In 1994, Utah installed jukeboxes at Brigham Young University's Lee Library and at the University of Utah to supply academic libraries throughout the state with the UMI ProQuest system.

PRE-WEB PUBLISHER HOSTED DATABASES

As publishers began to host their databases on their own servers, libraries responded with cautious enthusiasm, though it didn't solve the PC/Mac problem; and Mac users grew increasingly vociferous about their second-class status. And there was still concern that it might not be possible to maintain acceptable response times as use of the Web grew. Early licenses were all over the place–some allowed access on a single terminal, some only in one building. Some based pricing on the FTE of the Chemistry Department and others on the library's acquisitions budget. When asked about a state-wide license, publishers had no clue as to what to say. Nor did libraries know what it would be reasonable to offer.[26]

Decisions focused on the interface–SilverPlatter, CAS, EBSCO. For the first time, content was not necessarily the driving force in reference purchases. Databases were still mostly indexes, but other titles started cropping up. A full-text facsimile of the *Pennsylvania Gazette*. Complete works of philosophers. Perseus, for material on ancient and modern Greece.

In early aggregated full-text databases, a search might yield 20 citations, maybe two of them with full text. This was for many users more frustrating than no full text at all. But the balance has gradually shifted. Databases now are seen by users not just as an alternative to the reference collection. They now seem to many users a sort of pre-packaged rival to the whole idea of coming to the library to research a paper.

As use of electronic sources has risen, queues at reference desks have dwindled. ARL stats show that circulation transactions began to drop in 1996 and reference stats in 1998. In 2000, both figures were for the first time below 1991 levels. Between 1991 and 2002, the number of reference transactions dropped by 26%.[27]

Libraries gradually canceled print indexes. There was a belief though, that important print journals could never be cut. Nor did it yet seem feasible to consider doing without any major reference work in print solely because the library also had electronic access. Partly this was due to a queasy feeling about the permanence and stability of online sources. And partly, perhaps, because use statistics were so hard to come by and so little standardized that it seemed as yet unwise to put much confidence in their accuracy.

DATABASES ON THE WEB

As librarians began to hear about the Web, it was somewhat difficult to envision just what this thing was or how it would work. You needed to see it. But it very soon became clear that the Web would be a godsend. Libraries were quick to move databases from CD-ROM or tape loads to Web interfaces. Finally, the PC/Mac problem was solved for most users.

Web search engines don't yet offer the same level of sophistication as non-Web interfaces–a cause for consternation among some librarians, though users seem largely oblivious. Users also seem alarmingly willing to settle for the content found online and to skip retrieving journal articles not available online. Librarians had thought that users, especially researchers, would always want comprehensive searches, but now we wonder.[28]

In "everything's a serial" mode, one-time book and reference set purchases are being replaced with annual database subscriptions.[29] This makes it mathematically certain that unless expenditures go up very fast, the number of titles purchased will go down.[30] For years research libraries have been cutting both book budgets and journal subscriptions to cover price increases in journals. Today, many are also cutting to pay growing (but unfunded) technology infrastructure bills, and to pay database subscriptions.[31]

New reference products are emerging in subject areas and formats for which libraries may not have previously budgeted major sums. It is difficult to see how libraries will afford humanities and fine arts resources currently being developed; many of these will clearly be costly endeavors priced in the arena formerly dominated by scientific and business titles.

CONVERGENCE

The line between reference and full text has blurred as rapidly increasing amounts of full text are linked to indexes and from one text to another. New online collections offer access to printed monographs and to primary source materials, and may include encyclopedias, biographical sources, dictionaries, and specialized subject reference works.

Many printed reference titles were important to us as a way to keep track of what's in other books or in journals. The ability to search full text, though, turns every collection of online texts into a reference collection and provides an automatic concordance for every title.[32] Titles can no longer be tidily separated into "reference works" and "general collection."

In the past, a reference simply pointed the way. Now users expect to be taken there. As a result, electronic statistics are rising at a quite spectacular rate, while print reshelving statistics are dropping. At the Marriott Library, reshelves were down 9% in 2001-2002 and another 3% in 2002-2003. This year's figures are dropping at a rate of 9-10%; and the decline is almost entirely in reference and bound journals.[33] Some reference departments are pushing the printed reference collection off towards the stacks, in order to place user workstations and users who may need assistance close to the desk. Perhaps it is not too much to hope that one day those users who have since the advent of the first libraries been frustrated by non-circulating titles might be permitted to take a few of these home. Maybe even overnight.

CONCLUSION

What will be the next step in the evolution of reference collections? It seems evident that there will continue to be reference librarians, though perhaps they will use some other title. Reference collections, though, might be a less certain bet.

Why will we move away from "reference collections"? Partly because, given the convergence among formats, we can't recognize a reference book when we see one. Nor can its electrons be pinned down to a "reference collection."

Why will we still need "reference librarians"? Because users frequently need more, rather than less, assistance to find needed sources and information. The needle in the haystack was hard enough to find when there was only one haystack. Now the number of haystacks is multiplying.

Too many choices can be even less appealing to a library user than too few. There are many examples of this with printed collections. We have always known that many college students complain with their feet–and take themselves off to their local public library. And at my library, with nearly two million volumes in our library, the students complained that they couldn't find anything to read. So a Browsing Collection was instituted. Less choice of titles has made for more choice in leisure reading.[34]

Too much information has, with online sources, become a core issue. Libraries (as well as Amazon.com, Google, and Microsoft[35]) are exploring federated search engines and portals, and are increasingly integrating full text within other, broader contexts.

Technology has made people more independent when it comes to their research and reference needs. But there will always be users who welcome assistance. These users either cannot find what they need on their own, or they want to be certain that their results are conclusive and complete–and the best way to do that is likely to continue to be to consult a reference librarian.

REFERENCES

1. *Oxford English Dictionary*. 2nd ed. 1989 (ed. J. A. Simpson and E. S. C. Weiner), Additions 1993-7 (ed. John Simpson and Edmund Weiner; Michael Proffitt), and 3rd ed. (in progress) Mar. 2000- (ed. John Simpson). OED Online. Oxford University Press. <http://dictionary.oed.com>.

2. The author enquired among users as to their definition of "reference." The most common answer was, "It's the books the librarians lock up and won't let me take home and it is very irritating."

3. Michael H. Harris. *History of Libraries in the Western World*. 4th edition. (London, The Scarecrow Press, 1995): 10-63. As another example of a persistent issue, Harris noted that intellectual freedom hadn't made much headway. Assurbanipal's librarian is reported to have said "I shall place in it whatever is agreeable to the king; what is not agreeable to the king, I shall remove from it."

4. Lionel Casson. *Libraries in the Ancient World*. (New Haven, Yale University Press, 2001): 97-132. Casson lists the advantages of the codex form. It holds more–several rolls fit in one codex; and readers can move about easily within the text, book marking as needed. Their covers make them easier to transport and sturdier; and the title can be written on an edge. He also described the 15th century book wheel, holding about 15 books, each chained to its own small shelf.

5. Lawrence J. McCrank, "Medieval Libraries," in Wayne A. Weigand and Donald G. Davis, Jr. *Encyclopedia of Library History*, (New York: Garland, 1994):429.

6. Bill Katz, *Cuneiform to Computer: A History of Reference Sources*. (London, The Scarecrow Press, 1998): 2.

7. Harris: 91.

8. Fred Lerner, *The Story of Libraries: From the Invention of Writing to the Computer Age.* (New York, Continuum, 1998)97.

9. Samuel Rothstein, "The Development of the Concept of Reference Service in American libraries, 1850-1900," *The Reference Librarian* 25-26(1989). First published in *Library Quarterly* (1953)14.

10. Samuel Rothstein, "The Development of Reference Services through Academic Traditions, Public Library Practice and Special Librarianship (1955)," *The Reference Librarian* 25-26(1989)65.

11. Katz: 9. In January 2004, there were 258 dated from 1400-1700, 439 from 1700-1800, 14,813 from 1800-1900, and 100,927 from 1900-1006.

12. Mary Biggs and Victor Biggs, "Reference Collection Development in Academic Libraries: Report of a Survey," *RQ* 27 #1 (1987): 77.

13. Frank B. Rogers, "Computerized Bibliographic Retrieval Services," *Library Trends* 23(1974/75): 74-76.

14. M. Lynne Neufeld and Martha Cornog, "Database History: From Dinosaurs to Compact Discs," *Journal of the American Society for Information Science* 37(4):183.

15. Joan Stoddart, now Associate Director of the Eccles Health Sciences Library, University of Utah.

16. Carol M. Tobin, "The Book that Built Gale Research: The *Encyclopedia of Associations,*" in James Rettig, ed., Distinguished Classics of Reference Publishing. (Phoenix, Oryx Press, 1992): 94.

17. J. E. Straw, "From Magicians to Teachers: the Development of Electronic Reference in Libraries: 1930-2000," *The Reference Librarian* 74(2001):1-13.

18. Dorothy B. Lilley and Ronald W. Trice, *A History of Information Science: 1945-1985.* (San Diego, Academic Press, 1989).

19. Edwin M. Perry, "The Historical Development of Computer-Assisted Literature Searching and Its Effects on Librarians and their Clients," *Library Software Review*, 11(1992) 18-24.

20. The author is indebted to Ann Marie Breznay, Marriott Library, who searched the library archives for relevant documents, compiled a time line, and provided her usual high level of editing, proof-reading, and moral support. As did a number of Marriott Library colleagues.

21. John R. M. Lawrence, "The Bibliographical Wonder of the World": *The National Union Catalog,*" in James Rettig, ed., *Distinguished Classics of Reference Publishing.* (Phoenix, Oryx Press, 1992): 170.

22. The author particularly remembers a reference CD-ROM in Hebrew. It came with a small plastic black box which had to be attached to the back of the PC. The directions on how to do this were in Hebrew. This was a problem.

23. Donald C. Dickinson, "The Way It Was, the Way It Is: 85 Years of the *Guide to Reference Books,*" *RQ* 27#2(1987): 220-225.

24. Michael Noe, *Marriott Library CD-ROM Database Network Report.* (Salt Lake City, Marriott Library, 1990).

25. Kenning Arlitsch, Ann Marie Breznay, and Ruth Hanson, *Information Systems Handbook.* (Salt Lake City, Marriott Library, 1995). Four editions, 1995-1997, also online at the Marriott Library Gopher for those who knew what a Gopher was.

26. David Densmore of the Institute of Physics mentioned recently to the author that he recalls an early visit to the University and being asked what it would cost to get all the IOP journals online. He said he had no idea what to say, as no one had ever asked

that; and IOP did not suppose there was a library which would want every one of its journals. So he went away and thought up "the Z package" over lunch.

27. Association of Research Libraries, "Service Trends in ARL Libraries," http://www.arl.org/stats/arlstat/graphs/2002/2002t1.html.

28. At Marriott Library, informal surveys by Barbara Cox show that reshelf stats are falling about as rapidly for journals which are not available electronically as they are for journals which are available.

29. Second Edition of the *Oxford English Dictionary* is available in print–twenty volumes for $895 on Amazon. For the library, though, it is now a subscription–priced for a large institution at $4,166 a year. Worth every penny of it, too.

30. Take as an example Safari Books. This product aggregates relatively inexpensive but high demand titles such as "JavaScript by Example." The University of Utah pays $6,598 for 170 titles and 3 simultaneous users. The per use cost is going down. The overall cost is going up.

31. Landesman, Margaret, "The Cost of Reference," *Library Journal*, 11/15/2001 Supplement, Vol. 126 Issue 19, 8.

32. Katie Hafner, "A New Way of Verifying Old and Familiar Sayings," *New York Times*. February 1, 2001. G8. This article shows how JSTOR, used as a concordance, is useful in researching the origins of the saying, "There's no such thing as a free lunch." An earlier researcher used it in the same way to look for the earliest uses of "hopefully" as an adjective. It also works for "impactful" as a new and unwelcome adjective.

33. University of Utah Marriott Library statistics. Ian Godfrey.

34. Barry Schwartz, "A Nation of Second Guesses," *The New York Times*, January 22, 2004. A.27. Schwartz is the author of *The Paradox of Choice: Why More is Less*.

35. John Markoff, "The Coming Search Wars," *The New York Times*, February 1, 2004.

The company [Microsoft] has also been pushing hard to find new sources of information to index, beyond material that is already stored in a digital form. In December, it began an experiment with book publishers to index parts of books, reviews and other bibliographic information for Web surfers.

And Google has embarked on an ambitious secret effort known as Project Ocean, according to a person involved with the operation. With the cooperation of Stanford University, the company now plans to digitize the entire collection of the vast Stanford Library published before 1923, which is no longer limited by copyright restrictions. The project could add millions of digitized books that would be available exclusively via Google.

Out of the Stack and into the Net: International Perspectives on Academic Reference Resources

Gaynor Austen
Carolyn Young

SUMMARY. The transition of academic library reference resources from print to electronic format has been characterised by a growing level of strategic decision making by librarians, as mediated searches were replaced by end-user CD-ROM formats, only to be superseded by online user access. The experience of Australian university libraries, which were early adopters of these changes, is outlined. Particular factors which impacted on this transition in other English-speaking countries (the United Kingdom, United States, Canada, and South Africa) are also described. The formation of purchasing consortia has been crucial in all countries in facilitating this transformation of reference collections. *[Article copies available for a fee from The Haworth Document Delivery Service: 1-800-HAWORTH. E-mail address: <docdelivery@haworthpress.com> Website: <http://www.HaworthPress.com> © 2005 by The Haworth Press, Inc. All rights reserved.]*

Gaynor Austen is Director, Library Services (E-mail: g.austen@qut.edu.au); and Carolyn Young is Associate Director, Library Services (Information Resources) (E-mail: c.young@qut.edu.au), both at Queensland University of Technology, Brisbane, Australia.

The authors wish to acknowledge research assistance by Fiona Doyle and Robyn Tweedale, QUT, and information on the South African experience provided by Hilda Kriel, University of Pretoria.

[Haworth co-indexing entry note]: "Out of the Stack and into the Net: International Perspectives on Academic Reference Resources." Austen, Gaynor, and Carolyn Young. Co-published simultaneously in *The Reference Librarian* (The Haworth Information Press, an imprint of The Haworth Press, Inc.) No. 91/92, 2005, pp. 23-38; and: *The Reference Collection: From the Shelf to the Web* (ed: William J. Frost) The Haworth Information Press, an imprint of The Haworth Press, Inc., 2005, pp. 23-38. Single or multiple copies of this article are available for a fee from The Haworth Document Delivery Service [1-800-HAWORTH, 9:00 a.m. - 5:00 p.m. (EST). E-mail address: docdelivery@haworthpress.com].

Available online at http://www.haworthpress.com/web/REF
doi:10.1300/J120v44n91_03

KEYWORDS. Reference collections, electronic resources, library consortia

INTRODUCTION

The past twenty years have been a most stimulating time to be a librarian. It has been a roller-coaster ride from substantial print-based reference collections, whose mysteries were evident only to the most experienced of reference librarians, through to end-user database searching and "Google for everyone with access to a PC." Which of us has had a moment to stop for breath and reflect back upon the ride so far? What has this experience, with all its "highs" and "lows," meant for the development of the academic library reference collection?

While the rate of change has varied for academic libraries in different parts of the world, the current and ongoing transition from print reference collections to electronic has been a global experience. The changes in Australian academic library reference sources have been emblematic of this transition.

THE AUSTRALIAN EXPERIENCE

The uptake of electronic formats has been faster in Australia than many other countries. This "early adopter" strategy has been due to a combination of libraries' ongoing financial problems, a long-term focus on the information needs of remote students, and an accompanying rapid uptake of technology by Australians compared to other nationalities. However, Australian trends do, in general, reflect those of libraries across the English-speaking world.

One factor which has actively driven the early transition of Australian university library reference collections from print to electronic has been the substantial fluctuation of the Australian currency against its overseas counterparts, and, in particular, throughout the 1990s, the deterioration of its value against currencies of the United States and Europe, from which the vast majority of university reference materials (generally 80-90%) are sourced. In October 1996, one Australian dollar was worth 80.55 U.S. cents. By November 2000, it had fallen to 51.25 U.S. cents. Subsequent recovery has been only marginal. Table 1 outlines this relevant decline in more detail.

TABLE 1. U.S. Dollar and UK Pound Value of AUS Dollar

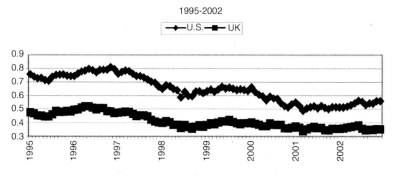

(Graph derived from internally derived QUT figures.)

This dramatic decline in the buying power of the Australian dollar required concerted action by many university libraries if they were to maintain reference collections that were both viable and financially affordable. Many were faced with this problem at the very time when vendors were introducing electronic alternatives to traditional print formats and, in many cases, seeking to sell these to libraries as "add-ons" to their print subscriptions. For many of these university libraries, the payment of additional charges to add electronic access to their current print reference subscriptions was out of the question. Yet, electronic options clearly provided significantly improved access, not only for on-campus students but especially significant in the Australian context, for remote students with little or no access to the library's print reference sources. An inevitable result was that many of Australia's university libraries chose to move immediately to decouple the print/electronic bundle, preferring the "electronic only" option for purchasing reference resources. As a result of this, the transition amongst their scholars and researchers to the electronic reference environment was greatly accelerated.

Australia's emphasis on distance education is another factor leading to its early transition to electronic resources. Australia is a very large country geographically, but one with a relatively small population (about 20 million). Most of this population is grouped in several substantial cities along the Eastern seaboard, with smaller pockets on the southern and western seaboards. The great majority of its universities are similarly located within this area. Traditionally, the scattered population in the rest of the country has been served for university education through "external" or "distance" studies, originally offered by selected universities through correspondence courses. Australia has been a leader in this field. Australian higher education libraries have for many years demonstrated a commitment to the development of information literate students and graduates. In a print environment, it is extremely difficult for distance-based students to undertake their own information searching and retrieval. Requests for information on a topic were traditionally mailed or phoned to a reference librarian, who undertook the search on behalf of the student, subsequently mailing relevant material to the student to enable them to complete the assignment. The advent of electronic databases accessible electronically provided the opportunity for transition from this "spoon-feeding" approach, facilitating the distance student's ability to develop information seeking skills on a par with those of campus-based students. As access to computers and the Internet has spread to more remote areas of the country, and as bandwidth to these areas has improved, this possibility has become a reality for a large number of non-metropolitan based university students and scholars. As reference sources available to students electronically increase, so *all* students, whether campus based or remote, are more readily able to identify and access the information essential for course completion.

In the 1970s and 1980s, Australia's remoteness from the major publishing houses of Europe and USA meant delays in accessing the latest reference publications and journal issues. Normal sea mail delivery of issues to Australia usually meant a three month delay between the time the issues were available in North American or European libraries and the time they were available in Australian libraries. Few Australian libraries could afford the price for airfreight delivery. Even in the most prestigious Australian academic libraries, library budgets were not, and still are not, in the same league as those of most major U.S. universities.

These factors led Australian academic libraries to move quickly to adopt the new opportunities in reference collections. Such adoption did not begin in an orderly, rational fashion. It happened rather opportunistically, responsive to innovations in products and technology, with one eye on improved service to the client and the other on the value of the Australian dollar. As time went along, and librarians became more accustomed to the new electronic environment, the libraries were able to be strategic and plan more consciously.

In the late 1970s and early 1980s, academic libraries were using dial-up online database search services, such as Dialog and MEDLINE, to search indexing and abstracting services online. These tools offered a search capability across databases, which was far superior to that for print equivalents. A few expert librarians were trained in the secrets of Boolean logic and conducted these expensive searches on behalf of the client. The client–mostly academics or researchers–was encouraged to sit alongside the reference librarian, changing the search strategy as the search results clacked out on the teletype. In Australia, the price of accessing Dialog was multiplied by the cost of the real time international telephone call from Australia through to the U.S.-based Dialog headquarters.

The introduction of CD-ROM products onto the Library market in the late 1980s was warmly welcomed as an alternative to this expensive, and consequently rather exclusive, service. Indexing and abstracting services were the first such products available. In 1987, Australian academic libraries were subscribing to CD-ROM products such as *Business Periodicals Index, Applied Sciences and Technology Index, Library Literature*, and *ERIC*. The Australian Bureau of Statistics had also published its latest census data on CD-ROM. This census data was a forerunner of many later electronic full-text reference products to be added to the reference collection. Wherever possible, academic libraries (especially those on multiple campuses) negotiated site licences with product vendors to network these CD-ROMs and to make them available beyond the library walls and across the university. Students, who had previously largely been excluded from dial-up Dialog type computer searching of indexes and abstracts, became enthusiastic users of the new CD-ROM services. Many academic libraries set up small labs near their Information desks for students to use the CD-ROM databases. Reference librarians were still at hand to guide students in searches, just as they remained in proximity to the print reference collection. Reference librarians adapted their reader education training on indexes and abstracting services to include the CD-ROM services as well as print.

By the late 1980s, academic libraries in Australia and elsewhere had embraced CD-ROM database reference products where these could be afforded. CD-ROM indexes and abstracting services offered a search capacity that was unrivalled by their print equivalents. Users could search across titles, abstracts and keywords, and combine search terms. They could conduct a single search across several years at a time instead of one year at a time on the print version. Importantly, most students, especially the younger ones, loved the interactive technology.

The Queensland University of Technology (QUT) Library's Annual Report for 1989 reads: *"Major acquisitions of CD-ROM databases occurred, offering students at all levels unprecedented capacity to locate information in support of assignments and research projects. By year's end, the Library was offering 20 CD-ROM products directly to students and staff. These included the first full-text CD-ROM publication, signalling the Library's entry into the storage and use of true electronic publishing."* The Library had just bought its first encyclopaedia on CD-ROM. The arrival of CD-ROMs in the Library coincided with the peak of mediated online searching services. Librarian mediated dial-up online searching services quickly declined over the next few years.

By 1990, many more CD-ROM abstracting and indexing products became available on the market. Academic libraries subscribed to those services which they used most heavily and, to cover the cost, many were obliged to cancel the subscription to the print version of these titles.

This set the stage for the next progression. In the early 1990s, the first full-text journal CD-ROMs were on the market. One of the first purchased at QUT was *Business Periodicals Ondisc*, shortly followed by ProQuest's *Social Sciences Index*. The merging of indexes and full text on disk met the strong user desire to match index search results with the articles. So many students wanted to use these full-text databases, the Library had to set up a half hourly student bookings system for *Business Periodicals Index Online*.

By 1994, the CD-ROM wave had crested and was quickly overtaken by the Internet, as many of the key reference products which had been available on CD-ROM became available online. The concepts of the "Virtual Library" and the "Scholar's Workstation" suddenly became so much more real and achievable. Universities as a whole were grappling with the logistics and costs of providing easy student access to the Internet. Student computer labs around campuses were upgraded and linked to the Internet. Small labs of terminals for CD-ROM searching, often located adjacent to the reference desk and serviced by the reference librarians, were expanded and upgraded to PCs with Internet access. Issues of user access to CD-ROM campus networks and standalone CD-ROMs were replaced by problems of access to the online products from outside the campus. The difficulties of managing network access to large stacks of CD-ROMs, and searching one time range after another, were replaced by difficulties with authentication in the Internet environment. Issues of authentication and Internet access featured in Library negotiations with vendors and publishers and many took several years to resolve. University provision of Internet access for students enabled libraries to develop Internet access to information resources with some measure of confidence.

The introduction and trialing of electronic reference sources in Australian universities was greatly facilitated by activity through the 1990s by the Council of Australian University Librarians (CAUL). CAUL comprises the library directors of all 38 Australian university libraries. It was first formally constituted in 1965, and opened a permanent office in Canberra, the national capital, in 1995.

> *The Council of Australian University Librarians is dedicated to improving access by the staff and students of Australian universities to the scholarly information resources that are fundamental to the advancement of teaching, learning and research. Through an expanding program of information dissemination, coordination and consortial acquisition of electronic information services, it offers members tangible evidence of the benefits of working together.*[1]

CAUL began its program of consortial purchase, or brokering, of electronic resources for Australian university libraries with its involvement in administering trials for a federally-funded scheme through which, in 1994-96, the Australian government, which is the primary funding authority for Australian universities, provided A$2 million to Australian university libraries for licensing costs to enable the provision of trials of electronic databases. The first reference database trialed was *ISI Current Contents*, and this was followed by others, including *Academic Press IDEAL* and *IAC Expanded Academic ASAP*. Following the success of these trials, CAUL members agreed to continue the central coordination of subscriptions to new electronic services wherever feasible. As a result, CAUL has continued this function for Australian university libraries, as well as for the Australian government research arm (CSIRO), for New Zealand university libraries, and for other research libraries, these activities being funded by a levy on participants. Since 1994, some 32 electronic products, including a number of major reference resources, have been acquired consortially through this mechanism, with advantages to Australian universities such as improved access conditions and pricing models.

Most recently, the Australian Vice Chancellors' Committee, (the body representing the heads of all Australian universities) also stepped into this negotiating arena. After initial unsuccessful discussions with Elsevier Publishing, the AVCC did successfully broker a deal, in which most Australian universities participated, to provide nationwide access to ISI's *Web of Science* database. Recent special funding from the Australian federal government has enabled purchase of backsets of this resource for participating libraries.

With increasing public access to the Internet, more and more information resources became Internet accessible. Universities, government, and other organisations began to make information and publications available online from their Web pages. Reference librarians began searching the Web for answers to ready reference questions they had previously answered from their print reference collections. Dictionaries, encyclopedias, handbooks and manuals, statistics, almanacs, directories, standards, and catalogues of other libraries have all become available online over the past decade. As William Katz noted in the introduction to his latest edition of the standard *Introduction to Reference Work, "In another decade or so print reference works will disappear entirely, particularly when the retrospective indexes are put online. Note though, this does not mean all print, but primarily reference works which are much easier to use online."* [2]

The Queensland University of Technology Library has tracked its uptake of electronic information resources compared to print acquisitions. In 1996, expenditure on all electronic information resources consumed 15% of the Library's expenditure on serials. By 2002, this had risen to 58% of total serials expenditure and 37% of the total Library acquisitions budget.

The era of electronic reference collections is now truly upon us.

LOCAL FEATURES AFFECTING OTHER MAJOR ENGLISH-SPEAKING COUNTRIES

As already outlined, the Australian experience of this transition from print to electronic reference collections was typical of the change across the English-speaking world. In all countries investigated, the formation of purchasing consortia has greatly assisted this process. However, while the experience of other countries in general paralleled that of Australia, particular circumstances in each, such as the relative economic climate and the degree of government assistance available, have affected both the means and the speed of the transition that occurred.

United Kingdom

Throughout the United Kingdom, university libraries have been fortunate to have access to the assistance and funding provided through the

Joint Information Systems Committee (JISC) of the UK Higher Education Funding Councils, which was founded to promote the development of electronic information in UK universities. Whilst not specifically established to service libraries, the development of electronic library resources has always constituted one of the major foci of JISC activity.

The Joint Information Systems Committee was established in 1993, and has, since that date, been actively involved in facilitating the purchase of electronic resources for UK academic libraries, at times providing seeding funds to pilot consortial purchase activities developed through a number of agencies. This facilitation role has enabled a number of deals to be struck by libraries for the purchase of online reference resources at more affordable prices than would have been possible individually. Some of these agreements apply to only some universities, while some are nationally based. A JISC Model Contract and Model Licence are used for many of these negotiations. A considerable number of contracts for indexing and abstracting tools in a variety of disciplines have been negotiated via this method. These initiatives have also recently been extended into the full-text journal arena through the NESLI (National Electronic Site Licence Initiative) and NESLi2 programs.

JISC, however, is not the only purchasing consortium activity occurring amongst UK academic libraries. Negotiations for research libraries have also been undertaken during this period by the Consortium of University Research Libraries, while other regionally-based networks have assisted their members' transition to electronic reference sources through consortial deals.

The relative strength of the British pound throughout this transition period has been one factor that contrasts to recent currency exchange rate deterioration in many other countries. This, together with the infrastructure and seed funding for many initiatives available through JISC, has meant that the print to electronic transition in UK universities has been relatively more controlled than has been the case in regions where factors have been less favourable.

United States

It is impossible to discern any one approach or model for the transition of reference collections from print to electronic across the USA. The number of universities involved, and the fact that the basic funding model for universities is either state or privately based, rather than centrally funded by the federal government, makes the circumstances very different from those applying in Australia, or in most other countries under discussion.

In a presentation to the JULAC Task Force Consortia Seminar, Hong Kong, in 2001, Arnold Hirshon, Executive Director of NELINET, referred to the U.S. picture as "a mosaic, not one best practice or model," identifying the following differences in approaches to funding e-resources across the country:

- *no single funding or distribution model across the states*
- *many states provide little or no central funding*
- *funding may be one time rather than recurring*
- *funding levels differ greatly for different types of library*
- *funding is in a constant state of flux*
- *total allocation is less important than per capita spent*
- *funding patterns [are] based on local politics*[3]

As a consequence of the size of the U.S. library market, and its proximity to major database vendors, American universities have been able to more effectively negotiate deals which facilitate the transition to electronic reference materials than has often been the case in those countries with smaller purchasing power, or those more distantly located from major markets. The basic trend, however, has been the same, as libraries band together to develop market power and to advocate their own cases more effectively.

As in other countries, library consortia have become effective lobbying instruments in negotiating e-resource deals. Collective buying power has been used to overcome vendor practices that are inimical to the interests of individual libraries. Examples of such collective approaches to the acquisition of electronic resources exist across the country. Hirson's own organisation, NELINET, is a prime example. Formed as a program of the New England Board of Higher Education, it serves over 650 member libraries across six New England states and negotiates individual deals on numerous e-reference products. Another typical major consortium is OhioLINK, a state-funded consortium of the libraries of 83 colleges and universities, together with the State Library of Ohio. One of its major programs is the brokering of access to electronic resources on behalf of its members. In an article discussing OhioLINK's activities in this area, Tom Sanville commented:

> . . . *the economics of group purchase are far superior to the role of the individual library as an economic island . . . Consortium pur-*

chasing enhances vendor revenue and profits while lowering library unit cost of purchase. Many consortia have experienced this phenomenon, saving anywhere from 20% to 70% when buying as a group compared to accrued individual library prices. . . . OhioLINK has found that in many cases only a small increment in spending is needed to achieve group wide access.[4]

Many U.S. academic libraries, in fact, belong to more than one consortium, each bringing particular advantages both in electronic resources purchasing and in other consortial activities. Smaller local consortia have also been shown to produce very tangible results for their members.

Canada

The Canadian university environment also differs from that in Australia, as the principal funding source for these institutions is provincially, not federally, based. Thus, Canadian university libraries have, throughout the period of rapid growth in online reference sources, cooperated in regional- or province-based consortia to negotiate affordable access to appropriate sources. Many of these consortia centre on academic library needs, though some are inclusive of the broader library community of the region. Whilst most such consortia were not founded solely to facilitate collaborative purchasing, this has become a major part of the operations of many of these organisations. Examples of such organisations include The Electronic Library Network (ELN) of British Columbia, the Council of Atlantic University Librarians (CAUL), Novanet in Nova Scotia, the Ontario Council of University Libraries (OCUL), the Libraries Committee of La Conference des recteurs et des principaux des universites due Quebec (CREPUQ), and the Council of Prairie and Pacific University Librarians (COPPUL).

COPPUL is a typical example of such joint efforts. The Council is a consortium of 22 university libraries located in Manitoba, Saskatchewan, Alberta, and British Columbia. Its Web site states, *"Member libraries cooperate to enhance information services through resource sharing, collective purchasing, document delivery, and many other similar activities."*[5] The organisation itself was first formed in 1967 to facilitate resource sharing. Since the 1990s, consortium purchasing has become an increasingly important part of its activities. Its current list of negotiated products, both reference and full text, includes 48 separate licenses and products. The Ontario Council of University Libraries (OCUL) similarly cites collective purchasing as one of its principal activities. The range of its currently licensed reference resources range from the *Grove Dictionary of Art* to *CINAHL*, from *PsycInfo* to *SciFinder Scholar*.

Most recently, Canadian academic libraries have been able to significantly increase their access to electronic publications, including online reference tools, via the Canadian National Site Licensing Project. The project has been funded by a C$20 million grant from the Canada Foundation, which partially supports access for the 64 university participants to electronic material, primarily in scientific, technical, and medical disciplines. The remainder of the funding to purchase such online resources is met by the project participants. Access to the multidisciplinary reference tool *Web of Science* is one of the licences funded through this program.

Like Australian academic libraries, those in Canada have suffered during this period from a currency value, which has fallen in relation to strong U.S. and European currencies. And again, as in Australia, there is evidence that strong consortial networks have been a major factor in improving the affordability of electronic reference sources for university libraries across the country.

South Africa

The educational environment in South Africa is unique amongst major English-speaking countries. The country contains a significant highly literate group but also a substantial illiterate population. These significant differences in literacy levels are also marked between races, and between urban- and rural-based populations. The previously weak school system for indigenous South Africans, and the prevalence of an oral, rather than written, culture has exacerbated these differences.

As commented by Darch, Rapp, and Underwood:

> *The library and information sector is characterised by pockets of excellence, and relative technological sophistication, while the majority of citizens, many of whom live in rural areas or townships, do not have access to even the most rudimentary library and information services.*[6]

In addition, South Africa's academic institutions vary substantially in their resource bases, the former elite institutions such as the Universities of Pretoria, Cape Town, and Witwatersrand being traditionally far better resourced than their counterpart institutions originally intended to service "black" and "coloured" populations. The latter did receive overseas funding during the apartheid era, but little of this funding penetrated to the university libraries.

As a consequence of generally stretched financial resources in the newly democratic structure, South African university libraries have been slower than those in many other English-speaking countries in being able to take advantage of the opportunities to transform their reference resources from print to electronic format. In this context, some of the factors which have acted to slow the adoption of such transition are:

- Lack of telecommunication bandwidth in much of the country
- Relatively high communication costs
- Lack of infrastructure in non-urban areas
- Relatively widespread computer illiteracy
- The divide between rich and poor universities, and the current trend to institutional mergers
- Low budgets for material acquisition
- A deteriorating exchange rate, relative to the currencies in which electronic resources are generated

As with most academic library communities, the South African transition to electronic reference began in the 1980s, when the better-resourced institutions acquired the Dialog service. The transition to electronic material was made at different tempos across various institutions and discipline areas. At the University of Pretoria, for example, subject specific reference collections were converted to electronic format well before this occurred within the general reference collection. However, in many cases this conversion, because of the factors outlined above, has been slow.

Darch, Rapp, and Underwood commented in 1999:

In general, South African academic libraries are still in the process of positioning themselves for the kind of consortial purchasing of electronic information products that is now common in North America and other parts of the world. South Africa is a new market for most vendors, both because South African academic libraries are still largely print oriented, and also because most of the libraries cannot afford to buy electronic products outside a consortial environment.[7]

Consortia are the major negotiating bodies for South African libraries in transforming their print reference (and general) collections to electronic format. These consortia are generally regionally based. Two of the most successful have been GAELIC (founded in 1996 and partly funded by the Andrew W. Mellon Foundation), based in the province of Gauteng and including the Universities of Pretoria and Witswatersrand, and CALICO (founded in 1992), based in the Cape Town area and including the Universities of Cape Town and Stellenbosch. Most recently, the South African site licensing initiative is seeking to extend electronic resource purchasing, including full-text journal databases, on a national basis.

The pricing models being used by online resource vendors are, on the whole, unrealistic in the current South African economic environment. Libraries there are trying to address this through their consortial-based negotiations. They are also actively involved in advocacy to the government regarding issues of affordable high bandwidth connectivity across the country. Changes in such factors will be essential if South African libraries are to be able to capitalise on the advantages of such online reference resources–easier searching and accessibility, improved coverage, and greater connectedness across academic products. Existing models will not suffice. South African libraries are hoping to "leap frog" some of the interim solutions adopted elsewhere, possibly moving to an online environment based on mobile and wireless technologies.

WHERE TO NOW?

Students and staff are now able to meet most of their information needs from a selected, authoritative, online reference collection, but of course, many will routinely bypass this in favour of a Google search. A key challenge for the reference librarian is how to make these authoritative online reference collections a readily accessible, attractive, and easy to search alternative for the devotees of general Internet search engines. Stacy-Bates has outlined the design characteristics of good quality ready-reference Web pages through her study of over one hundred academic libraries in the Association of Research Libraries (ARL). She concludes, *"As distance education efforts and the use of the Internet as an information source increase, librarians must offer high-quality reference services through the Web to remain a meaningful research option for our patrons."*[8]

Another pressing challenge for librarians is the issue of what to do with the remaining print reference collections. Are they providing users with the same readily accessible, attractive, and up to date information resources that our users expect from electronic reference resources? Have they been weeded of those information resources now better provided in electronic form, for example the indexing and abstracting service back runs? Have key resources that are easier to use in print been identified and kept up to date? Finally, in a more complex and hybrid world of reference resources with some available in print and some available electronically, have academic library managers put in place adequate training and retraining programs in place to keep the skills of reference librarians at peak quality to provide our patrons with the very best professional service?

A further very relevant issue relates to the future viability of the very concept of a university reference collection. As clearly expressed by Susan Fales, Assistant University Librarian at Brigham Young University:

> *With the advent of societies providing their journals in full-text, coupled with an excellent search engine to these journals . . . the question becomes where is the need for mediation in the reference process and with a traditional reference collection? Information seekers have the opportunity to go directly to many of these resources, without a traditional reference collection existing at all.*[9]

There are no signs that the speed of transformation in academic library reference services is likely to abate. The transition of reference collections from print to electronic format will form only part of this transformation, as user behaviour continues to change. A recent research paper released by the Microsoft Corporation indicated that, amongst the 18-24 year old cohort of the United States population, 84% own a computer, and 25% own more than one, while college students spend an average of 11 hours per week online.[10] Such statistics suggest that 24x7 access to online resources will soon become the norm, providing even more opportunities to capitalise on these new reference formats. We are, without doubt, moving into a "brave new world" of interactive, real time provision of reference information and services to the users of academic libraries.

REFERENCES

1. Dianne Costello, "More, Better, Cheaper: The Impossible Dream?" *Information Technology and Libraries* (September, 1999) 154.

2. William A. Katz, Introduction to *Introduction to Reference Work.* 8th ed. (Boston: McGraw-Hill Higher Education, 2002).

3. Arnold Hirson, "Of Consortia and Caucus-Races: Consortial Programmes, Services and Roles and Their Effect on Member Libraries" (JULAC seminar, Hong Kong, May, 2001). Also available online at http://www.cityu.edu.hk/lib/julac_P2.ppt.

4. Tom Sanville, "Use Levels and New Models for Consortial Purchasing of Electronic Journals" *Library Consortium Management: An International Journal* 1 (1999) 3.

5. Council of Prairie and Pacific University Libraries, http://www.coppul.ca/index.html.

6. Colin Darch, Joan Rapp, and Peter G. Underwood, "Academic Library Consortia in Contemporary South Africa" *Library Consortium Management: An International Journal* 1 (1999) 25.

7. Darch, Rapp, and Underwood (1999) 26.

8. Kristine K. Stacy-Bates, "Ready-Reference Resources and E-mail Reference on Academic ARL Web Sites" *Reference and User Services Quarterly* 40 (2000) 72.

9. F.C. Wilkinson, and L.K. Lewis, "Reference Materials: Stalking the Wild Electron" *Against the Grain* (September, 2000) 16.

10. Microsoft Corporation, "Educating the 21st Century Citizen," white paper issued August 2003, http://www.microsoft.com/education/?ID=21stCenturyCitizen.

Electronic vs. Print Reference Sources in Public Library Collections

Jeanne Holba Puacz

SUMMARY. The evolution of electronic sources has had a significant impact on reference collections in libraries, and public library reference collections are no exception.

Evaluating, selecting, and organizing sources to meet the needs of public library users has always been a fundamental role of public librarians. However, now they have the added responsibility of evaluating electronic resources and deciding whether the electronic sources will supplement or replace traditional paper reference sources. Issues of authority, accessibility, cost, comfort, and user education must be carefully weighed during this evaluative process. *[Article copies available for a fee from The Haworth Document Delivery Service: 1-800-HAWORTH. E-mail address: <docdelivery@haworthpress.com> Website: <http://www.HaworthPress.com> © 2005 by The Haworth Press, Inc. All rights reserved.]*

KEYWORDS. Reference collections, electronic sources, public libraries, virtual libraries

---

Jeanne Holba Puacz is Library Consultant and Adjunct Faculty, University of Illinois, Urbana-Champaign (E-mail: jpuacz@uiuc.edu).

[Haworth co-indexing entry note]: "Electronic vs. Print Reference Sources in Public Library Collections." Puacz, Jeanne Holba. Co-published simultaneously in *The Reference Librarian* (The Haworth Information Press, an imprint of The Haworth Press, Inc.) No. 91/92, 2005, pp. 39-51; and: *The Reference Collection: From the Shelf to the Web* (ed: William J. Frost) The Haworth Information Press, an imprint of The Haworth Press, Inc., 2005, pp. 39-51. Single or multiple copies of this article are available for a fee from The Haworth Document Delivery Service [1-800-HAWORTH, 9:00 a.m. - 5:00 p.m. (EST). E-mail address: docdelivery@haworthpress.com].

doi:10.1300/J120v44n91_04

INTRODUCTION

Anne Lipow, in her keynote address at the 1999 Information Online & On Disc Conference, made the astute observation that "reference librarians who are not in denial know that doing business as usual isn't working the way it used to."[1] Electronic resources have had and continue to have a serious impact on reference services, sources, and collections. Many traditionally paper reference sources are migrating to the electronic format. While there are distinct advantages to the electronic format, there are also definite disadvantages. Ultimately, the particular needs of an individual library's patrons must be the key factor in any collection development decisions.

GOAL OF THE REFERENCE COLLECTION

Some arguments in the print versus electronic format battle remain constant regardless of library type; however, it is possible to narrow the scope of the debate to a particular library type by focusing on the goal of the reference collection. The goal of any reference collection should be to accurately and authoritatively meet the needs of its users. Since users vary greatly by library type, so too will their needs. Unlike academic, special, and school libraries, there are fewer limitations as to which members of a given community can use the resources of the public library; therefore, public libraries are generally acknowledged to have a wider variety of patron needs than any other type of library. "Clients are not only students and teachers, but laypersons, of different ages and backgrounds who may wish to gather information for practical purposes."[2]

Directory, geographic, career, legal, health, and tax information, consumer guidance, homework, and research paper assistance are some common public library queries. Although frequent, these queries by no means represent the whole spectrum of questions faced by public librarians. Likewise, these assumptions about the general needs of public library patron should not replace careful evaluation of the actual needs of a particular public library's users.

Reference librarians in public libraries, through experience at the reference desk, often develop a sense of their users' needs. Thus, these same librarians are well suited to the task of evaluating sources for possible inclusion in the reference collection. It is necessary to evaluate the possible sources of information on various levels, including format, authority, accessibility, ease of use, and cost. Format has become a more interesting factor in today's world of electronic sources. Some sources may only be available in either paper or electronic format. Other sources may come in both forms and it is usually necessary to compare and choose the superior version. It is imperative to remember that the sources should be evaluated in terms of the patrons who will be using the information; their needs, preferences, and comfort levels should be considered. A source that would be considered appropriate at an academic library may not be considered so at a public library.

The phrase electronic resources can encompass a wide variety of media types. Free and fee Web sites, Web accessible databases, DVDs and CD-ROMs all fall into the category of electronic resources. DVDs and CD-ROMs, however, may have limited usability. It is widely acknowledged that the capabilities of Web-based resources in capacity, currency, and accessibility surpass the capabilities of DVDs and CD-ROMs. Therefore, when possible, public libraries may wish to consider the online source instead. However, smaller libraries that do not have the monetary or equipment resources to support online sources may still be well served by DVDs and CDs. Likewise, when the source is only available in limited formats, disk formats should not be discounted.

IMPLICATIONS OF ELECTRONIC SOURCES

When an electronic source is deemed superior and chosen for the collection, the librarian continues to have responsibilities to the users. The source may necessitate formal or informal instruction in its use, particularly in a public library setting. Informal instruction may include, but is not limited to, demonstration to patrons, the creation of handouts, or the development and posting of an online guide to the source. The democracy of the Internet and the ease with which it is possible to publish information to the Web necessitate another facet of instruction. There are no editorial review processes in place to evaluate what is published independently to the Web; thus, it is even more important than in traditional research to evaluate findings for bias and inaccuracy and librarians should instruct their patrons in how to do so. Public librarians must see the Web and the capabilities it provides as opportunities for instruction. Patrons should be educated as to the possible misinformation available on the Web and should be taught the basic principles of evaluating Web sites.

Placement of and access to electronic sources also demand careful thought on the part of the librarian. If the source is Web based, as many fee and free electronic sources now are, then easy access to the source should be available via the library's home page. The home page can serve as a portal or gateway to "guide the user to the correct resources."[3] Librarians should consider the collection of Web sites and their arrangement into Web-based subject guides as a new phase of their traditional collection development duties. As with paper reference sources, electronic sources are regularly reviewed in various professional journals to assist librarians with these duties. Sites such as the Internet Public Library (http://www.ipl.org/) and the Librarians' Index to the Internet (http://lii.org/), which have as their ultimate goal to develop a "Yahoo! with values and a brain,"[4] are quality subject directories in their own right. These services can also assist librarians in choosing quality Web sites for in house subject guides developed to meet the needs of their own patrons. Subject guides added to a public library site might include such items as a homework help page for students, a frequently asked questions (FAQ) section for the library, and a general subject guide for traditional adult public library patrons. Electronic resources added to the library Web site must be maintained over time. The sources should be reevaluated periodically to determine their continued worth and those that are no longer deemed worthy should be weeded from the library site, just as paper sources are weeded from the traditional reference collection.

ACCESSIBILITY ISSUES

In addition to the organization and development of Web-based resources, the accessibility of for-fee sources to which the library subscribes must be considered. Superior accessibility of the electronic format has been loudly touted as a major benefit of such sources. Ideally, multiple users can access the same source concurrently, which is often impossible with paper sources. Also, libraries may have the right to make the sources available to their patrons remotely. When negotiating contracts for online sources, an important consideration is whether the vendor will allow the library to make the source available to patrons outside the library itself. Remote access should be investigated and made available, whenever possible, for all relevant sources.

Academic libraries have long recognized the value of remote access to resources and were quick to enable such access. Public libraries have lagged behind somewhat in this arena.[5] Lack of funding and staff expertise may have impacted the ability of libraries, particularly public libraries, to provide this service. Remote access has since become far less difficult to implement. Reasonably priced services such as EZproxy (http://www.usefulutilities.com/) allow even those public libraries with limited technical competencies to provide remote access to their users.

Increasingly, public library patrons expect that they should be able to access information regardless of their physical location. Patrons can and should have the right to choose where they are most comfortable pursuing their information needs, and public libraries should accept and meet the remote access challenge. Access to quality subject guides, local and remote database access, and electronic question services, combine to create a virtual library that is available to patrons regardless of the time or their location.

The library catalog is the essential reference source in any library collection and all but the smallest libraries now use electronic catalogs. It is widely accepted that the electronic catalog format is superior to the old card catalog format. The additional access points of an electronic catalog and the ability to manipulate search results increase the possibility of locating quality matches. However, at the public library, some patrons may even dispute the worth of the electronic catalog. Patrons who are not comfortable with computers see the electronic catalog as an impediment to access rather than a facilitator. Obviously, this is not reason enough to consider eliminating the electronic catalog and reverting to cards. Rather, public librarians should recognize this problem and try to seize any available opportunities for instruction in the use of the electronic catalog. During instruction, patrons should begin to see some clear advantages of the electronic format.

READY REFERENCE SOURCES

Ready references questions, or queries for brief, factual information, are common in most libraries and are acknowledged to be especially frequent in public libraries.[6] It is generally agreed that some ready reference questions are answered more quickly with traditional paper reference sources than with electronic sources. In some areas this remains true; however, the continual evolution of electronic resources and the continued development and improvement of the interfaces to those sources will positively impact their overall usability in the ready reference realm.

Directories, a common ready reference tool, provide examples of both superior paper and superior electronic sources. It is difficult for an electronic source to match the speed and ease of locating a listing in the current local telephone directory, the paper copy of which is often shelved within easy reach of the reference librarian. Similarly, Polk City Directories provide quick and easy access to significant information about local residents and businesses. Polk City Directories are now available electronically but, often due to budget constraints, many public libraries opt for the paper format. Additionally, when retained, the print copy provides excellent historical information about the area. Due to continual updates, this historical perspective is unavailable from electronic sources. If the directory request is not for local information, the usability of paper sources decreases significantly. Maintaining a collection of paper telephone directories for the United States was a longstanding goal of many public library reference services. However, this endeavor was often fraught with difficulty. It was next to impossible to have complete coverage; directories were expensive; they took up an incredible amount of space, and maintaining currency was a constant battle. Online directory sources overcome many of these difficulties and thus allow superior access to directory information. Both fee and free Web-based directory sources are available. While free Web sources may be adequate for the needs of most patrons, the increased access points of fee-based sources, such as Reference USA (http://www. referenceusa.com/), establish them as superior; thus they should be considered for selection.

Maps and mapping sources, too, have excellent resources in both paper and electronic formats. Traditional atlases, particularly due to their size, are often easier and clearer to use in the paper format. Mapping sources, however, such as those freely available from Yahoo! Maps (http://maps.yahoo.com/) and MapQuest (http://www.mapquest.com/) or, for a fee from Microsoft Streets & Trips (http://www.microsoft. com/streets/default.asp), are not available in any other format and therefore must be used electronically. These sources, which provide users the ability to map any United States address and to obtain driving directions, are a wonderful addition to the standard geographical sources. Far simpler than attempting to map a route with only an atlas, these sources facilitate travel planning and research for both the librarian and patron. It must be noted that these sources, particularly the free versions, have been found to have some inconsistencies. It is wise to counsel patrons to consult more than one mapping service and then compare the proposed routes. Comparing the proposed routes to a paper atlas from a reputable publisher is also wise.

There is always demand in public libraries for general dictionaries, quotation books, and thesauri. Some quality free Web dictionaries do exist, such as that available from Merriam Webster (http://www.m-w. com/). However, it must be noted, that only the 10th edition of Merriam Webster's Collegiate Dictionary is available free of charge at this time. Librarians should use caution when using such sources on the Web. Many of the Web products that are currently available for free may not be of the highest quality. They may, instead, be outdated editions of previously published paper sources that are no longer under copyright and have now been digitized and posted to the Web. Although this does not mean that all of the information posted is incorrect, it does imply that the information may be antiquated and incomplete.

Automotive repair sources, such as the Chilton's and Mitchell Manuals, are incredibly popular and well-used items in any public library reference collection. Unfortunately, these books are somewhat complicated to use, large and unwieldy in format, and have a tendency to lose pages over time due to pilfering by users unwilling to make photocopies. The electronic alternatives now available from Chilton's (http://www.chiltonsonline.com/) and ALLDATA (http://www.alldata.com/) are definitely worth public library evaluation. Increased access points, ease of preservation, and possibilities for remote access are some of the many positive considerations. The major drawback of these sources, at this point, is the cost of subscription.

Biographical inquiries, particularly about celebrities, are regularly made at the reference desks of public libraries. Traditional paper sources such as *Who's Who in America*, *Current Biography*, and *Contemporary Authors* are excellent resources for such queries. Gale has compiled these and many other valuable biographical resources into an online database called Biography Resource Center (http://www.galegroup.com/BiographyRC/). This excellent database, produced and maintained by a reputable publisher, indexes biographical sources and often links to the full text of the articles. Various search strategies are supported, thus significantly increasing the access points provided by the paper sources. Unfortunately, this database, which is an incredible resource for public libraries, requires a subscription and may be too expensive for some. Libraries should investigate the option of gaining access to this source through a consortial agreement. A free Web source of fairly reliable, if brief, biographical information does exist at http://www.biography.com; A&E maintains this site in association with their Biography television series. Although the depth of coverage cannot compare to Biography Resource Center, this free site does provide adequate coverage, especially for current celebrities.

RESEARCH RESOURCES

The public library collection is not designed to meet the demands of academic research. However, many students turn to the public library for assistance. Whether it is out of familiarity or convenience, students from grammar school through college arrive at the public library looking for sources that may be, strictly speaking, beyond the scope of the public library. It would be impractical for a public library to attempt to maintain a large collection of scholarly and research journals. However, in an effort to meet the needs posed by student researchers, public libraries should consider subscribing to an electronic general periodical index. An electronic periodical index has a number of advantages over a similar item in paper. In addition to increased access points and the ability to search multiple years concurrently, currency of the electronic sources is far superior. In addition many of the electronic indexes provide or link to the abstract or the full text of the articles. A Web accessible database of full-text articles, that covers both popular and scholarly topics, greatly expands and enhances the coverage and scope of the average public library collection. These databases are available from such vendors as Gale, EBSCO, and ProQuest. In addition to adding valuable content to the collection, such databases greatly facilitate access to the necessary articles. Although these general databases alone are not sufficient for the more thorough needs of true academic research, they meet and exceed the needs of many student researchers.

Also, such general periodical databases serve far more users than just student researchers. They provide access to ultra current information that may not yet be covered by any monographic sources in the library's collection. Likewise, they provide current information that can update the information available in the library's collection in more traditional sources. Current information about businesses, companies, health, medical treatment, and consumer guidance, to name just a few areas, is readily available to patrons via such databases.

In an effort to meet the general information needs of public library users and to address the basic research needs of younger students, public libraries should investigate electronic encyclopedia sources. Electronic encyclopedia sources often provide valuable enhancements to which the print versions cannot compare. The inclusion of multimedia and links to additional resources not only improves the content of the source, but also makes the source highly appealing to younger, computer savvy users. While some reputable encyclopedia information is available for free on the Web from Britannica Concise (http://www. britannica.com/) and Encarta (http://encarta.msn.com/), the value of an online encyclopedia subscription should not be overlooked. Many encyclopedia vendors also offer subject and age specific products. Public libraries are wise to evaluate all products to determine which most closely match the needs of their users. Vendors may also offer reduced pricing for libraries that subscribe to multiple resources.

General periodical databases and encyclopedias such as those described above are incredibly valuable to the patrons of public libraries and significantly expand the scope of a public library's collection. Unfortunately, they also require a significant financial commitment. This commitment may put them outside the grasp of many public libraries. The worth of these sources should prompt public libraries to actively investigate alternative means of access. An exciting and effective means of access for many public libraries comes in the form of consortial agreements. Consortia may be at the state, regional or local level, or may be defined by library type. Multiple libraries, by joining together, may be able to afford more resources than any of them could separately. Consortia are also often offered discounts from vendors due to their "bulk buying" power. The INSPIRE project (http://www.inspire.net/) in Indiana and the POWER Library (http://www.powerlibrary.net/) in Pennsylvania are excellent examples of increased access provided by library consortium.

FREE WEB SOURCES

Reputable publishers, such as universities, non-profit organizations, and governments produce and maintain valuable Web resources, and often make them available to the public for free. These Web sites usually provide easier and far timelier access to requested information. Federal and state governments make many frequently requested items, such as tax forms and legal codes, readily available via their Web sites.

The federal government maintains many excellent and freely available Web-based databases. The government supports databases that cover government, legal, educational, agricultural, and medical topics, to name just a few. The content from these databases is often repackaged and the interface enhanced before being sold by for profit database vendors. The original data with the government interface is generally available without charge.

Public libraries regularly field requests for legal forms and often have a substantial number of "do it yourself" legal form books and guides in their paper reference collections. Patrons often assume that a similar number of quality legal forms will also be available for free on the Web. At this point, this is not the case. Some legal forms are available online, but many sites charge a fee to access and print the forms. Correct forms can also be difficult to locate and problems, such as finding the right topic but for the wrong geographic location and vice versa, are regularly encountered. Gradually, forms are becoming available for free online, generally due to the efforts of state governments. The forms that have been posted to the Indiana Supreme Court Self-Help Legal Center (http://www.in.gov/judiciary/selfservice/index.html) are an excellent example of this evolving access.

Statistical information, popular in public libraries with students and trivia buffs alike, is also available on the Web, at no cost, from the U.S. government. Census information is easily located and, often, is ready to be manipulated by the user to quickly determine similarities and differences in the population. Statistical Abstract of the United States (http://www.census.gov/prod/www/statistical-abstract-us.html), a standard ready reference source in paper, is available free on the Web. However, browsing this source in paper is, at this juncture, considerably easier than browsing the source online.

Several excellent geographic sources are provided free of charge on the Web from the United States government. The depth of coverage for U.S. place names provided by the USGS Geographic Names Information System (http://geonames.usgs.gov/gnishome.html) is astounding, as is the level of information freely available on foreign countries from the CIA World Factbook (http://www.cia.gov/cia/publications/factbook/index.html). The Columbia Gazetteer of the World (http://www.columbiagazetteer.org/), a respected resource for geography research and reference, has an excellent Web version. Unfortunately, the price of this product may put it beyond the reach of many public libraries.

Career research, a popular topic in public libraries, has been truly enhanced by the development of electronic sources. The Occupational Outlook Handbook (http://www.bls.gov/oco/home.htm), long a standard at every reference desk for job hunters and students with career research projects alike, is freely accessible from the Bureau of Labor Statistics home page. Classified ads from local and distant newspapers are often easily accessed and used free of charge via newspaper Web sites. Job hunters and prospective employers can also access large job databases to search various fields or geographic areas concurrently.

Public libraries have traditionally provided access to expensive financial research tools such as Value Line and Morningstar. While such information is available online, it is not available without a subscription. There are also some Web sites that freely provide a limited amount of company and financial information. Yahoo! Financial (http://finance.yahoo.com) is just one example of a site that provides direct links to company information and free, if slightly delayed, stock quotes. Obviously, such free sites are not a substitute for the analysis provided by the specialized publications. However, the quick access to current information is a valuable addition to the financial resources of any public library.

Genealogists and genealogy queries are rife in public libraries. Traditionally, many of the resources needed by genealogists were available only in paper or microfilm and only in local history archival collections. The Web has had a significant impact on genealogy research; not only are many traditional resources now available in digital formats from libraries and database vendors, but amateur historians and genealogist are also publishing their findings to the Web. Excellent and reliable resources are available for free from such genealogy experts as The Church of Jesus Christ of the Latter-Day Saints (http://www.familysearch.org/), and for a fee via such databases as HeritageQuest from ProQuest (http://www.heritagequest.com/) and AncestryPlus from Gale (http://www.gale.ancestry.com/). Quality free resources are often available from the independently published Web sites of amateurs; however, independently published sites require more thorough evaluation due to the lack of editorial review.

LIBRARY CREATED RESOURCES

Rather than rely solely on electronic resources produced outside the library, public libraries would be wise to consider the creation of their own Web accessible sources, particularly in the area of local history. As more and more information becomes available to patrons remotely, libraries should consider what parts of their collections are truly unique. Many public libraries maintain large local history, genealogy, and archival collections. The content of these collections is often unavailable anywhere else. It stands to reason that such valuable material would be in regular demand. However, the very uniqueness that encourages demand may also limit availability. Fragile and rare archival materials often have restricted use and are not available to remote patrons via interlibrary loan. The advent of the digital age can significantly loosen these restrictions.

Proactive public libraries should work to digitize their valuable local history resources and then make them accessible remotely via the Web. This process concurrently preserves and makes available the items. Digitization ensures that a high-quality copy will be available for posterity and enhances the survival chances of the original. Use of the original can be severely limited because a high-quality surrogate is available to researchers. The use of the digital surrogate by both local and remote patrons can be encouraged and facilitated by the library. Digitization makes it possible for public libraries to share their local history collections via their Web sites. Although small libraries may be concerned that such digitization projects are beyond their means, many grants are available to help supplement the costs of the process. Additionally, software that is already available in many libraries, such as Microsoft Access and FrontPage, can be used to organize and post such resources to library Web sites.

CONCLUSION

In depth discussion supports and validates the obvious; combined use of print and electronic reference sources is both relevant and necessary in public libraries. It is a "mistake . . . to assume the need for information is finite and that it can be fully satisfied in any single medium."[7] There are pros and cons to each format. Librarians must carefully evaluate the needs of their patrons and determine which sources, regardless of format, are most appropriate to fill those needs. It is foolish to assume that online sources are on the verge of replacing all traditional reference sources; however, it is also foolish to deny the importance of the electronic format. Electronic sources are constantly evolving; therefore, this issue is and will remain in flux. Ongoing re-evaluation of sources, their available formats, and the needs of patrons is necessary if public libraries are to maintain useful collections. It must be stressed that electronic resources, particularly the Web, have raised the expectations of patrons. Libraries and librarians must grapple with the issue of "how to bring the library to where the users are rather than how to bring the users to the library"[8] if they hope to remain relevant in the future.

REFERENCES

1. Anne G. Lipow, *Serving the Remote User: Reference Service in the Digital Environment*, January 1999, http://www.csu.edu.au/special/online99/proceedings99/200. htm (July 12, 2003) Keynote Address.

2. William A. Katz, *Introduction to Reference Work: Volume II, Reference Services and Reference Processes*, 8th ed. (Boston: McGraw Hill, 2002), 130-131.

3. Kathleen M. Kluegel, "Electronic Resources for Reference," in *Reference and Information Services: An Introduction*, 3rd ed. edited by Richard E. Bopp and Linda C. Smith (Englewood, Colorado: Libraries Unlimited, 2001), 119.

4. Karen G. Schneider, "Creating a Yahoo! with values," *Library Journal: Net Connect* 127, i.12 (2002): 37.

5. Michael Rogers, "Proxy Servers in Wide Use," *Library Journal: Net Connect* 126, i.1 (2001): 7.

6. Katz, 277.

7. Kathy Niemeier, "The Medium Must Match the Message," *The Reference Librarian* 15 (Fall 1986): 217-23, quoted in Ken Winter, "From Wood Pulp to the Web: The Online Evolution," American Libraries 31, i. 5 (2000): 70.

8. Anne G. Lipow, *Are you ready for real-time remote reference? New question-handling skills and library policies needed to move the desk (and you) to the web.* Paper presented as part of the Reference Work Session at the annual conference of the International Federation of Library Associations and Institutions, Boston, MA, August 16-25, 2001.

Digital versus Print:
The Current State of Reference Affairs
in School Libraries

D. Jackson Maxwell

SUMMARY. This article examines the current state of digital versus print reference collections in school libraries. Issues addressed include an overview of adoption practices, acceptance and use of digital materials, and implications for the future. The article compares findings from multiple sources to provide an in-depth examination and understanding of the qualities and characteristics that school libraries share. The sources include current literature, research findings, and the observations and experiences of an information specialist in the role of participate observer. Survey and analysis of this data will provide a triangulation of information that will form the basis of the study. *[Article copies available for a fee from The Haworth Document Delivery Service: 1-800-HAWORTH. E-mail address: <docdelivery@haworthpress.com> Website: <http://www.HaworthPress.com> © 2005 by The Haworth Press, Inc. All rights reserved.]*

KEYWORDS. Reference, reference books, digital resources, electronic resources, library, digital libraries and school libraries

D. Jackson Maxwell is Information Specialist and Educational Consultant, Memphis City Schools in Memphis, TN (E-mail: maxwellj01@k12tn.net).

[Haworth co-indexing entry note]: "Digital versus Print: The Current State of Reference Affairs in School Libraries." Maxwell, D. Jackson. Co-published simultaneously in *The Reference Librarian* (The Haworth Information Press, an imprint of The Haworth Press, Inc.) No. 91/92, 2005, pp. 53-68; and: *The Reference Collection: From the Shelf to the Web* (ed: William J. Frost) The Haworth Information Press, an imprint of The Haworth Press, Inc., 2005, pp. 53-68. Single or multiple copies of this article are available for a fee from The Haworth Document Delivery Service [1-800-HAWORTH, 9:00 a.m. - 5:00 p.m. (EST). E-mail address: docdelivery@haworthpress.com].

doi:10.1300/J120v44n91_05

THE DIGITAL REVOLUTION

It took radio 40 years and television 13 years to reach an audience of 50 million in the United States, the Internet accomplished this feat in just 4 years.[1] Each new generation of information delivery systems disperses and is adopted by the populace in an ever-shorter space of time. The rapid acceleration in the development and adoption of digitally based information resources by business and the general public has left school libraries scrambling to catch up.

INTRODUCTION

I have been intimately involved with libraries and education for over twenty years. I have served as a teacher, professor, librarian, researcher, writer, and educational consultant. During this time I have been a part of the digital revolution–from automation to online searching to virtual librarianship. It has been my observation that school systems are some of the last organizations to adopt new technologies. School libraries, as a part of these organizations, are no exception. Through my experience and research, I have come to realize that school libraries loom as one of the profession's last, great challenges in committing and converting to digitization and digital resources.

There are a number of reasons for this situation that include budgetary factors, collection development priorities, availability of technology, obsolescence concerns, administrators, and the librarians themselves. As a result, the acceptance and use of digital technologies have been slow to be adopted and fully implemented. Unless changes are made soon, the problem will only get worse as the delivery of reference information increasingly becomes tied to technology.[2] However, to fully understand the reasons behind this "digital lag" one must closely examine the larger educational picture.

This qualitative study provides insight into the use of digital versus print resources in school libraries. The article compares findings from multiple sources to provide an in-depth examination and understanding of the qualities and characteristics that school libraries share.[3] The sources include current literature, research findings, and the observations and experiences of an information specialist in the role of participate observer.[4] Survey and analysis of this data will provide a triangulation of information that will form the basis of the study.[5,6]

CURRENT SCHOOL LIBRARY COLLECTIONS

While library core reference collections remain primarily print based, digital resources are beginning to become available in most school libraries.[7] This transformation has been made possible by a hodge-podge of generally uncoordinated local, state, and federal initiatives.

A Brief History

Local support for building digitally based school libraries is as diverse as there are school districts in the nation. In some instances, school boards have provided guidance and funding for system-wide plans to digitize. In other cases, individual librarians and schools have led in the digitization drive through the use of operating funds, grants, fundraisers, corporate sponsorships, and community partners in developing a digital collection.[8]

Statewide programs have helped schools by creating a base for establishing electronic, networked libraries.[9,10,11,12] Increasingly, states are taking the lead in getting all of their schools and libraries online. For example, Tennessee, through the ConnecTEN initiative, provided Internet connections for every public school in the state via a single network.[13] This initiative placed the initial network connection in the library and from there branched out to classrooms and the rest of the school.

Federal programs such as Goals 2000 and similar legislation have provided the impetus for moving school libraries toward digitization through the promotion of technology in schools.[14,15] Funds from these programs can provide the rudimentary equipment and tools to make digitization of reference collections possible. However, the extent to which this has occurred depends on individual states, districts, and schools and how they have chosen to take advantage of these opportunities.

Print Resources

School libraries rely heavily on print materials for both their shelf and reference collections. Due to the traditional design of these libraries, print-based materials both reference and otherwise remain an essential part of smaller libraries' collections.[16] The following is an overview of print-based reference materials found in school libraries and their use.

Core school library reference collections, like other small library collections, include encyclopedias, dictionaries, first fact books, atlases, almanacs and materials in a similar vein that provide broad overviews or quick assistance in locating often requested facts and information.[16] Many of these books come in multi-volume sets (e.g., encyclopedias) and/or must be updated every few years (e.g., almanacs). Reference books are kept in a special section of the library and are usually short-term or non-circulating–their use is primarily reserved for in the library.

Other primary sources include periodicals. These collections consist of both current and back issues. Like the core reference collection, the multiple copies allow a large number of students to peruse copies simultaneously. Additionally, multiple copies allow students to each have individual copies to serendipitously discover ideas and facts for research assignments through browsing.[17]

Digital Resources

According to The Digital Library Foundation,[18] digital libraries are "organizations that provide the resources, including the specialized staff, to select, structure, offer intellectual access to, interpret, preserve the integrity of, and ensure the persistence over time of collections of digital works so that they readily and economically are available for use by a defined community." School libraries are in the process of digitizing and are gaining access to a plethora of digital equipment and resources. However, each school library is subject to a number of factors both within and outside of the librarian's control. The following is an overview of digital devices that are widely in use for referencing and information retrieval in school libraries.

The Internet has provided educators with access to a wealth of reference sources never before available in the school library. Educational Web sites like the Community Learning Network (http://www.cln.org), Scholastic (http://teacher.scholastic.com), and enumerable others supply students and teachers with ready access to information and reference sources on virtually any topic. For example, rather than search the print reference and professional collections to prepare a lesson, teachers can go to an online site like LessonPlanZ (http://lessonplanz.com). Here educators find ready made lesson plans on virtually any subject that are specially designed for their content area and grade level. Additionally, the Internet allows students and teachers to access nontraditional reference sources such as full-text manuscripts like those found in Project Gutenberg (http://www.promo.net/pg/) that include titles not found in the library's print collection. E-mail allows students unprecedented access to primary information sources such as professionals in many fields through "ask-an-expert" sites (e.g., http://www.eduref.org; http://www.ask.com; or http://www.askanexpert.com). In these ways, the Internet and e-mail have helped to erase some of the geographic isolation of school libraries and librarians.[19] One draw back is that, although the Internet and e-mail are excellent resources, the onus for instruction on identifying reliable and valid reference materials has fallen even more heavily on librarians.

A growing number of states and school systems have created or subscribe to electronic libraries.[20,21] Electronic libraries bundle together a variety of digital resources such as online magazines, journals, serials, newspapers, reference sources and other literature that can be reached from a single access point or portal.[22] An advantage of electronic libraries is that the package cost is discounted (by as much as 95%) and often assumed by the state or school district rather than by a single entity.[23] Thus, distribution and access charges to these materials are less expensive than print equivalents.[24] For example, the Tennessee Electronic Library (http://www.state.tn.us/sos/statelib/tel/) makes thousands of educational periodicals, reference sources, and primary documents available via the Internet to school libraries. EBSCOhost is one of the largest private subscription services. This service allows access to indexes and abstracts of nearly 3,000 magazines with full-text access to about 1,200 and includes flexible searching techniques with a number of options to download information.

CD-ROMs have impacted school library reference collections. CD-ROM versions of encyclopedias, dictionaries, thesauruses, first facts, atlases, and almanacs are readily becoming accepted substitutes for print versions. One reason for this is that the CD-ROM versions of these reference standards are typically available for a fraction of the cost of print versions. Additionally, site licenses allow these materials to be accessed through any computer on the school network. Like the Internet, students prefer the flexibility of keyword searching as offered by CD-ROMs.[25] Peripherals such as scanners, digital copiers, digital cameras, and laser printers have made the transfer of this information quicker, cleaner, and more accurate than previous transcription methods allowing librarians to provide timely responses to reference requests.

Print versus Digital Resources

Print and digital resources each have their own unique advantages and disadvantages.[26] Print items are stand alone, not requiring special equipment nor training on the equipment to use.[27] Print resources have the advantages of browsability (beyond keyword searching), readability, and portability.[28] Computer-based technology exponentially increases school libraries' access to reference materials. Digital reference materials are usually flexible to use allowing for multiple searching options, networking schemes, and ease of accessing.

Depending on the school library policy, print reference materials can be checked out and taken to the classroom or home overnight for the students to use at their leisure. This process is more complicated for digitally based reference materials that require the acquisition of specific rights that permit circulation. Although digital resources such as CD-ROMs provide cleaner and crisper images than their paper counterparts, the user must possess the necessary equipment to view these digitally based resources. On the other hand, while many digitally based reference tools (e.g., Web sites) can be easily updated, this is not the nature of print materials.[29]

One unresolved digital issue is with the Internet in school libraries and the debate over free and unrestricted access versus filtering "inappropriate" sites.[30] Filtering has proven to be an ongoing issue for electronic resources.[31, 32] For example, a school librarian can easily peruse a print-based reference source to check for appropriateness based on age, comprehension, and reading level. Determining these traits for online sites which often have many links can be much more difficult. While school librarians can set predetermined search paths to avoid certain sites, this inhibits browsing, spontaneity, and discovery learning. School systems that employ blanket filtering of Internet connections risk blocking user access to many needed and acceptable reference sources. This debate has slowed the digitization of school library collections. Federal, state and local judicial and administrative bodies under the dictates of loco parentis and the Children's Internet Protection Act (CIPA) are in the process of resolving this conflict.[33,34]

At a time of shrinking educational budgets, online- and digitally-based resources can be an inexpensive means to expand and update school library reference collections. Subscribing to electronic databases is less expensive than purchasing the same material in print.[35,36] Some print reference items are available in full-text format and for free on the Internet.[37] In addition to less cost per title, less staff time is involved in providing these, they require less space, and are more flexible to access.[38] Some library systems have created their own portals of bundled resources of free online information and reference sources that clients can access through a single point.[39,40] Despite these digital advantages,

Quandt's[41] research indicates that due to publisher and user preferences, print copies of scholarly materials will continue to be available even as most of these materials appear online.

MITIGATING FACTORS

Beyond the physical qualities of print and digital reference materials, school libraries for the foreseeable future will remain largely print based due to a number of more subjective reasons. These reasons include librarians' level of expertise with technology, availability of technology, collection development priorities, the principal factor, change theory, and financial concerns on all levels.

School Librarians

School librarianship is a solitary practice. School librarians are isolated physically and often philosophically from their peers. The majority of school libraries are managed by a single library professional, who is nominally responsible to a school principal and an administrator at the board of education. Many decisions, such as converting print to digital, are primarily at the discretion of the librarian.

Stafford and Serban[42] found that librarians operating in a digital reference environment needed to acquire a specific set of skills that include librarian/client interfacing skills, information technology skills, information retrieval skills, organizational and instruction skills, and knowledge of both print and digital reference resources. To attain the personal and technology skills, and for these to be accepted and implemented, appropriate training is critical.[43,44,45,46,47,48] Without training, few educators are able to master technology and Internet integration on their own let alone teach students to use them.[49,50] Moreover, Marcum[51] reports that the requirements of comprehending and performing professionally in this increasingly technology-based, interactive environment will remain a challenge for the foreseeable future. As the duties of school librarians evolve and change over time requiring new expertise (e.g., digitized reference services), training for librarians will need to remain available and be ongoing in nature.[52] School librarians must then provide hands-on instruction for students and faculty. This training should include the use of technology tools and search strategies in the school digital environments they are using.[53]

Two other factors impacting acceptance and use of the Internet and electronic resources are age and gender.[54] Library professionals are predominately female and aging.[55,56] According to the American Library Association, 92% of school librarians are female and 57% of all librarians were age 45 or older.[57] Research indicates that older females are less likely than their male peers and younger females to be familiar with and use computer-based technologies.[58,59,60,61,62] The combination of the prevailing gender and age composition of library professionals makes the likelihood of the acceptance and use of new technologies particularly acute. De Ruiter[63] found for educators to accept and use electronic resources, librarians need to demonstrate the value of the Internet, offer training in navigating and searching skills, and provide Web links to quality sites. In addition, for acceptance to occur, individuals must believe that the potential rewards for adoption outweigh the expected efforts required of adoption.[64] When these efforts are made, use of digital reference materials and accompanying equipment are increased.

Technology

The tools and technology required to make digital reference collections possible are expensive. Simonson and Thompson[65] found that no more than two or three students could use the same computer simultaneously without a depreciable loss of effectiveness. Providing adequate numbers of computers, Internet connections, CD-ROMs, DVD players, DVDs, peripherals (e.g., printers, scanners), information storage and backup, training, systems support, and maintenance all cost money.[66] When budget cutting becomes necessary, library funding often suffers and technology expenditures as a part of this budget are no exception.[67] Updates and expansions of available technology is often pushed back or cut. In addition to cost, conversion from print to digital can be a difficult and time consuming process requiring not only the librarian but the users as well to learn a whole new set of search and referencing skills.[68]

Even if technology is available, connectivity can be an issue. Moyo[69] stresses the need to have appropriate technological infrastructures to permit universal and equal access is key to the overall scenario. The age and capabilities of equipment can limit its practical abilities virtually assuring that every school library is at a different level of connectivity.[70] Each digital tool and resource has unique searching characteristics. Without proper training, clients may waste time learning how to operate, search, and connect to the reference resource they desire.[71] Finally, a single or extremely limited access points are not sufficient. School librarians and teachers need to have access to technology immediately when and where it is needed.[72,73]

Collection Development

Collection development priorities are another issue. In my experience, the needs of the students, faculty, and the community, accrediting institutions, and district and state mandates all demand expenditures meet specified requirements that may or may not include the conversion of print resources to their digital equivalents. For this to occur, school librarians need to make stakeholders aware of the importance of digital reference materials. As with developing any new collection, librarians should engage in strenuous lobbying efforts at all funding levels to ensure stable, long-term commitment to ensure digitization.[74]

Obsolescence is another collection development reality faced by school librarians.[75] In the past, librarians have spent large percentages of their budgets developing phonograph record, eight-track tape, filmstrip, videotape, videodisk, and floppy-disk collections only to see these "latest" technologies fade into obsolescence and then discarded. Not only did school libraries have to pay for the new technology-based collections but more importantly the equipment to run it all-the-while maintaining the digital files to provide a migration path when these technologies become obsolete.[76] These are reasons why some school librarians are reluctant or slow to commit to digitizing their reference collections. While CDs, CD-ROMs, and DVDs are the current technologies, there are always reports of a new technology (e.g., MP3) just over the horizon that will soon replace these. The cost of replacing whole sections of the library collection plus their operating equipment often leads librarians to select the print medium over digital.

The Principal Factor

The Lance, Welborn, and Hamilton-Pennell[77] study found that a key indicator of school achievement levels is dependent upon the condition and funding of the school library. The principal is usually the key person in determining how the school's financial pie is divided. How much money a school library has to create and expand digital reference collections is at the principal's discretion. The principal sets the tone for the school that in turn influences the direction the school takes and the materials it contains.[78] For example, programs such as Accelerated Reader (AR) dictate that a large percentage of the budget is committed to purchasing print materials that students can check out. Digitized reference materials do not fall into this category and therefore, under these conditions, are not an administrative priority.

Change Theory

Finally, change is often resisted and education is subject to this rule.[79,80] Librarians, teachers, and to a lesser degree students are more familiar with the print versions of reference materials, have grown accustomed to using them, and are often reluctant to embrace digital equivalents. To overcome resistance and to increase the use of digital resources, both advertising and integration of digital resources needs to be strengthened and stressed.[81]

To facilitate acceptance and use, school librarians need to introduce digital resources to users and demonstrate how these can be used in educational contexts. Converting to digital collections requires libraries to play a continuing role in helping people manage the new literacies of the Information Age in a context that respects the traditional literacies on which they were built.[82] Until digital reference sources are fully accepted, libraries may need to continue purchasing both digital and print versions to appease readers' preferences.[83]

CONCLUSION: LOOKING TOWARD THE FUTURE

The development, implementation, and use of digital resources by school libraries and librarians on a national level have been uneven.[84] However, eventual digitization of libraries and their reference collections on some level is inevitable. While for the foreseeable future both formats of reference materials will coexist, the goal for librarians will be to fully implement and integrate the new digital resources into routine school library service. In referencing, Jackson[85] indicates that librarians will need to continue "doing what they do best, integrating and synthesizing print, microform, and electronic sources by using memory, intuition, knowledge, and just plain persistence." In the end, fiscal considerations will most likely lead to the complete conversion of school library collections to electronically-based information systems. Once the equipment and infrastructure has been acquired and connected, updating and expanding reference collections using digital resources is less expensive than purchasing print equivalents.[86]

The current challenge for school librarians is to discern what are the best resources to answer any given reference inquiry.[87] Digitization, especially via the Internet, is beginning to decrease the isolation and develop interactive communities of even the most physically isolated librarians.[88] E-mail facilitates school librarians' communication with peers on all levels including seeking assistance in answering reference queries to how to begin the process of converting from print to digital collections.

Research is progressing on establishing digital reference collections and how they can be best utilized in servicing library clientele.[89,90] This information will be of increasing value as more school libraries adopt and integrate digital resources into their reference practice. Beyond this, library systems are beginning to offer live online, 24/7 reference services to their clients.[91,92] With schools and their partners already offering homework hotlines and extended tutoring, after-hours library reference service could easily become a reality. Borgman[93] states that computer and telecommunication networks are making physical visits to the library less necessary. In the future, students will be able to go online, e-mail or telephone a reference query and immediately gain access to library resources and information they need.

It was merely twenty years ago in the 1980s when most libraries were beginning to adopt their first generation computers for online and referencing services. From these humble first steps, electronic libraries have come a long way in a very short time. While a digital lag still exists between school libraries and other types of libraries, digitization of school library reference collections and the educational institutions that support them is just over the horizon. In spite of all the mitigating factors, digital reference collections and virtual school libraries will become a reality in our time.

REFERENCES

1. B. Hambly, "Numbers," *Time*, (1998): 152, no. 4, 19.

2. J. Kutzik, "It's EGATS All Over Again! Behind the Scenery in Reference Services," Library Mosaics, (2003): 14, no. 2, 14-16.

3. R. K. Yin, *Case Study Research: Design and Methods* (Newbury Park, CA: Sage, 1994).

4. M. Zelditch, "Some Methodological Problems of Field Studies," *American Journal of Sociology*, (1962): 67, no. 5, 566-576.

5. I. Seidman, *Interviewing as Qualitative Research: A Guide for Researchers in Education and the Social Sciences* (New York, NY: Teachers College, 1991).

6. V. L. Banyard, & K. E. Miller, "The Powerful Potential of Qualitative Research for Community Psychology," *American Journal of Community Psychology*, (1998): 26, no. 4, 485-505.

7. C. L. Borgman, "The Invisible Library: Paradox of the Global Information Infrastructure," *Library Trends*, (2003): 51, no. 4, 652-674.

8. L. Kniffel, "Gates Expands Access Mission during Alabama Visit," *American Libraries*, (1998): 20, no. 4, 16-19.

9. S. J. Farmer, "NetDay Links Schools and Volunteers to Information Highway," *Technology Connection*, (1996): 26, no. 5, 39-40.

10. E. Niendorf, "ConnecTEN Builds Roads for Schools to Information," *Nashville Business Journal*, (1996): 12, no. 13, 37, 43.

11. C. Watkins, "Chapter Report: Take the Tele- out of Communications," *American Libraries*, (1997): 28, no. 11, 8.

12. D. J. Maxwell, & L. DeMeulle, "The ConnecTEN Initiative: A Comparative Study of Policy Intent and Teacher Perception," *Tennessee Education*, (2000/2001): 30/31, nos. 2/1, 5-16.

13. D. J. Maxwell, "ConnecTEN Training for Teachers: A Cautionary Tale Describing a Statewide Technology Initiative," *Tennessee Education*, (1999/2000): 29/30, nos. 2/1, 23-31.

14. *Goals 2000: Educate America Act*, Public Law H. R. 1804, 103rd Cong. 2nd Sess. (1994). Online: http://www.ed.gov/legislation/Goals2000/TheAct/intro.html.

15. G. Flagg, "ALA News: Sharp Increase in Internet Use at Public Libraries," *American Libraries*, (1998): 29, no. 1, 11,15.

16. B. Kelling, C. Moirai, & W. Reister, "A Core Reference Collection for a Small Public Library," *Tennessee Librarian*, (2002): 53, no. 3, 19-25.

17. S. Wiegand, "Incorporating Electronic Products into the Acquisitions Workflow in a Small College Library," *Library Collections, Acquisitions, & Technical Services*, (2002): 26, no. 4, 363-366.

18. *Digital Library Foundation*, "A Working Definition," (2003). Online: http://www.diglib.org.

19. A. Goulding, "Online Communication: For Good or Evil?" *Journal of Librarianship and Information Service*, (2002): 34, no. 4, 183-185.

20. C. H. Candee, "The California Digital Library and the eScholarship Program," *Journal of Library Administration*, (2001): 35, (1/2), 37-59.

21. L. Moyo, "Collections on the Web: Some Access and Navigation Issues," *Library Collections, Acquisitions, & Technical Services*, (2002): 26, no. 1, 47-59.

22. M. Goldner, "Go portal," *Library Hi-Tech News*, (2003): 20, no. 1, 24-26.

23. L. Moyo, "Collections on the Web: Some Access and Navigation Issues," *Library Collections, Acquisitions, & Technical Services*, (2002): 26, no. 1, 47-59.

24. R. E. Quandt, "Scholarly Materials: Paper or Digital?" *Library Trends*, (2003): 51, no. 3, 349-375.

25. A. K. Shenton, & P. Dixon, "Models of Young People's Information Seeking," *Journal of Librarianship and Information Science*, (2003): 35, no. 1, 5-22.

26. E. Bryant, A. Kim, R. Miller & N. Ward, "A Different Sort of Publishing," *Library Journal*, (2002): 127, no.19, 8-12.

27. B. Kelling, C. Moirai, & W. Reister, "A Core Reference Collection for a Small Public Library," *Tennessee Librarian*, (2002): 53, no. 3, 19-25.

28. S. Wiegand, "Incorporating Electronic Products into the Acquisitions Workflow in a Small College Library," *Library Collections, Acquisitions, & Technical Services*, (2002): 26, no. 4, 363-366.

29. E. Bryant, A. Kim, R. Miller & N. Ward, "A Different Sort of Publishing," *Library Journal*, (2002): 127, no. 19, 8-12.

30. J. Barry, "Where the Appropriate Things Are: The Rehabilitation of Internet Filters in Libraries," *Tennessee Librarian*, (2002): 51, no. 1, 4-25.

31. J. Grubb & A. Bond, "Internet Filtering: A Pilot Study of Tennessee Public Librarians' Attitudes," *Tennessee Librarian*, (1999): 50, no. 4, 26-39.

32. S. B. Hagloch, "To Filter or Not: Internet Access in Ohio," *Library Journal*, (1999): 120, no. 7, 50-51.

33. J. Grubb & A. Bond, "Internet Filtering: A Pilot Study of Tennessee Public Librarians' Attitudes," *Tennessee Librarian*, (1999): 50, no. 4, 26-39.

34. B. Goldberg, "Supreme Court Upholds CIPA," *American Libraries*, (2003): 34, no. 7, 12-14.

35. L. Moyo, "Collections on the Web: Some Access and Navigation Issues," *Library Collections, Acquisitions, & Technical Services*, (2002): 26, no. 1, 47-59.

36. L. Aiguo, "Calis: Acquiring Electronic Resources," *Library Collections, Acquisitions, & Technical Services*, (2003): 27, no. 2, 261-267.

37. B. Kelling, C. Moirai, & W. Reister, "A Core Reference Collection for a Small Public Library," *Tennessee Librarian*, (2002): 53, no. 3, 19-25.

38. D. W. King, P. B. Boyce, C. H. Montgomery & C. Tenopir, "Library Economic Metrics: Examples of the Comparison of Electronic and Print Journal Collections and Collection Services," *Library Trends*, (2003): 51, no. 3, 376-400.

39. M. Goldner, "Go portal," *Library Hi-Tech News*, (2003): 20, no. 1, 24-26.

40. M. Rowlatt, & M. Allcock, "Delivering Joined-up Access to Local and National Information in the United Kingdom," *Library Hi-Tech News*, (2002): 19, no. 9, 10-11.

41. R. E. Quandt, "Scholarly Materials: Paper or Digital?" *Library Trends*, (2003): 51, no. 3, 349-375.

42. C. D. Stafford, & W. M. Serban, "Core Competencies: Recruiting, Training, and Evaluating in the Automated Reference Environment," *Journal of Library Administration*, (1990): 13, nos. 1/2, 81-97.

43. D. J. Maxwell, & L. DeMeulle, "The ConnecTEN Initiative: A Comparative Study of Policy Intent and Teacher Perception," *Tennessee Education*, (2000/2001): 30/31, nos. 2/1, 5-16.

44. J. Edwards, "CAI and Training Needs," In *Proceedings of the National Conference on Professional Development and Educational Technology* (Washington, DC: Information Dynamics, 1980).

45. M. Gallo & P. Horton, "Assessing the Effect on High School Teachers of Direct and Unrestricted Access to the Internet: A Case Study of East Central Florida High School," *Educational Technology Research and Development*, (1994): 42, no. 4, 17-39.

46. M. Stuckey, "Schools Working Together–It Just Makes Sense," *Momentum*, (1995): 26, no. 4, 8-10.

47. L. Knapp, & A. Glenn, *Restructuring Schools with Technology* (Boston: Allyn & Bacon, 1996).

48. M. Simonson, & A. Thompson, *Educational Computing Foundations* (3rd ed.) (Upper Saddle Creek, NJ: Merrill/Prentice Hall, 1997).

49. J. Werner, "Reaching Out to the World: Training Teachers to Integrate Telecommunications into Special Education Classrooms," In *Proceedings of the 14th Annual National Conference of the American Council on Rural Special Education*, (1994). Online: ERIC Document Reproduction Service No. ED 369 595.

50. L. Buchanan, "Planning the Multimedia Classroom," *MultiMedia Schools*, (1996): 3, no. 4, 17-21.

51. J. W. Marcum, "Rethinking Information Literacy," *The Library Quarterly*, (2002): 72, no. 1, 1-26.

52. K. L. Holloway, "Developing Core and Mastery-level Competencies for Librarians," *Library Administration & Management*, (2003): 17, no. 2, 94-98.

53. N. H. Seamans, "Student Perceptions of Information Literacy: Insights for Librarians," *Reference Services Review*, (2002): 30, no. 2, 112-123.

54. D. J. Maxwell, "Technology and Inequality within the United States School Systems," *Journal of Educational Thought*, (2000): 34, no. 1, 43-57.

55. E. Kerslake, "Women and Librarianship: A Review Article," *Journal of Librarianship and Information Science*, (2002): 34, no. 1, 53-56.

56. M. J. Lynch, "Reaching 65: Lots of Librarians Will Be There Soon," *American Libraries*, (2002): 33, no. 3, 55-56.

57. *American Library Association*, "Library Profession Faces Shortage of Librarians," (2003). Online: http://www.ala.org/ala/pio/piopresskits/recruitpresskit/libraryprofession.htm.

58. E. Gardner, "Human-oriented Implementation Cures Phobia, *Data Management*, (1985): 46, 29-32.

59. R. Corston & A. M. Colman, "Gender and Social Facilitation Effects on Computer Competence and Attitudes Toward Computers," *Journal of Educational Computing Research*, (1996): 14, no. 2, 171-183.

60. G. George, R. Sleuth & C. G. Pearce, "Technology-assisted Instruction and Instructor Cyberphobia: Recognizing the Ways to Effect Change," *Education*, (1996): 116, no. 4, 604-608.

61. C. Fiore, "Awaking the Tech Bug in Girls," *Learning and Leading with Technology*, (1999): 26, no. 5, 10-17.

62. A. Hewitson, "Use and Awareness of Electronic Information Services by Academic Staff at Leeds Metropolitan University–A Qualitative Study," *Journal of Librarianship and Information Science*, (2002): 34, no. 1, 43-52.

63. J. De Ruiter, "Aspects of Dealing with Digital Information: 'Mature' Novices on the Internet," *Library Trends*, (2002): 51, no. 2, 199-209.

64. E. M. Rogers, *Diffusion of Innovations* (New York: Free Press, 1992).

65. M. Simonson, & A. Thompson, *Educational Computing Foundations* (3rd ed.) (Upper Saddle Creek, NJ: Merrill/Prentice Hall, 1997).

66. A. Blau, "Access Isn't Enough," *American Libraries*, (2002): 33, no. 6, 50-52.

67. G. M. Eberhart, "Recession, 2003: More Cutbacks and Closures," *American Libraries*, (2003): 34, no. 7, 20-25.

68. S. Goddard, "Library Automation or Making Life Easier, the Hard Way," *Library Mosaics*, (2003): 14, no. 3, 17.

69. L. Moyo, "Collections on the Web: Some Access and Navigation Issues," *Library Collections, Acquisitions, & Technical Services*, (2002): 26, no. 1, 47-59.

70. A. Blau, "Access Isn't Enough," *American Libraries*, (2002): 33, no. 6, 50-52.

71. L. Aiguo, "Calis: Acquiring Electronic Resources," *Library Collections, Acquisitions, & Technical Services*, (2003): 27, no. 2, 261-267.

72. D. J. Maxwell, & L. DeMeulle, "The ConnecTEN Initiative: A Comparative Study of Policy Intent and Teacher Perception," *Tennessee Education*, (2000/2001): 30/31, nos. 2/1, 5-16.

73. M. Gallo & P. Horton, "Assessing the Effect on High School Teachers of Direct and Unrestricted Access to the Internet: A Case Study of East Central Florida High School," *Educational Technology Research and Development*, (1994): 42, no. 4, 17-39.

74. J. Dilevko & K. Dali, "The Challenge of Building Multilingual Collections in Canadian Public Libraries." *Library Resources & Technical Services*, (2002): 46, no. 4, 116-137.

75. D. Dillon, "Songs of the Dodo: Information Extinctions, Innovation, and Ecosystem Change," *Journal of Library Administration*, (2001), no. 3, 67-78.

76. B. Baruth, "Missing Pieces that Fill in the Academic Library Puzzle," *American Libraries*, (2002): 33, no. 6, 58-63.

77. K. C. Lance, L. Welborn & C. Hamilton-Pennell, *The Impact of School Library Media Centers on Academic Achievement* (Castle Rock, CO: Willow Research and Publishing, 1993).

78. P. Bayley, "The Reflective Principal: Back to Square One," *Principal*, (2000): 79, no, 3, 45-46.

79. M. Fullan, *Change Forces: Probing the Depth of Educational Reform* (Bristol, PA: Falmer Press, 1993).

80. C. P. Etheridge, D. Horgan, T. Valensky, M. L. Hall & L. Terrell, *Challenge to change: The Memphis Experience with School-based Decision Making* (Washington, DC: National Education Association, 1994).

81. L. Aiguo, "Calis: Acquiring Electronic Resources," *Library Collections, Acquisitions, & Technical Services*, (2003): 27, no. 2, 261-267.

82. A. Blau, "Access Isn't Enough," *American Libraries*, (2002): 33, no. 6, 50-52.

83. D. W. King, P. B. Boyce, C. H. Montgomery & C. Tenopir, "Library Economic Metrics: Examples of the Comparison of Electronic and Print Journal Collections and Collection Services," *Library Trends*, (2003): 51, no. 3, 376-400.

84. K. Calhoun, "From Information Gateway to Digital Library Management System: A Case Study," *Library Collections, Acquisitions, & Technical Services*, (2002): 26, no. 2, 141-150.

85. M. G. Jackson, "The Great Reference Debate Continued–With a Manifesto," *American Libraries*, (2003): 34, no. 5, 50-52; p. 52.

86. S. Kalyan, "Non-renewal of Print Journal Subscriptions that Duplicate Titles in Selected Electronic Databases: A Case Study," *Library Collections, Acquisitions, & Technical Services*, (2002): 26, no. 4, 409-421.

87. W. Fisher, "The Electronic Resources Librarian Position: A Public Services Phenomenon?" *Library Collections, Acquisitions, & Technical Services*, (2003): 27, no. 1, 3-17.

88. G. Burnett, "The Scattered Member of an Invisible Republic: Virtual Communities and Paul Ricoeur's Hermeneutics," *The Library Quarterly*, (2002): 72, no. 2, 155-178.

89. C. H. Candee, "The California Digital Library and the eScholarship Program," *Journal of Library Administration*, (2001): 35, (1/2), 37-59.

90. J. Pomerantz, S. Nicholson & R. D. Lankes, "Digital Reference Triage: Factors Influencing Question Routing and Assignment," *The Library Quarterly*, (2003): 73, no. 2, 103-120.

91. N. K. Maxwell, "Introduction to Live Online Reference," *Library Technology Reports*, (2002): 38, no. 4, 5-14.

92. J. V. Richardson, "The Future of Reference: The Intersection of Information Resources, Technology and Users," *Reference Services Review*, (2003): 31, no. 1, 43-45.

93. C. L. Borgman, "The Invisible Library: Paradox of the Global Information Infrastructure," *Library Trends*, (2003): 51, no. 4, 652-674.

Reference Publishing
in the Age of Also

John M. Morse

SUMMARY. Reference publishing is in an era of competing technologies: print and electronic. For large multivolume reference books, the transition from being primarily a print resource to being primarily electronic is well advanced, perhaps nearly complete. For many smaller reference books, such as dictionaries, thesauruses, and almanacs, the transition is less advanced; in fact, it seems likely that print and electronic editions of such works may coexist for years to come. There are good reasons for this to happen, but this situation also poses challenges to librarians, publishers, and patrons. This article reviews some of the aspects of this transitional era in terms of what has been learned so far and what may develop in the future. *[Article copies available for a fee from The Haworth Document Delivery Service: 1-800-HAWORTH. E-mail address: <docdelivery@haworthpress.com> Website: <http://www.HaworthPress.com> © 2005 by The Haworth Press, Inc. All rights reserved.]*

KEYWORDS. Dictionaries, reference works, online dictionaries, print technology, Merriam-Webster dictionaries

---

John M. Morse is President and Publisher, Merriam-Webster, Incorporated, 47 Federal Street, PO Box 281, Springfield, MA 01102 (E-mail: jmorse@merriam-webster.com).

[Haworth co-indexing entry note]: "Reference Publishing in the Age of Also." Morse, John M. Co-published simultaneously in *The Reference Librarian* (The Haworth Information Press, an imprint of The Haworth Press, Inc.) No. 91/92, 2005, pp. 69-81; and: *The Reference Collection: From the Shelf to the Web* (ed: William J. Frost) The Haworth Information Press, an imprint of The Haworth Press, Inc., 2005, pp. 69-81. Single or multiple copies of this article are available for a fee from The Haworth Document Delivery Service [1-800-HAWORTH, 9:00 a.m. - 5:00 p.m. (EST). E-mail address: docdelivery@haworthpress.com].

doi:10.1300/J120v44n91_06

INTRODUCTION

The next 10 to 15 years will be the age of "also." [W]e're going to have print, we're going to have books. We're going to have better magazines and more magazines; better newspapers and different newspapers. We're going to have TV and we're going to have satellite. We're going to have computers. We are going to have computers that are TV. We're going to have DVD. We're going to have lots of things. Will there be some falling outs? You bet. . . . But for the next 10 to 15 years we'll also have a bunch of things going on, all at the same time. And that's fine. There isn't a best answer for things, anymore. There's not a best way to have transportation. There's not a best way of communicating. There's not a best way for anything. There are just good ways.

–Richard Saul Wurman[1]

Richard Saul Wurman has coined a number of useful terms for describing life in the Information Age, most famously *information anxiety* and *information architect*, but from a publisher's point of view perhaps his most useful contribution has been the idea that we live in an Age of Also, where print and various forms of electronic media coexist and flourish. Publishing in Wurman's Age of Also can present both a reassuring and a frustrating prospect. It is reassuring in its suggestion that familiar, and often effective, ways of conveying information will not be taken away from us, but also frustrating because the complicated reality described in this vision often works against the bold new initiatives that we might like to undertake.

As frustrating as such a stage may be, it is probably inevitable. Certainly the occurrence of such a transitional stage is consistent with the very useful schema for understanding the life cycle of a technology that was presented by Raymond Kurzweil in his series of articles in the "Futurecast" column in *Library Journal* between August 1991 and October 1993.[2]

Kurzweil's schema was described in the January 1992 issue in an article entitled "The Future of Libraries Part 1: The Technology of the Book." In that article he identifies seven distinct stages in the life cycle of a technology: the *precursor* stage, during which the prerequisites of a new technology exist; the *invention* stage, when the new technology is brought to life; the *development* stage, during which it becomes more robust; the *maturity* stage, when it takes on a life of its own and looks as if it will last forever; the *false pretenders* stage, when upstart technologies begin to appear to threaten the established technology; the *obsolescence* stage, in which the older technology is supplanted by a newer technology and goes into gradual decline; and finally the *antiquity* stage, by which time a technology is interesting mostly for its nostalgia value.[3]

In thinking about reference works and the competing print and electronic technologies, it seems clear that print is probably somewhere near the end of the false pretenders stage or the beginning of the obsolescence stage. Kurzweil's description of the false pretenders stage will strike many people as an apt description for the current print versus electronics struggle:

> Here an upstart threatens to eclipse the older technology. Its enthusiasts prematurely predict victory. While providing some distinct benefits, the newer technology is found on reflection to be missing some key element of functionality or quality. When it indeed fails to dislodge the established order, the technology conservatives take this as evidence that the original approach will live forever.

Kurzweil tells us that this stage is usually short-lived, but that the next stage, obsolescence, during which the older technology lives out its remaining years in gradual decline can comprise five to ten percent of the life cycle of the technology. If we see the precursors of print technology in the library of scrolls at Alexandria in the second century B.C., more than two thousand years ago, then we should have a hundred to two hundred years during which print and electronic technologies will exist side by side. This kind of rough calculation could easily be way off, but it suggests that Wurman's estimate–that our Age of Also will extend for the next ten to fifteen years–may be quite reasonable.

Until that transition is complete, reference publishers and reference librarians will live in a hybrid world populated by both print and electronic reference sources. For some large and expensive sources, the transition will be short or perhaps is already complete. For other smaller and less expensive sources, the transition will be either mercifully or agonizingly slow, depending on one's perspective. What follows are some thoughts about what this Age of Also looks like as seen from the perspective of a publisher whose company has been on the front lines of this transition.

LESSONS LEARNED TO DATE

The Age of Also began for Merriam-Webster in July of 1996. That was when Merriam-Webster launched its new Web site, Merriam-Webster Online (http://www.Merriam-Webster.com). A principal feature of that site was something that was still unusual at the time: free access to the databases of commercially important products, in this case *Merriam-Webster's Collegiate Dictionary* and *Merriam-Webster's Collegiate Thesaurus*. This was a risky move, as sales of print editions of the *Collegiate Dictionary* constitute a considerable portion of Merriam-Webster's revenue, but there were compelling reasons to take the risk.

Although the number of Web users had only recently passed 10 million in 1996, we understood, even if imperfectly, that the Web was more of an opportunity than a threat. We knew that there was an interest in online reference materials because, since 1995, we had been providing a reference area to America Online subscribers, a service we still provide today. And we knew that there were people who were determined to get their language information from a free Web site and that our company's mission included finding ways to meet that demand.

Today, traffic on that Web site has grown to nearly 100 million page views a month, with almost all of the traffic consisting of look-up requests for dictionary or thesaurus entries. In addition we have introduced two new subscription sites, http://Merriam-WebsterUnabridged.com, offering access to the full text of our unabridged dictionary, *Webster's Third New International Dictionary*, as well as a collection of other Merriam-Webster reference sources, and http://Merriam-Webster.Collegiate.com offering access to the text of the new Eleventh Edition of *Merriam-Webster's Collegiate Dictionary* and other Merriam-Webster reference sources.

We have become reference publishers with both print and electronic publishing programs, and as such we have already learned several important lessons about publishing in the Age of Also.

Online Use Does Not Necessarily Threaten Print Sales

The speed with which multivolume print encyclopedias were almost wholly supplanted by electronic encyclopedias offers a powerful lesson about the disruptive potential of new technologies. New technologies create demand for new kinds of content, and they allow new players to offer new products that can overtake older, well-established products. Yet publishers should be careful how they apply this lesson. The fate of high-priced, multivolume reference works does not appear to be a good predictor of smaller, less expensive reference works.

Today the predominant way that people receive information about language is still though print dictionaries. This situation is partly explained by price. The truly disruptive moment in dictionary publishing came in 1847, when George and Charles Merriam published a new edition of Noah Webster's unabridged dictionary and lowered the price from $25.00 to $6.00 a copy, thus making dictionaries an affordable household item, and the highly competitive nature of dictionary publishing has kept prices low ever since.

However, the main reason for the persistence of the print dictionary is convenience. Today's college-level desk dictionary is a superbly well-engineered product, in which the best features of print technology are perfectly matched to a user's ability. Thumb notches take the user to the desired alphabetical section; guide words across the top of the page narrow the search; boldface headwords set flush left in each column identify the exact entry. A selection of typefaces, including boldface, italic, and small capitals, developed over the centuries help signal the significance of each word on the page. Ongoing printing and papermaking technology create heightened black-white contrast and crisp letters, making even small type legible to most eyes. A modern-day print dictionary, combined with a set of human eyes and the human brain, is one of the most effective information storage and retrieval devices ever invented. As one editor at Merriam-Webster once put it, the print dictionary is the original handheld device.

Or consider this: Depending on how you count, *Merriam-Webster's Collegiate Dictionary* includes between a million and two and a half million separate pieces of information. Most people can find the one piece of information they seek in less than thirty seconds, often in as little as ten seconds. In addition, because of the print dictionary's ability to lay out a large amount of data for review at one time, it offers browsing and fuzzy-logic retrieval options that are not available from any electronic dictionary at this time. Put simply, well-designed one-volume reference books are a tough act to follow.

There are, of course, many advantages to electronic editions. Most obviously, online dictionaries and dictionaries installed on the hard drive offer obvious convenience when one is working at a computer. In addition, there are unique advantages to computer access, including a more attractive and easy-to-read display of the data, powerful search options, spelling assistance, and often audio pronunciations. And there is the cost consideration. The cost of the CD-ROM version of our unabridged dictionary, *Webster's Third New International Dictionary*, is roughly half the cost of the print edition, and a year's subscription for an individual to the Web site offering that dictionary, http://Merriam-WebsterUnabridged.com, is roughly half of that.

Hence, we anticipate that electronic dictionaries can and will improve in many interesting and attractive ways and will become more popular, ultimately even more popular than print dictionaries. But for now, we remain in the Age of Also, in which print and online coexist. To some extent, online usage may reduce use of the print product, but we also have reason to believe that online sometimes stimulates use of the print product. We certainly have abundant anecdotal evidence of online users attesting to their ongoing use of print dictionaries and their intention to buy a Merriam-Webster print dictionary because of their pleasure with the online edition.

The Job of the Dictionary Appears to Be Unchanged as Users Go Online

This observation may seem rather unremarkable, but when we first started our Web site, we were uncertain whether people would bring different needs and expectations to an online dictionary. Were we including the words that people most wanted to look up? Were we providing the kinds of information about those words that people most wanted to find? Were we speaking in a language that was appropriate for most users? We believed we were doing a good job, but we had little hard evidence to support our view.

That changed when we went online. One of the greatest benefits of going online was that we learned what the most frequently looked-up words in the dictionary are. To the surprise of some, the most frequently looked-up words are not the newest words, not the latest high-tech words, not the cool new slang. The most frequently looked-up words are the slightly difficult and somewhat learned vocabulary that we frequently encounter in contemporary speech and writing–words like *ubiquitous, paradigm, oxymoron, serendipity, hubris, esoteric, epiphany*, and *synergy*.

Also high on the list of frequently looked-up words are usage questions, such as *effect/affect* and *ensure/assure*. Spelling is seldom a big issue for our online users, although they had some trouble getting the right number of *p*'s and *z*'s in *paparazzi* at the time of Princess Diana's death and in getting the two *n*'s in *millennium* as we approached January 1, 2000.

Words from current news stories are frequently among the most looked up. Since 1996, almost every major event has carried terminology that people seek to understand in greater detail. The range of words looked up is striking, from simple *chad* to the highly technical *per curiam decision* of the 2000 election controversy, from the obvious terms such as *perjury* and *impeach* of the Clinton scandals to the surprising *succumb* and *surreal* in the days following September 11, 2001.

Through lists like these, and the thousands of e-mails we receive each year from visitors to the site, we are developing a better idea of what people want from language reference sources, and especially online reference sources.

1. They want to fine-tune their understanding of the meanings, the uses, and the connotations of the words they hear. They may already be somewhat familiar with the words, but they want to improve and add depth to their understanding.
2. They want more information, not less. To date, no one has complained that the definitions are too long or include too much detail. On the other hand, Web site visits are short. Having found the information they seek, most users return quickly to the task that they were working on.
3. They want information about a broad range of words. On any given day, hundreds of thousands of words are looked up, yet even the most frequently looked-up words constitute a small fraction of the total look-ups.
4. They want guidance about usage, not so much in the form of do's and don'ts but in the form of usage examples associated with each definition.
5. They want help with hard-to-spell words. They are still faced with the old problem of how to look up a word whose spelling they don't know, and they appreciate the help that a good search engine can provide in this matter.
6. They don't like phonetic symbols, and they much prefer recorded pronunciations.

The good news for dictionary publishers is that the information that users seek is precisely the information that we are able to provide. There is nothing on this list that goes beyond the capacity of today's dictionary publisher to create and provide, especially in electronic editions of the dictionary.

Online Reference Products Need to Improve in Quality

The charge has been made that online dictionaries today offer little more than access to the print editions. This charge ignores many of the improvements introduced in electronic dictionaries, such as spelling help, audio pronunciations, more user-friendly text displays, and hot-linked cross-references. Still, in many ways, the charge is valid. Online reference sources have not taken full advantage of the electronic medium in which they are delivered, and electronic dictionaries, both online and off-line, could and ought to be better. The list that appears above is a road map to providing the next generation of products, and some of those improvements can appear only in electronic editions. For example, providing example sentences for each definition could double the size of a print dictionary but could easily be accommodated online.

So far, however, truly significant improvements in product quality have proved difficult to implement. Most online reference sources are based on databases that were originally conceived for print display, a format that allows discrete pieces of information to be displayed within a larger information-rich visual field. In a dictionary, for example, one sees not only an individual entry, but an entire page and, most importantly, surrounding entries that may provide significant relevant information. In an electronic product, entries are viewed in isolation, and that richness is lost. Only a complete redesign of the structure of these databases will address problems like this.

Workable Revenue Models Are Slowly Emerging

Unfortunately, without a revenue source for online development, reference publishers will continue developing mostly for print products, and online development will be mostly restricted to making print-product databases available on the Web. This is an understandable state of affairs for the early days of the Age of Also, but we need to find ways to move beyond this state.

In this regard, the most interesting change of the past several years is that individuals are increasingly willing to pay for content. A case in point is our subscription Web site, http://Merriam-WebsterUnabridged.com, which offers access to our unabridged dictionary, *Webster's Third New International Dictionary*. This Web site was launched in March of 2002 and has become very successful with individual users. In fact, in the last twelve months, more individuals bought access to *Webster's Third* through a Web site subscription than through a book purchase.

Interestingly, the same shift of business has not occurred for institutional customers, including libraries. Pricing could have something to do with this, although pricing for schools and libraries was set very low in comparison with other online resources. What is more likely is that consumers have seen a value in online access to an unabridged dictionary that librarians are slower to acknowledge. While this slowness to embrace new technology is frustrating, it may still be valid. To rephrase the words of Richard Wurman, there is no best way to look words up in a dictionary; there are only good ways, and looking them up in a print dictionary is still a pretty good way.

Nevertheless, schools and libraries are becoming subscribers to Merriam-WebsterUnabridged, and the pace at which we are gaining new institutional subscribers has quickened in 2003. This is encouraging, as increasing revenues are the best motivation for making the needed investment in product improvements.

PREDICTIONS

A futurist looking at the field of reference publishing a decade ago might well have predicted that by now we would have moved beyond the point where we find ourselves today. However, the Age of Also presents many complicating factors, and one ought not to take the rate of change to date as an indicator of the extent to which–or the rate at which–change will occur in the future. As Raymond Kurzweil reminded us in another of his Futurecast essays, "in the development of technology we overestimate what can be accomplished in the short term and underestimate what can be accomplished in the long term."[4] In keeping with the spirit of that remark, one can make these predictions:

The Age of Also Will Persist

Publishers, librarians, patrons, and consumers are well served by print reference books. Unless there is a compelling reason to switch from print to electronic, the transition will be gradual. Powerful search engines and multimedia enhancements provided that compelling reason for encyclopedias. To date, however, no truly compelling reason has emerged for dictionaries, thesauruses, almanacs, or other traditional one-volume reference books.

The situation is illustrated by one reference librarian I know who recently elected not to buy a new print edition of the *McGraw-Hill Encyclopedia of Science and Technology*, feeling that his patrons expect to find that kind of information on the Web. In his view, there will be little future interest in print editions of any multivolume encyclopedia. However, this same librarian includes only print editions of core one-volume reference books in his reference collection. To this librarian, there is no contradiction in that choice. There is no best way to look up information; there are only multiple good ways.

Product Improvements Will Lead to Greater Use of Online References

As outlined above, we have a good idea of what improvements people would like to see in dictionaries, and the special opportunity that we have with electronic dictionaries to meet those needs. In addition to those stated needs, we can also begin developing electronic dictionaries with a richer network of hyperlinks between entries and also new interfaces that create more opportunities for browsing. And as we begin to respond to those needs, buyers and users of dictionaries will be more motivated to prefer the electronic edition to the print.

Whether or how soon these improvements are made depends on a number of factors. First, users will have to demand quality. Individual consumers will play a role in this, but there is a crucial role for librarians. Librarians should hold online reference providers to the same standards they set for print publishers. If librarians would not send a patron to a 100-year-old print thesaurus, they should not refer the patron to the same text on the Web. A principal feature of one of the successful free dictionary Web sites is the 1913 revision of our 1890 edition of *Webster's International Dictionary*. While this dictionary includes a few scattered updated entries, it has not been revised in any significant way by a professional lexicographer since 1913. One wonders how many library patrons access this dictionary because their library does not provide online access to a more up-to-date edition.

Second, publishers need to respond to calls for quality. The nature of the electronic medium allows publishers to respond to requests for kinds of information that we would not have been able to satisfy in the past. We should embrace this opportunity. The Age of Also should be an Age of Experimentation. We need to heed the lessons from the encyclopedias: the venerable are the vulnerable. And innovation is the cure.

The Economic Factor Will Vary in Its Impact

The third factor is the emergence of a workable revenue model that will justify the investment that some of these improvements require. That model will emerge when libraries can achieve a cost savings by switching to an online edition. Once again, the large multivolume reference books lead the way, and smaller, less expensive print products seem harder to displace. In fact, cost savings are available even for smaller reference products when multiple copies are bought or when online products offer a suite of reference sources, as in the case of the Merriam-WebsterUnabridged Web site, which offers our unabridged dictionary, the new edition of the *Collegiate Dictionary*, the *Collegiate Thesaurus*, the *Collegiate Encyclopedia*, and our Spanish-English dictionary. Still, the fundamental fact is that many fine high-quality one-volume reference books are available for very reasonable prices. The cost of these reference books is not a serious problem for most libraries, so the economic advantage of electronic delivery may not be a compelling factor for these publications.

User Preference Will Ultimately Rule

The essential quality of a dictionary, as with most one-volume reference books, is that it be easy and convenient to use. The print dictionary has thrived in large part because it is so easy to use. However, our conceptions of ease and convenience are shaped by our environment and are open to change. As we integrate electronic access to information more fully into our lives, from our home computers to our PDAs, our cell phones, and even our kitchen appliances, our notion of convenience and ease of use may come to embrace electronic access almost to the exclusion of print. One can foresee a day when, quite apart from any issue of cost or product quality, users prefer electronic dictionaries because it feels more natural to look things up that way. At that point, librarians may be compelled to provide additional online access to core reference sources within libraries simply to respond to patron requests.

The Virtual Reference Room Will Become a Reality

Many reference sources, including Merriam-Webster reference sources, are now being published in a form that can be delivered via remote access to every cardholder at home, every staff member, every patron at a computer, and every student and faculty member on a campus. Many libraries have started moving in this direction, but again progress seems slow. We have often been surprised in speaking to librarians to discover how many librarians are reluctant to part with the notion that reference services are something delivered within the four walls of the library. From that point of view, online access to an unabridged dictionary may seem like no more than one piece of hardware (a computer monitor) replacing another (a big book on a stand). And yet clearly there is a larger opportunity for libraries to become reference portals serving their communities. This concept poses challenges, as both publishers and librarians will need to be realistic about each other's revenue needs and resources, but we should be moving in this direction. If we don't, commercial virtual reference rooms available on a subscription basis only to those who can afford them are a predictable development, and one that would inevitably widen the digital divide. In this regard, both publishers and librarians are vulnerable as well as venerable.

CONCLUSION

Navigating our way through this Age of Also will be a tricky business for both reference librarians and reference publishers. Publishers will need to pursue policies that ensure the availability and quality of both print and online references. Premature withdrawal of support for print products may shortchange traditional users, create short-term opportunities for a competitor, and lead to a loss of revenue needed for creating products. However, publishers must also give particular support to new investment in electronic products, as that user base is in place today and is growing.

Similarly, librarians need to focus on meeting users' needs and preferences, which will not remain static during the Age of Also. The inevitable shifts will add complexity to the librarian's job, and issues of print versus electronic must not wind up diminishing attention to the quality of the information. And librarians need to be advocates. The move to the virtual reference room, for instance, will not come about without strong voices making the case for a new way of conceiving of the role of the library.

Most importantly, librarians need to be educators. If navigating in the Age of Also is a challenge for publishers and librarians, it is even more so for consumers and patrons. Librarians need to be aware of the entire range of reference options that are available, and they should make a point of educating print-oriented patrons (and colleagues) about electronic alternatives, as well as reminding those who are online-oriented about print alternatives. The spirit of this age is choice, but choice is only valuable when it is an informed choice, and responsible reference publishers will encourage librarians to put themselves forward as an important resource in making that choice.

REFERENCES

1. Richard Saul Wurman. "Understanding in the Age of Also," *Ubiquity* 1, no. 3 (March 6, 2000), http://www.acm.org/ubiquity/interviews.html (accessed September 28, 2003).

2. The entire series of articles can be found at KurzweilAI.net, http://www.kurzweilai.net/meme/frame.html?main=/meme/memelist.html?m%3D13 (accessed September 28, 2003).

3. Raymond Kurzweil, The Futurecast, "The Future of Libraries Part 1: The Technology of the Book," *Library Journal*, January 1992, 80.

4. Raymond Kurzweil, The Futurecast, "The Future of Libraries Part 2: The End of Books," Library Journal, August 2001, http://www.kurzweilai.net/meme/frame.html?main=/articles/art0261.html (accessed September 28, 2003).

From the Womb to the Web:
Library Assignments
and the New Generation

Necia Parker-Gibson

SUMMARY. Subject faculty members and students often have different expectations for selection of appropriate sources for assignments, and the Internet makes this problem that much more complex. Community, context, and content all play roles in the evaluation of information. Distinguishing search engines from databases and understanding jargon play a part in students' successful negotiation of evaluation, citation, and integration of information of all types. Campuses are receiving pressure to increase information literacy among students. Exacting description of assignments, definitions of terms, and collaboration between subject faculty and librarians are considered key to success of programs. *[Article copies available for a fee from The Haworth Document Delivery Service: 1-800-HAWORTH. E-mail address: <docdelivery@haworthpress.com> Website: <http://www.HaworthPress.com> © 2005 by The Haworth Press, Inc. All rights reserved.]*

KEYWORDS. Evaluation, citation, faculty, graduate students, undergraduates, assignments, expectations, community

---

Necia Parker-Gibson is Social Sciences Librarian and Library Instruction Coordinator, University Libraries, University of Arkansas, Fayetteville, AR 72701 (E-mail: neciap@uark.edu).

[Haworth co-indexing entry note]: "From the Womb to the Web: Library Assignments and the New Generation." Parker-Gibson, Necia. Co-published simultaneously in *The Reference Librarian* (The Haworth Information Press, an imprint of The Haworth Press, Inc.) No. 91/92, 2005, pp. 83-102; and: *The Reference Collection: From the Shelf to the Web* (ed: William J. Frost) The Haworth Information Press, an imprint of The Haworth Press, Inc., 2005, pp. 83-102. Single or multiple copies of this article are available for a fee from The Haworth Document Delivery Service [1-800-HAWORTH, 9:00 a.m. - 5:00 p.m. (EST). E-mail address: docdelivery@haworthpress.com].

Available online at http://www.haworthpress.com/web/REF
© 2005 by The Haworth Press, Inc. All rights reserved.
doi:10.1300/J120v44n91_07

INTERNET EXPERIENCE
IS NOT INFORMATION-FLUENCY

The Internet provides college students massive, often indigestible amounts of information, usually at the speed of T1 connections. Studies suggest that the Web is the preferred starting place for research for a majority of students.[1] While the number of available reputable Web sites has increased, with an increase in the number of scholars willing to publish their research in electronic journals or via their own pages, so has the sheer number of sites, including many of questionable research value, with a resulting "net" dilution of the quality of the Web as a whole. There is an enormous quantity of misinformation available. For example, one study of sixty medical "articles" published on the Web found that 80 percent of the sources gave wrong information about the treatment of childhood diarrhea.[2] The context of information-seeking–which includes not only the individual, but the community[3]–has been altered by the ubiquitous nature of advertising for computers and Web products; the presence of computers in labs, dorm rooms, and homes; the frequent isolation of individuals[4] as they sit in front of a computer in their dorm rooms or off campus; the sheer variety and volume of potential sources; the variety of interfaces; and uncertainty about "what the professor wants" (WPW) when a research paper is assigned.[5]

When they begin any library assignment, lower division students frequently don't understand what is required for an academic paper in terms of authority, content, relevance, or other ways of attaching value to information, particularly when they are confronted with a research paper. Scholars have their own practices and habits developed over time, and often don't realize that undergraduates have often not yet developed their own; underdeveloped research habits may persist throughout a college career, but the tendency is particularly noticeable before the senior year.[6] Faculty members frequently express frustration with the quality and type of sources cited in lower division papers and speeches. They comment on the fact that the students don't recognize differences between a scholarly article and an amateur's Web site, or know when it is appropriate to use one or another as a source. Subject faculty members also complain that students don't understand the boundaries inherent in quoting from sources and where the line between applying someone's work and stealing it is drawn.

CHALLENGES

Faculty members who assign library research projects often hold several implicit assumptions. They assume that students will:

1. use library resources, including books and scholarly journals;
2. be able to distinguish between free Web site documents and scholarly publications, such as journal articles;
3. be able to identify scholarly databases available through library Web sites (operating definition: provided by libraries, by subscription, indexing a significant number of peer-reviewed publications) to identify appropriate materials;
4. be able to use databases (and are aware of which databases to use) that are key in the particular field of study, such as MLA for literature;
5. use materials that are on the shelves in the library (i.e., the "stuff in the stacks") rather than just what is available electronically;
6. be able and willing to evaluate materials they have found and decide what is appropriate for a particular project.

Faculty members' frustration over the common lack of understanding of these points by the average undergraduate has been evident for a long time, but has been exacerbated by the Internet, as students are prone to start any type of research assignment by using Internet sources and often without consulting traditional sources.

MORE FACULTY ASSUMPTIONS

Many faculty members start with the assumptions of scholars–that a field is more or less self-revelatory. They presume that students will know how to develop and dig into a research question, find the names of the top scholars and the major schools of thought or arguments,[7] and that students will understand both discipline-specific vocabulary and research or library vocabulary. Gloria Leckie remarks that:

> Within the university, faculty are considered the experts in their chosen fields, and so the characteristics of faculty research . . . can be thought of as the "expert researcher" model. The model requires a long process of acculturation, an in-depth knowledge of

the discipline, awareness of important scholars working in particular areas, participation in a system of informal scholarly communication, and a view of research as a non-sequential, non-linear process with a large degree of ambiguity and serendipity. The expert researcher is relatively independent, and has developed his or her own personal information-seeking strategies (e.g., a heavy reliance on personal contacts and citation trails). Libraries may or may not play a large part in these strategies, and librarians are rarely thought of as key people in the research process.

Unfortunately, this expert model does not work well when applied to novices (i.e., undergraduates), who most often have none of these characteristics. . . . They do not think in terms of an information-seeking strategy, but rather in terms of a coping strategy. Research is conceptualized as a fuzzy library-based activity that is required of them to complete their coursework. In other words, the novice is very far from the expert model.[8]

Although standard reference tools in print, such as *The Blackwell Companion to Major Social Theorists*, or sources that define jargon, could give students an overview of a field, most faculty members don't consider suggesting such items to students–they may not be aware that they are in the collection, or they may rarely talk about specific resources with the students, or they may just consider such sources too elementary. While many faculty members are what Jacqueline De Ruiter refers to as "mature novices" in relation to electronic sources–individuals who rely on a printed source (rather than a Web site) to which they can return as needed and consult to find a reliable answer to a particular question[9]–they often don't encourage their students to seek these tools, and relatively few students think to look for them, unless guided. Additionally, many students' preference, especially for those living off-campus or working at a distance, is for electronic sources that they may access remotely,[10] so that many sources that are on the shelves are not used as often as they might be. Some faculty members recommend new electronic resources to students as they become available, but others don't, depending in part on the level of the students and the discipline, and on what faculty members use themselves, and how often. Faculty members who are enthusiastic users and early adopters of particular databases are more likely to recommend them to students, as when the library subscribed to JSTOR a number of years ago and suddenly had students asking for it at the desk ("Dr. Adams sent me to use Jester?!").

Even though reference books are a first recommendation in most library research handouts, Barbara Fister notes that excellent (3.2 GPA or better, in her study) students actually do not consult these, although some of the students she interviewed did use them later, to clarify terms or chronology.[11] Rather than starting students with basic sources, it is more common for the faculty member to suggest the name of a scholar, and then expect the student to be able to go forward from that point ("Vince Tinto has done a lot in this area–have a look at his work" is one remark overheard recently), or to suggest a bibliography. But many students have no idea how to proceed; many of them type "Tinto" into Google and hope for the best rather than starting with the local online catalog or with ERIC, or another related database, not realizing that much of Vincent Tinto's work relates to colleges as communities and a community's influence on retention and academic achievement, and that a subject-specific database is going to be the most fruitful and straightforward place to start. While typing "Tinto" into Google might bring them some success, it might be confusing as well; a search with just his last name retrieved more than eight thousand hits in Google, but a simple author search in ERIC yielded thirty-eight hits (as of June 30, 2003), a much more manageable set. Some of the Web hits were for speeches or presentations that he is going to give or has given; the set also included his address and vita at Syracuse.

In a more recent article, Barbara Fister points out that many of the students do not have a grounding in what used to be considered basic research ideas–for example, the fact that most scholarly books have an index that allows one to locate topics within the content![12] Nor do many of them understand that scholarly writing arises out of a discussion or context of its own–that many fields have multiple schools of thought, or that each publication is, in theory, intended to develop the field, and that many published ideas are controversial and subject to argument.[13] Thus, even the students who begin by locating a few relevant articles on a topic may not recognize that the articles may only represent one aspect of the scholarly dialogue, or be able to construct an intellectual "scaffolding" to integrate the information into their own synthesis of the topic.

The major dichotomy between students and faculty is that they often have not only different expectations but different purposes when approaching a library assignment, especially a research paper, and electronic and Web resources just increase the divergence, because electronic text is often only scanned by students rather than read, and many of the resources available online provide a different level and quality of content than traditional books or journals. Some faculty members have the simple goal of exposing their students to the library and to the discipline's literature, but many also have the expectation that the production of a research paper will be something that the students will find valuable, albeit in a less tangible, almost holistic way. They view it as an opportunity for growth, a creative outlet, and a chance for the students to think for themselves. By contrast, the average undergraduate views the Internet as a source of convenient, if not comprehensive, support for information needs or entertainment. They are grade-driven, and want to know what is required to receive an A, a B, and so on.[14] The demands on their time mean that their primary focus is on the near goal, completing the paper, in order to reach the main goal, completing the degree. They will more than likely prefer to use electronic databases, electronic full text if available, and the Web if allowed, for the sake of convenience and time saved. The quality of their exposure to the literature of the discipline developed in this way may not meet the faculty member's expectations.

Many librarians are working with faculty members to improve library assignments, which occurs most commonly on a one to one basis. Evan Farber speaks of the difficulty of convincing a group of people inherently conservative of their resources (primarily time) that it is necessary to work towards information literacy; it is natural that such trends develop from personal contact and through individual relationships.[15] Exceptions to this rule of thumb include a program developed by Pixey Anne Mosley, who presented a session illustrating effective library assignments to faculty members at Texas A&M University.[16] Other institutions that provide workshops for faculty on construction of library assignments include Ball State University, University of California, Hayward, and University of California, Berkeley. Other institutions, including Claremont College and Aquinas College, provide handouts of assignment tips. While not directly dedicated to library assignments, collaborative relationships such as learning communities, Freshman Interest Groups (FIGs) and other avenues create opportunities to help faculty members and students understand library resources; one example is the seminars developed at "a large Eastern university" [Penn State]–that were created to help integrate teaching about library resources and information literacy into the syllabuses for new learning communities, as one of a series of ten workshops on the development of those cadres.[17]

HOW ARE GRADUATE STUDENTS AND FACULTY ACCLIMATING TO THE INTERNET?

Harry Kibirige and Lisa DePalo[18] found that the use of search engines to find information correlates with frequency of Internet use for all classes of academic users–that is, daily use of the Internet correlates with the heavy use of search engines; less frequent Internet use correlates with a higher use of databases. However, for many faculty members, the Internet is primarily viewed as a place to institute another branch of the invisible college. Communication between scholars continues to be increasingly by e-mail, through discussion lists, or by way of other electronic fora, while at the same time conferences and associations allow discussion and networking face to face.[19] Graduate students, at least in some disciplines, are socialized into their own faculty's ways and methods of using the Web. Rather than influencing the faculty member's methods, even heavy Internet users are commonly drawn into the departmental practices, except when there is already a culture in place that allows transference of methods or habits from junior to more senior members, and only if the technology required is both available and supported, as in a computer sciences department. Otherwise, graduate students adopt and use whatever materials and tools are considered proper in the disciplinary setting and, for the most part, they use the Web to create and maintain their own social or research connections and to collect data.[20]

CHALLENGES OF CONTEXT AND UNDERSTANDING

Some authors, including Juris Dilevko and Lisa Gottlieb, find books essential to the undergraduate research experience, particularly if students start with them:

> Books, because of their historical and contextual scope, are invaluable generators of ideas–ideas that can then be investigated in greater detail through academic journal literature. If the order is reversed–if the study of journal literature comes before reading books–undergraduates may often be overwhelmed by the level of technical detail in journals and risk missing the forest for the trees.[21]

By extension, someone who starts with the Internet rather than with books or journals is not only potentially missing the forest for the trees, they may well be so detached from the scholarly context of a discipline as to be "out to sea." Thomas Mann suggests that books provide structure for ideas that is lacking in most other sources that detach information from its context:

> First, there is a hierarchy in the levels of awareness that we have of our world, from data to information to knowledge to understanding to wisdom. Each level is more complex than the previous in that each integrates more and greater kinds of awareness. Information can exist in relative isolation; it becomes knowledge only when it is perceived as corresponding to, or cohering with, larger generalizations that are shared by other people. And knowledge itself reaches the level of understanding only when the reasons or causes underlying its appearances become grasped and articulated. Here is the important point, and there is no getting around it: If the higher levels of knowledge and understanding are going to be grasped, they require greater attention spans than do the lower levels of data and information. The book format is by far the best means that the human race has yet devised for communicating to itself knowledge and understanding, as opposed to unintegrated data and information.[22]

Dilevko and Gottlieb found, with their online survey, that students on their campus *self-report* that they will use books and other printed materials if the printed materials provide the best information on a topic for a particular assignment.[23] Recent studies such as those by the Pew Charitable Trust and the Digital Library Foundation, suggest that the Internet presence is not in fact overpowering printed resources, at least at advanced levels in a discipline: 68 percent of faculty and 61 percent of graduate students in the Digital Library Federation study used printed sources exclusively; and faculty members used books extensively for teaching.[24] However, undergraduates were reported to use proportionately fewer printed materials. Even in the Dilevko and Gottlieb study, students frequently used Web sources. Students and faculty members consider the ability to access online resources an important motivation to their use of "the library" (that is, of materials subscribed to or purchased by the library, in this case).[25] And studies, such as one by Oppenheim and Smith,[26] have found fewer and fewer printed sources cited over time, in citation studies. Anecdotal evidence from a number of faculty members at the University of Arkansas, including Rebekah Huss, the coordinator of the undergraduate speech class (a required course in the College of Arts and Sciences that registers from eight hundred to a thousand students per semester), and limited examination of the bibliographies turned in by a few students in a few sections of that class suggest that the students will only use printed sources from the Libraries' shelves only if required to do so by the instructors or professors. I had hoped to examine most of the bibliographies from this semester's speeches to get a fuller understanding of what the students *actually* used, but most of the students did not turn in their bibliographies at the end of the class. Perhaps they suspected that their sources would be found lacking under scrutiny; in fact, in those examined, many students ignored very explicit instructions about source requirements. This is all part of a cycle–students are more motivated to do research that requires the use of library resources if they are insisted upon by the faculty members; faculty are more likely to be happy with the quality of sources used if the students use the library's databases and materials.[27]

FACTORS THAT IMPACT INTERNET CONTENT

The common commercial insistence that "everything can be found on the Web," is not only not true, it will never be true.[28] Laurel Clyde discusses some of the reasons that this is likely: the fact that most search engines do not retrieve materials that exist in other than the top twenty-five languages, (and translations into English are spotty at best), that some forms of Web materials, such as Flash files, are not indexed by common search engines, and that the algorithms used may never find some concepts that are taken out of context.[29] Also, what becomes electronically available through reputable scholarly publishers is based on a complex dynamic and depends in part on the control of products and profits that the publishers can protect and exercise through licensing.

Wallace Koehler's study suggests that the half-life of a Web page is approximately two years, although pages in some domains may be more stable–i.e., .edu sites and .gov sites are less likely to disappear than are .com sites, and navigation pages are more stable than content pages.[30] Web sites often disappear without trace (sometimes known as "404ing"), go out-of-date, or are otherwise unavailable. Many important works will never be published on the Internet, for various reasons, including the potential problems with plagiarism and copyright violation inherent in such publication. Students' reliance on what is questionable because of poor evaluation skills or lack of time and the Web's ephemeral character, even for reputable materials, is a continued challenge.

FACULTY ASSIGNMENTS

Library assignments from faculty members tend to err in one of three directions. Very simple assignments that may be completed by use of any "good enough" resource, rather than being complex enough to allow students to develop useful skills; very complex assignments, especially those that are ill-defined or involve undefined jargon, that the students find demoralizing or dumbfounding rather than useful; or assignments that involve so many higher level skills or incorporate so many of the faculty members' assumptions about the students' understanding of what is required that the students in effect can't comply with instructions–or don't realize that they are not in compliance. For example, unless the directions on what constitute appropriate sources for an assignment are both explicit and restrictive, a request for five cited sources is likely to generate papers with five cited Web sites.

The easiest assignments that are Web-appropriate are short answer, definitions of terms, multiple choice, or fill-in-the-blank questions, and questions involving brief statistics. These questions work as long as the question (and answer) are closely defined or delimited, ("When was the Hoover Dam dedicated?" or "Who were the members of Roosevelt's Cabinet in 1940?") rather than ambiguous, such as "How many Japanese cars were manufactured in 1999?"[31] Web sources are decent at answering these (providing the students can judge the accuracy of what is supplied, at least indirectly by the reputation of the site, for example). For faculty, some Web sites that mimic their printed counterparts in source and reputation, such as the Encyclopaedia Britannica Online, the Merriam-Webster Collegiate Dictionary, or the U.S. Census Bureau or other government Web sites are considered not only acceptable, but even preferable, as sources for certain assignments. One social work professor often asks her students to find law and legislation, policy statements and statistics from state and national government Web sites. She expects that they will need such answers professionally when in the field or in offices where they might not have the printed sources or subscription electronic resources available, but are likely to have Web access. She wants them to be able to find the most current information of that type. This is an area where accurate content exists and the use of certain Internet resources is logical and reasonable.

Assignments that involve short works or speeches are another area where Internet resources may be fruitful for students. The Web can be a source of literary or historical texts or speeches–presuming that the material has been rendered correctly. One difficulty here, especially in the humanities, is that it is not uncommon that the faculty member's intention is that the text to be analyzed should be from a particular edition or version of the work–which may include annotations or other content or be important because of paper, type, illustrations, or binding quality. "Copies" available on the Internet may not match requirements, and of course many works are not online at all. Again, an assignment of this type will need to be very explicit about appropriate sources. At some libraries, texts and speeches may be accessed through subscription databases such as *Early English Books Online*, or other relevant sources, such as *Vital Speeches of the Day* through various aggregators, but often students don't realize this, or recognize that a version from Early English Books Online is much more likely to be an accurate representation of the work than a stray Web site. For documents from databases, it should be noted that the optical character readers or scanners used to transcribe documents do not always work flawlessly. Several articles that I have recently printed out and read from aggregator databases included significant errors–humorously, one article repeatedly referred to "reference surf" and what their duties were (reference *staff*), and another rendered "these" as *theft*.

Assignments that center on the use of electronic resources are of varying value. Very often, the core of the students' time is spent learning to navigate, and getting "the answer" is sometimes secondary. Whether this is reasonable depends on the expectations of the faculty members making the assignment and the expectations and understanding of the students undertaking it. Faculty members who assigned students questions about material in *The Perseus Project* (http://www. perseus.tufts.edu), which is admittedly an extensive and complex electronic publication, for example, found these challenges:

> The combined data from the participating institutions point to four themes in the impact of Perseus:
>
> 1. Perseus amplifies and augments teaching and learning. Perseus brought much new content to courses, not only in texts but in images and maps that were easily integrated. . . . More importantly, Perseus made possible new kinds of student learning

(e.g., philological and visual investigations), even by students who knew no Greek.

2. Perseus requires a substantial physical infrastructure invest-ment. *At every site, hardware and network problems caused frustration for faculty and students, and laboratory staff had to be trained to support faculty and student access* [emphasis added].

3. Perseus demands new conceptual infrastructures for teach-ing and learning. Substantial commitments of time are re-quired from instructors–to create assignments and augment lectures with Perseus–and from students–to learn how to ac-cess materials and follow leads without being overwhelmed by the volumes of information available. . . . Instructors also must learn how to judge and react to electronic assignments.

4. Perseus is bringing systemic changes to the field of classics. There are several indicators that Perseus is beginning to change the way that classics is taught and studied. . . . New faculty posi-tion announcements in classics now list computer experience as a requisite.[32]

While students generally respond favorably to electronic resources of all kinds, every new electronic resource has a corresponding learning curve. Assignments that involve electronic resources involve learning curves for both the faculty member(s), and the students. If the assign-ment itself is complicated, or contains jargon that the students are not familiar with, confusion follows. One psychology professor assigned his students to do a "compare and contrast" of *PsycInfo*, *MEDLINE*, and *PubMed*, in terms of the form of authors' names, subjects, depth of cov-erage, and so on. While this is actually a useful assignment, and illus-trates the impact of indexing and software choices on the workings of databases, students involved express significant frustration, as many of them have never considered such elements in their searches.

Another factor in assignments that involve electronic resources is the alertness of particular faculty members to software and hardware changes. For example, one faculty member who assigns a search strat-egy worksheet every year consistently refers to *PsycInfo*, the form we subscribe to, as *PsycLit*, and asks the students to use it at the CD-ROM station that hasn't been available at our campus for years. Naturally, the students are dismayed not to find the title they seek in the database list, nor the product they expect in the form that they were told to use, but re-peated promptings have not resulted in a changed assignment sheet, so we keep explaining the changes to the students that actually ask about the problem, and hope that the others make the connection.

An added burden to students' understanding of an assignment is the fact that database software changes, sometimes abruptly, and different databases have different features. As we have discovered with titles as diverse as *Agricola*, *Lexis Nexis Academic*, and *America: History and Life*, and particularly as database providers rise and falter, and database subscriptions change, these assignments can be frustrating for all, especially when some databases can be linked to local holdings and some cannot, some databases link citations to full-text resources such as JSTOR and some do not, and some articles must be sought out on the shelves, in other databases, or on microform. Explaining these distinctions is often almost as difficult for librarians and faculty as understanding them is for the students. This is multiplied when students use other local or distant libraries, usually familiar to them, that may have other versions of the database or different databases entirely. It is challenging for the students to determine what makes the public library's version of a database different from the academic library's version, and if and when it matters that they may be different.

Research papers are less promising territory when Web sources are the primary support. They require reflection and intensive integration of material and are not well supported by spotty or sketchy sources. Research papers are the most likely type of assignment to generate indiscriminate quotation or cut-and-paste techniques, even in the best of circumstances (as has been said of term papers for years, well before the Internet intervened). More than one faculty member has discovered that an entire paper, beautifully illustrated and formatted, has been turned in after being taken in chunks or even as whole cloth from the Internet, without attribution or even a noticeable qualm.[33] Students confronted in such a situation are often mystified and defensive, as though nothing posted on the Web could possibly *belong* to anyone. The assumption that the information of all kinds found on the Web–individuals' correspondence, databases, and electronic primary works–is free for the taking is probably one of the greatest impediments to the teaching of correct attribution.[34]

It is important for librarians to know that while nearly half of faculty members surveyed at Tufts University in a study by Peter Hernon and Laura R. Walters[35] think that faculty members should be the ones to teach about evaluation of sources, academic honesty, research misconduct, and plagiarism, almost 42 percent thought that the responsibility should be the *shared duty* of librarians and faculty. Few students surveyed in the study questioned the accuracy of any documents, in print or on the Web, but were confident that the library wouldn't hold anything that wasn't true.[36] The presence of the Internet and the tendency of students to start with it increases their need to be able and willing to evaluate sources, but makes that process more complex. If we focus our instruction solely on evaluation of Internet sources (as may be tempting when we have limited time with the students), we may inadvertently keep them aimed at on the Web as a resource, and unconsciously disadvantage printed sources that much further.[37]

CHALLENGES FOR UNDERGRADUATES

Helping students distinguish among search engines and databases is a difficult task. In undergraduate library instruction, one of the consistent underlying assumptions that the students express is that search engines and databases are equivalent; i.e., they ask "What search engine should I use to find material on this topic?" Illustrating to students that databases are full of records (as with the online catalog), abstracts, or even full-text articles *intentionally collected* for a particular purpose or discipline, including books, journals, magazines, newspapers, and conference proceedings, among others, and in particular from scholarly publications, is challenging. The fact that databases are commonly part of the "invisible Web" not accessed by search engines, and not free to all,[38] is something that most students never consider. Students aren't commonly aware that search engines are algorithmic software programs that index parts of the visible Web (perhaps as little as one fifth to one half of theoretically available sites on the Web, according to Anna Clyde[39]), without, for the most part, touching the information in subscription databases or anything proprietary or guarded by password. Search engines or Web directories may or may not have indexed or collected resources on a particular topic, and the resources thus collected may or may not be scholarly. For research projects, using a relevant database to find citations for a project, compared to searching the Internet, is like casting from a dock where you have paid a fee to fish in a heavily stocked lake compared to fishing in one of the Great Lakes. The odds of finding something useful are much better, and the proper "bait" of the most useful indexing terms can often be looked up in thesauri.

Search software defaults create difficulties for student searchers regardless of the platform. Edward Proctor relates two major failures of users' understanding of Boolean logic–that although the major search engines have been set up to have a default AND between terms, searchers who ignore the consequences of default "ORing" in site-specific search engines (e.g., the Field Museum of Natural History in Chicago, http://search.fmnh.org) end up with far more hits and far less relevance than was desired;[40] and Proctor observed over years of doing mediated searches in various databases and while assisting end users with database and Web searching that both faculty members and students frequently failed to grasp that adding a term to a search *reduces* size of the retrieval set. While databases can be set to a default AND, (Proctor did just that with databases to which his library subscribed), and students can be alerted to the consequences of OR, AND, and NOT in both databases and search engines (one must capitalize them in Google, which is another tip not commonly recognized), few users read help screens to improve their results–they give up and try another database, engine or other source.

Students, particularly undergraduates, have a difficult time distinguishing between articles in journals and materials from other forms of publication. This skill was complex enough to teach in the days when students walked to the stacks to find printed sources; now it is much more complicated. The features that help us identify journals, such as named authors, cited sources, and specific headings and formatting, are straightforward to librarians, but not to the average student, or even to some graduate students. Further, unless scholarly journals are specifically required for the assignment, the students may or may not track them down. Thus, the delineation of the assignment and the subject vocabulary is crucial. If the professors define what they mean by a "scholarly journal," "a professional journal," or just "journals," or by such a term as "primary source," then their students will be ahead of the game, especially if they are also provided examples. It is helpful if the faculty members explain that the electronic versions of articles in scanned PDFs from journals that are in full-text databases are effectively identical to the printed versions (when they are). And even though there are some electronic journals available on the Internet, making sure that the students understand that there is often a difference in what is commonly available through the public Internet and what is accessible through Web-based library database subscriptions is important. Most of the databases are branded with headers, footers, and other identifying marks, which, along with the presence of the other elements of a recognizable journal, is one way to get oriented to scholarly sources in hyperspace.

CHALLENGES FOR GRADUATE STUDENTS

Increasingly, research reports, government documents, and articles or other "viewdata" are being published electronically on the Web. Although allowing their work to be published as preprints on the Web has caused some authors to have their work rejected as a simultaneous submission, providing their own articles on a personal Web site after other publication is not uncommon, if allowed under copyright agreements. In some cases, the full article is not there, but the citation, abstract and bibliography are made available. Graduate students who search the Web for material on their topic frequently run across these abstracts or publications. Citing them, if available in full, and using the abstract or bibliography if not, is more problematic than using abstracts and references from printed sources. In particular, with the ephemeral character of the Internet, the references examined today may not be available tomorrow. This exacerbates the classic problem for students writing theses or dissertations. If it's difficult to keep or track down and recreate full bibliographic entries for printed sources accurately, it's that much more difficult to cite materials correctly that are a moving, even a disappearing, target.

The presence of searchable electronic resources such as online catalogs, databases, and Web sites raises the ante for the literature review and makes it that much more difficult to know when the literature has been covered sufficiently. The lack of controlled vocabulary in some databases and on the Web, and the differences between controlled vocabularies in related databases, creates that much more confusion, as keyword searches may or may not generate the relevant documents or citations. As Christine Borgman points out in part of her discussion of metadata,[41] authority records, collocation, and other tools of organization and control are not only not generally present on the Web, but the "aboutness" of a work, in whatever format, in the mind of a researcher is not necessarily the same as that of the author, the editor, or indexer; the search words that would describe a particular document may never show up in that same document, abstract or title, so the habit of using restrictive keyword searching to attempt to reduce Internet results to a manageable number may zero out results in databases.

CHALLENGES FOR CAMPUS MANDATES

Various higher education commissions, accreditation boards, and other executive bodies have endorsed the need for college students to have training in using library resources as well as instruction in information literacy. The Association of College and Research Libraries (ACRL) developed the *Information Literacy Competency Standards for Higher Education*, which have been adopted or endorsed by such bodies as the American Association of Higher Education.[42] The process of integrating information literacy competencies and assessment into general education, developing programs, and paying for such initiatives on campuses that are already short on funding is too complex to detail here, although Thompson's[42] article has a good review of the literature on the topic, and certainly librarians like Cerise Oberman, Betsy Parks, and Lynn Cameron, among others, have had significant impact on their respective campuses in this regard. Suffice it to say that the availability of speedy Internet access and the need for evaluation of sources in terms of their provenance and content have scarcely been greater, and the need to integrate the discussion into the primary subject matter of all majors is intense.

Evaluation of content is a topic that can scarcely be covered in a single class, which is often how much time librarians may get for an entire semester. At Arizona State University, psychology faculty members Barry Leshowitz, Kristen Eignor DiCerbo, and Morris A. Okun used an entire semester to instruct students about information evaluation and get them beyond their preconceptions, using exercises, lecture, and peer teaching.[43] Admittedly, many research methods classes involve some similar techniques, but students commonly don't take a research methods class until junior year or later, if ever.

Making information literacy a part of campus-wide assessment, as has been done at James Madison University[44] and at other campuses is an important facet of the process. Collaborative outreach into the regular classes is most likely the only way to have the necessary impact on students' understanding and reasoning. Networking, getting acquainted with our respective subject faculty members, and working together to develop content to address these outcomes, is, as Thompson also states, even more important.

MAKING DISTINCTIONS EXPLICIT

Although faculty may still be the most effective transmitters of methods of information evaluation (since they have authority over and regular contact with the students), and they are more likely to be perceived as experts by the students, especially on issues such as plagiarism,[45] librarians can reach students directly in face to face consultations, in instruction, in tutorials–which some students may prefer[46]–by electronic means such as chat, (especially when push technology is available and we can "show and tell," and type examples and strategies even for distant students), and by expanding our efforts to work with faculty members to integrate information literacy into subject content by way of tailored practicums, exercises, and other forms of instruction. In particular, providing real-life examples of what is and is not a journal, a scholarly monograph, or a scholarly Web site may allow the students to begin to make those distinctions. Reinforcement from faculty in their assignments of what constitutes a credible source and in particular, what will be *accepted* as a source for specific projects, and the kinds of sources that will be rejected or result in point deductions, may alert the students to acceptable citation techniques and use of scholarly resources in the reward system that most of them understand. For librarians, making and keeping contact with faculty members to keep them aware of database changes and the new tools that are available, and negotiation of the type, complexity and required elements of assignments when possible, are all elements of helping students succeed in the electronic age.

REFERENCES

1. Kelley, Kimberly B., and Gloria H. Orr. "Trends in Distant Student Use of Electronic Resources: A Survey." *College & Research Libraries* 64, no. 3(2003) p. 190.

2. McClung, H.J., R.D. Murray, and L.A. Heitlinger. "The Internet as a Source for Current Patient Information." *Pediatrics* 101, (1998) no. 6:E2, cited in Wathen, C.N., and Jacquelyn Burkell. 2002. "Believe It or Not: Factors Influencing Credibility on the Web." *Journal of the American Society for Information Science & Technology* 53, no. 2:134.

3. Borgman, Christine L. *From Gutenberg to the Global Information Infrastructure: Access to Information in the Networked World.* Cambridge, MA.: MIT Press, 2000. p. 164-5.

4. Bodi, Sonia. "Ethics and Information Technology: Some Principles to Guide Students." *Journal of Academic Librarianship* 24, (1998) no. 6: p. 459.

5. Valentine, Barbara. The Legitimate Effort in Research Papers: Student Commitment versus Faculty Expectations. *Journal of Academic Librarianship* 27(2001), no. 2: p. 109.

6. Ibid., p. 109.

7. Bodi, Sonia. "How Do We Bridge the Gap Between What We Teach and What They Do? Some Thoughts on the Place of Questions in the Process of Research." *Journal of Academic Librarianship* 28, (2001) no. 3: p. 109.

8. Leckie, Gloria J. "Desperately Seeking Citations: Uncovering Faculty Assumptions About the Undergraduate Research Process." *The Journal of Academic Librarianship* 22 (1996) p. 202-3.

9. De Ruiter, Jacqueline. "Aspects of Dealing with Digital Information: 'Mature' Novices on the Internet." *Library Trends* 51 (2002) no. 2: p. 200.

10. Kelley and Orr, p. 180.

11. Fister, Barbara. "The Research Processes of Undergraduate Students." *Journal of Academic Librarianship* 18 (1992) no. 3: p. 168.

12. Fister, Barbara. "Fear of Reference." *Chronicle of Higher Education* 48, (2002) no. 40:B20.

13. Fister, Barbara. "Teaching the Rhetorical Dimensions of Research." *Research Strategies* 11 (1993) no. 4: p. 215.

14. Valentine, p. 109.

15. Farber, Evan. "Faculty-Librarian Cooperation: A Personal Retrospective." *Reference Services Review* 27 (1999) 3:229-235.

16. Mosley, Pixey Anne. "Creating a Library Assignment Workshop for University Faculty." *Journal of Academic Librarianship* 24 (1998) 1: 33-41.

17. Stefanou, Candice R. and Jill D. Salisbury-Glennon. "Developing Motivation and Cognitive Learning Strategies Through an Undergraduate Learning Community." *Learning Environments Research* 5 (2002) 1: 77-77.

18. Kibirige, Harry M., and Lisa DePalo. "The Internet as a Source of Academic Research Information: Findings of Two Pilot Studies." *Information Technology and Libraries* 19 (2000) no. 1: p. 14.

19. Borgman, p. 114.

20. Covi, Lisa M. "Debunking the Myth of the Nintendo Generation: How Doctoral Students Introduce New Electronic Communication Practices into University Research." *Journal of the American Society for Information Science* 51 (2000) no. 14: p. 1297-9.

21. Dilevko, Juris, and Lisa Gottlieb. "Print Sources in an Electronic Age: A Vital Part of the Research Process for Undergraduate Students." *Journal of Academic Librarianship* 28 (2002) no. 6: p. 389.

22. Mann, Thomas. "The Importance of Books, Free Access, and Libraries as Places–and the Dangerous Inadequacy of the Information Science Paradigm." *Journal of Academic Librarianship* 27 (2001) no. 4: p. 270.

23. Dilevko and Gottlieb, p. 386.

24. Peek, Robin. "The Internet's Role on Campus." *Information Today* 19 (2002) no. 11: p. 36.

25. Kelley and Orr, p. 183.

26. Oppenheim, C., and R. Smith. "Student Citation Practices in an Information Science Department." *Education for Information* 19 (2001) no. 4:299-323.

27. Kelley and Orr, p. 185.

28. Mann, p. 270.

29. Clyde, Laurel A. "Search Engines Are Improving–But They Still Can't Find Everything." *Teacher Librarian* 30 (2003) no. 5:44.

30. Koehler, Wallace. "Web Page Change and Persistence–A Four-Year Longitudinal Study." *Journal of the American Society for Information Science & Technology* 53(2002) no. 2: p. 170.

31. Borgman, p. 130.

32. Lessons Learned from FIPSE Projects IV-May 2000. http://www.ed.gov/offices/OPE/FIPSE/LessonsIV/tufts-greek.html, accessed 7/29/03.

33. Bodi, 1998, p. 462.

34. Kellogg, Alex P. "Students Plagiarize Online Less than Many Think, A New Study Finds." *Chronicle of Higher Education* 48 (2002) no. 23:A44.

35. Hernon, Peter and Laura R. Walters. "Student and Faculty Perceptions About Misconduct: A Case Study." Pp. 59-70 In Altman, Ellen, and Hernon, Peter. *Research misconduct: Issues, implications, and strategies.* Greenwich, CT: Ablex Corp., 1997. p. 61-2.

36. Ibid., p. 65-8.

37. Mann, p. 272.

38. Clyde, Anna. "The Invisible Web." *Teacher Librarian* 29 (2002) 4:47-50.

39. Ibid, p. 47.

40. Proctor, Edward. "Boolean Operators and the Naïve End User: Moving to AND." *Online* v26 (2002) 4: 34-38.

41. Borgman, p. 76-7.

42. Thompson, Gary B. "Information Literacy Accreditation Mandates: What They Mean for Faculty and Librarians." *Library Trends* 51 (2002) no. 2:220-3.

43. Leshowitz, Barry, Kristen Eignor DiCerbo, and Morris A. Okun. "Effects of Instruction in Methodological Reasoning on Information Evaluation." *Teaching of Psychology* 29 (2002) no. 1:5-10.

44. Cameron, Lynn. 1993. Assessment of Library Skills (at James Madison University). In *What Is Good Instruction Now?* Ann Arbor, MI: Pierian Press, 1993. p. 47-50.

45. Arcuri, Jennifer A. "Methods for Helping Students Avoid Plagiarism." *Teaching of Psychology* 29 (2002) no. 2:112.

46. Kelley and Orr, p. 187.

Cyberplagiarism and the Library: Issues and Solutions

Jennifer R. Sharkey

F. Bartow Culp

SUMMARY. Plagiarism by students in academic institutions is an old but continuing problem facing teachers and librarians. Although studies disagree on the Internet's effect on student plagiarism, the easy availability of electronic information creates a challenge for librarians, who must be ready not only to detect and deter plagiarism, but also to educate their patrons about it. The purpose of this contribution is to summarize briefly the nature, extent, and causes of plagiarism in its academic aspect, especially as it has been influenced by electronic information sources, and to review measures of its detection and deterrence. *[Article copies available for a fee from The Haworth Document Delivery Service: 1-800-HAWORTH. E-mail address: <docdelivery@haworthpress.com> Website: <http://www.HaworthPress.com> © 2005 by The Haworth Press, Inc. All rights reserved.]*

Jennifer R. Sharkey is Assistant Professor of Library Science/Information Integration Librarian, Purdue University Libraries UGRL (E-mail: sharkeyj@purdue.edu); and F. Bartow Culp is Associate Professor of Library Science/Chemistry Librarian, Purdue University Libraries CHEM (E-mail: bculp@purdue.edu), both at 504 West State Street, West Lafayette, IN 47907-2058.

[Haworth co-indexing entry note]: "Cyberplagiarism and the Library: Issues and Solutions." Sharkey, Jennifer R., and F. Bartow Culp. Co-published simultaneously in *The Reference Librarian* (The Haworth Information Press, an imprint of The Haworth Press, Inc.) No. 91/92, 2005, pp. 103-116; and: *The Reference Collection: From the Shelf to the Web* (ed: William J. Frost) The Haworth Information Press, an imprint of The Haworth Press, Inc., 2005, pp. 103-116. Single or multiple copies of this article are available for a fee from The Haworth Document Delivery Service [1-800-HAWORTH, 9:00 a.m. - 5:00 p.m. (EST). E-mail address: docdelivery@haworthpress.com].

Available online at http://www.haworthpress.com/web/REF
doi:10.1300/J120v44n91_08

KEYWORDS. Plagiarism, academic dishonesty, Internet, online reference tools, paper mills, electronic information sources

INTRODUCTION

Plagiarism has become a frequent item in the popular press in recent years; well-known authors have admitted to it, a college president has resigned because of it, and great newspapers have seen their reputations tarnished because their reporters have committed it. In addition, numerous anecdotal reports have given the impression that the Internet has dramatically increased the problem of plagiarism in schools and colleges. Librarians in academic institutions, especially those with instructional duties, need to be aware of the issues surrounding not only plagiarism in general, but especially as it pertains to the electronic resources they manage. In a 2002 *Reference Librarian* article, Jacqueline Borin stated "Reference librarians . . . have a role in combating plagiarism because libraries 'provide and promote the Internet as a research tool.'"[1]

WHAT IS PLAGIARISM?
DEFINITIONS AND SOME HISTORY

What is plagiarism? The Latin root for the word, *plagiare*, means to kidnap, and to many of those who have seen their words or ideas thus appropriated, there is that feeling that their child has indeed been stolen. The Modern Language Association Style Guide defines it by quoting Alexander Lindey: "It is the false assumption of authorship: the wrongful act of taking the product of another person's mind and presenting it as one's own."[2] The extent of a plagiaristic act can vary considerably, ranging from the most serious (copying or purchasing an entire paper) down to the omission of a few references or attributions in a brief written assignment. The particular aspect of plagiarism that arises in the context of electronically based information has been referred to as "e-plagiarism" or "cut-and-paste plagiarism," but is now more commonly called "cyberplagiarism." Of concern to educators at all levels are both its comparative ease and the vast information resources that potential cyberplagiarists have at their disposal.

Moreover, many educators are neither sure nor comfortable with how to deal with plagiarism, whatever its means of commission. In the preface to his elegant little book on the subject, *Stolen Words*, Thomas Mallon goes immediately and neatly to the heart of the problem:

> No, it isn't murder. And as larceny goes it's usually more distasteful than grand.
> But it is a bad thing.
> Isn't it?[3]

And later he writes: "We are also as uncomfortable dealing with charges against the long-dead great as we are with those against the living obscure. [We often, and mistakenly, see plagiarism as a crime of degree, an excess of something legitimate . . . "[4] This clearly illustrates the problem that teachers and librarians have when confronting plagiarism; many do not see it as a "bad" crime, and are reluctant to apply the full weight of their authority to punish it. Even in institutions with a clearly articulated policy on academic dishonesty, most faculty prefer to deal with incidents of plagiarism themselves or simply to ignore them.[5]

Another problem is that many instructors cannot clearly differentiate between copyright violation and plagiarism. While the former is clearly illegal, the latter may be legal, but it is clearly unethical. Copyright violations, while subject to interpretation based on fair use principles, pertain only to documented expressions; an egregious act of plagiarism such as the copying of an entire chapter or article can violate copyright statutes, but the smaller and more frequent acts of "cut and paste" plagiarism generally fly under the radar screen of copyright law.[6] Also, non-copyrightable concepts such as ideas and spoken words can be plagiarized, as can those writings which exist in the public domain.

HISTORICAL BACKGROUND

The notion of writings, ideas or utterances as the property of an individual is not new in Western civilizations, nor is the act of another individual appropriating them; however, the concept and connotation of plagiarism as a reprehensible act (even if only slightly so) did not arise until fairly recently. Beginning in the 17th century, when writing was becoming a means of earning a livelihood, it became more important to authors that their words not be co-opted by others. The first copyright statutes were enacted in England at the beginning of the 18th century, initially to protect the publisher's profits more than the author's; however, their effect advanced the emerging idea of an individual author's work as his or her property.

In colleges and universities, plagiarism was not considered a serious problem until the middle of the 19th century. Then, increasing enrollments and changing student attitudes ran headlong into a stultifying and outmoded pedagogy. Under pressure to produce an almost continuous stream of essays, many students came to rely on 19th century versions of term paper mills.[7] From those times until now, numerous studies have described–and decried–the various manifestations of academic misconduct (for a thorough annotated bibliography, see Anderson).[8]

RECENT STUDIES ON THE EXTENT OF PLAGIARISM IN ACADEME

The broader issue of academic misconduct, which includes plagiarism among other topics such as cheating on examinations, falsifying the results of research, and embezzling grant money has been thoroughly studied (for an overview of this broader subject, see Decoo).[9] These studies show that the incidence of academic misconduct is widespread, but their findings vary considerably, and the variety of methodologies applied make comparisons difficult. Furthermore, specific data on incidences of student plagiarism are generally buried within these larger studies. In the only large-scale study of its kind, McCabe and Bowers compared the cheating behavior of students at the same campus in 1963 and 1993, before the influence of the Internet became widespread. They found that the percentages of students who said they had plagiarized at least once were 30% in the earlier study and 26% in the later one.[10]

Disagreement also abounds on the extent and growth rate of plagiarism in academe since the advent of the Internet. While media accounts and some publications use the terms "plague" and "crisis," research has shown that there has not been nearly as steep a rise in incidences of plagiarism as indicated by anecdotal evidence.[11,12] The only multi-campus study to date that specifically focuses on Internet plagiarism has shown that, although a considerable minority (24.5%) of students commit Internet plagiarism "sometimes to very frequently," these figures are no higher than those reported earlier.[13] Similarly, campus surveys conducted at Stanford University in 1961, 1976 and 2003 even showed a slight decline in minor plagiarism from a high of 35% in 1961 to 28.2% overall (12.2% from print sources and 16% from Internet sources) in 2003.[14]

CAUSES OF PLAGIARISM

Research has found that the major reasons why students plagiarize center on ignorance and environment. Wilhoit states that most incidences are unintentional, and arise from ignorance of proper citation and attribution practices.[15] A special case of this arises with some foreign students; they are not only unfamiliar with Western strictures against plagiarism, but they may have been schooled to believe that copying the exact words of a mentor shows intelligence and respect.[16] Other reasons cited in student surveys are time and grade pressures.[17,18] A number of studies have shown that, when plagiarism is intentional, students are strongly influenced by their perceptions of their peers' behavior, the likelihood of their being caught, and the severity of the resulting penalties. The presence or absence of a climate or culture of academic integrity on a campus is seen as the most important determinant of student cheating.[19,20]

Some educators disagree with the "absolutist" view of plagiarism as expressed in many institutional code of ethics statements, and argue that the omission of quotation marks should not be treated the same as passing off a downloaded paper as one's own work.[21] Studies show that students understand the basic concept of plagiarism and believe that cheating is wrong; however, it is not clear if students are really aware of what constitutes plagiarism. The study by Ashworth and Bannister shows that most of the students surveyed had a difficult time clearly defining plagiarism.

> The tendency of certain students to conceive of plagiarism in a very literal, concrete sense offered a clear indication of the limits of their understanding: the verbatim use of an author's words obviously counts as plagiarism, but paraphrasing their argument in one's own language renders the offence in some way different, lesser. Similarly, the 'mosaic' technique of constructing an essay entirely from disparate but suitably referenced sources, one's own input being only to thread the material together, was not seen as wrong by several.[22]

In such an unsure environment, what can librarians do to help their patrons–both faculty and students–to avoid plagiaristic acts, either conscious or unintentional?

THE LIBRARIAN'S ROLE IN COMBATING PLAGIARISM: TRUANT OFFICER OR MENTOR?

Detecting Plagiarism

As plagiarism gains more attention across the country at all levels of education, librarians often find themselves being consulted as experts–experts in finding information, experts in detecting falsified information, and experts in helping students become information literate. While most librarians are willing to play these roles, we need to think about the broader picture to determine how librarians can influence an institution's system-wide efforts in combating plagiarism. As we all know, being everything to everyone causes stress, burnout, and a potential decline in service quality.[23] Staying attuned to the institution's overall efforts in addressing plagiarism and academic honesty can help us determine what is the most effective way to participate and support those efforts.

Today, there are multiple options for detecting plagiarized texts and papers. Doing a keyword search on any search engine or online database yields many hits ranging from lists of quick tips to free Web services to fee-based services. One of the most well known Web-based services is Turnitin.com. This site states, "[s]ince 1996, Turnitin has been helping millions of faculty and students in 51 countries to improve writing and research skills, encourage collaborative online learning, ensure originality of student work, and save instructors' time–all at a very affordable price."[24] Visiting the site provides a showcase of the various products and services they have to offer. Many high schools, colleges, and universities, subscribe to services like Turnitin.com to help them address the attempts of plagiarism by students. Other companies that provide similar services are Glatt Plagiarism Services and Essay Verification Engine.[25]

Detecting a plagiarist doesn't need to be done with a fee-based service. Often using a free search engine such as Google, AltaVista, HotBot, or Yahoo can yield the very Web sites that have been copied. Also, using the online databases to which a library subscribes can be beneficial in detecting copied articles that free search engines cannot find. The trick of using these online resources is to choose a search string that will give specific results instead of thousands of potential hits. In his article "Busting the new breed of plagiarist," Bugeja recommends several techniques when using electronic sources for detecting plagiarism.[26] Two key techniques he suggests are to "enter a long phrase from the first paragraph" and "identify and enter phrases that [arouse] your suspicion."[27]

How the identified phrases and word combinations from suspicious papers are searched greatly depends on the search engine or database being used. A resource like Turnitin.com or Google cannot successfully retrieve plagiarized passages from subscription databases.[28] Therefore, librarians' informational retrieval expertise can aid faculty by identifying and searching these resources for possible plagiarism. Bugeja suggests avoiding the use of Boolean logic when using search engines but to depend on this logic for online databases.[29] As more and more databases provide the full text of articles, reliance on each database's options for searching and limiting to full text will vary.

Using translation software to convert foreign text to English and copying verbatim is a unique type of plagiarism and quite difficult to track down. Stebelman suggests that using the "Find related articles" feature in various online databases is a technique to find this type of plagiarism.[30] With additional features being added to search engines, their translation features could also be used to translate foreign text on Web sites and then copied word for word. However, the "Find similar sites" option on many search engines like Google, Yahoo, and Alta Vista could likely identify plagiarized foreign sites.

In a recent *CQ Researcher* issue about plagiarism, several organizations are listed whose missions are to provide open forums about the various aspects of academic integrity and plagiarism such as detection and prevention.[31] The Center of Academic Integrity, affiliated with the Kenan Institute for Ethics at Duke University, is a consortium of universities and colleges across North America and "provides a forum to identify, affirm, and promote the values of academic integrity among students, faculty, teachers and administrators."[32] Other sites that deal with plagiarism and academic dishonesty provide articles, checklists, discussion groups, and curriculum kits.

Deterring Plagiarism

In an academic environment there are many ways librarians can support the University in fighting plagiarism. As librarians we support not only information retrieval but the whole process of research and development of information literacy skills from identifying a topic to finding resources to using critical thinking and analysis. Promoting information literacy includes teaching students about plagiarism. Brandt defines a basic model for librarians when addressing plagiarism:

1. Define it . . .
2. Show examples to make it clear . . .
3. Describe its consequences . . .
4. . . . promote its prevention . . .
5. Discuss it.[33]

One powerful way to incorporate this model into the curriculum is in the classroom. Teaching a semester-long course, collaborating with faculty, or doing a workshop or seminar provides opportunities to address plagiarism on multiple levels.

A dedicated information literacy course or the full integration of information literacy into a course's curriculum are ideal situations to address plagiarism on these various levels. Unfortunately, we don't all have these opportunities; many of us still conduct the "50-minute" one shot classroom visits and it is a struggle to fit everything into a specific class. However, close consultation with the instructor often identifies areas that librarians need to address in the classroom environment and what areas can be addressed through assignment modification. As information professionals, we are in a position to guide the professor in identifying what aspects of plagiarism we should emphasize when teaching his or her students.

When librarians conduct instructional sessions, it can be a challenge to develop an activity or exercise that will work within the given time frame and also achieve the goal of bringing greater awareness to students. While developing a handout or conducting a mini-lecture will provide the necessary information, these approaches are less effective in demonstrating the multiple aspects of plagiarism. A simple interactive exercise to address plagiarism is to have students form small groups and develop their definitions of plagiarism, create examples that support that definition, determine reasons why plagiarism occurs, and identify ways to prevent it. Each group should report back to the whole class and use the comments to initiate further discussion. Additionally, these comments can be recorded, specific points agreed upon by the whole class and then used to develop a non-plagiarism agreement form, which all of the students in the class would sign. Signed agreement forms can also help an instructor or professor when dealing with a case of plagiarism.

Another activity would be to present a case of plagiarism or a newspaper article reporting an incidence of plagiarism to the class. In small group discussions, students can address why they support or don't support the individuals involved in the case, discuss the punishment of the accused, and the consequences of actions by the individuals involved in the case. Students can each write a reflective piece about the case and their position.

Collaborating with faculty and key programs on campus can be a second major vehicle in plagiarism prevention. Being a detective for individual faculty is an easy way for a librarian to demonstrate knowledge and expertise. However, in reality, it is just a band-aid solution. One could be very quickly overwhelmed with requests to expose plagiarists. A broader approach such as working with instructors and professors when developing assignments, projects, and overall curricula addresses the many ways poorly designed assignments actually promote plagiarism rather than prevent it. Hinchliffe suggests that educators:

- Emphasize the processes involved in doing research and writing papers. Ways to do so include requiring topic proposals, idea outlines, multiple drafts, interim working bibliographies and photocopies of sources.
- Require students to engage and apply ideas, not just describe them.
- Require students to reflect personally on the topic or the processes of research and writing, either in the paper or as an additional writing assignment.[34]

Another preventative strategy is to "[l]et educators know how easy it can be to search for potentially plagiarized text."[35] Providing a workshop through your library can achieve this; alternatively, you can utilize your institution's professional development structure. For example, the Center for Instructional Excellence at Purdue University sponsors a development series for faculty and staff called the *Teaching Workshop Series*. This series provides opportunities for peers and colleagues to share their experiences and effective techniques or practices throughout the campus. Another venue is the *Focus on Teaching* program, which showcases instructional initiatives being developed and practiced by professors throughout the University. Other programs or departments that can be sponsors for workshops and seminars are the campus writing lab and campus copyright office. Another forum can be in local conferences, particularly the ones that promote teaching and technology.

LIBRARY WEB SITES ADDRESSING PLAGIARISM

Libraries and librarians are addressing plagiarism in multiple ways through their Web sites. Gary L. Anderson suggests "[a] well-written plagiarism guide can be an effective tool. It should define plagiarism. . . . quote the institution's policy on plagiarism and cheating, and illustrate what is and is not plagiarism."[36] Many library Web sites now offer informational guides for instructors and students on defining plagiarism, how to avoid it, and how to detect it. Below is a brief annotated list of selected Web sites created by academic libraries in North America. Additionally, the search engines Google, Yahoo, and Alta Vista provide lists of plagiarism Web sites in their writing or education sections.

Plagiarism and Cyberplagiarism
http://www.aquinas.edu/library/plagiarism.html

Provided by the Woodhouse Library at Aquinas College, this Web page provides information for both students and faculty about defining plagiarism and ways to prevent it. The information sources are a combination of other Web resources, print articles, and even seminar notes.

Plagiarism, Cyberplagiarism and Possible Solutions
http://library.smsu.edu/LIS/workshops/wplagiarism.shtml

A mini online workshop developed by the Southwest Missouri State University Libraries. This page, basically a list of online resources, provides access to various search engines, detection programs, and term paper mills and vendors.

eSearch: Spring 2002(1)–Dalhousie University Libraries
http://www.library.dal.ca/news/esearch5.htm

This is the feature article in the Spring 2002 issue of e-Search, an online newsletter produced by the Dalhousie University Libraries. The article entitled *Cyberplagiarism: The New Plague on Campus* overviews the library system's Web site resources for "avoiding, detecting and preventing plagiarism."

CyberPlagiarism: Identification and Detection
http://library.mtroyal.ca/instruction/02-03/plagiarism.htm

A resource list with some annotations guiding the reader to various resources and tools for doing what the title indicates–identifying and detecting cyberplagiarism. What distinguishes this resource list are the examples of unique phrases that can be searched online, helping an instructor determine what to look for in a potentially plagiarized paper. Also, on this page are quotes from journal articles about plagiarism and academic dishonesty. These quotes are cited at the end of the Web page.

Plagiarism Prevention Reference Resource
http://www.uwplatt.edu/~library/reference/plagiarism.htmlx

This reference resource, developed by the University of Wisconsin–Plattville Karrmann Library, is a brief article defining copyright and plagiarism, providing information on why students cheat, and ways to detect and prevent plagiarism. This article cites multiple resources to support the information provided as well as Internet resources giving information on online paper mills and plagiarism detection.

Plagiarism Resources and Services for Faculty at the Osterlin Library and How Do I Avoid Plagiarism?
http://www.nmc.edu/library/faculty/plagiarism/
http://www.nmc.edu/library/faculty/plagiarism/avoid.html

The Osterlin Library provides two resource guides, one for faculty and one for students. The faculty guide is entitled *Plagiarism Resources and Services A Guide for Faculty*. This well-developed guide provides a definition of plagiarism as defined by the college's handbook, ways to detect and prevent plagiarism, as well as extensive resources for more information on this issue. The student guide, *How Do I Avoid Plagiarism?* is a much shorter version of the faculty guide but provides key links to other resources for correct paraphrasing, appropriate citing of sources, and developing bibliographies.

Electronic Plagiarism Seminar
http://www.lemoyne.edu/library/plagiarism.htm

This seminar provides a comprehensive listing of subjects dealing with plagiarism such as detection, online paper mills, and guides for educators and students. The strength of this resource is the extensive use of Web resources. This Web site was created by Gretchen Pearson, Public Services Librarian, Noreen Reale Falcone Library, Le Moyne College.

Plagiarism in Cyberspace: Sources, Prevention, Detection, and Other Information
http://www.library.csustan.edu/lboyer/plagiarism/

This easy-to-navigate online resource includes extensive Web links to tools, Web sites, and articles about plagiarism in the electronic age. One of the unique articles cited is about high school students using hand-held devices, such as PDAs and calculators, for cheating on tests.

Guide to Plagiarism and Cyber-Plagiarism
http://www.library.ualberta.ca/guides/plagiarism/

This site developed by the University of Alberta Libraries is a well-structured guide that overviews the various aspects of plagiarism, including why students do it and how to prevent and detect it. It also provides numerous links to resources for faculty and students.

CONCLUSION

Plagiarism has been a part of the college and university environment since the 19th century and continues to be an issue today. Technology influences all aspects of librarianship and the academic learning environment; its tools challenge the classical perceptions of the ownership of expressions and ideas. While studies show that plagiarism has not reached "plague" levels, students will continue to steal passages, whether consciously or not, from all types of resources. The growing availability of online resources cultivates unintentional plagiarism with their easy accessibility. Librarians can apply their expertise by instructing students, collaborating with faculty, and developing online resources. As knowledge managers, librarians have an important role in educating their patrons about the meaning and dimensions of plagiarism and how best to deter and avoid it.

REFERENCES

1. Jacqueline Borin. "E-problems, E-solutions: Electronic reference and the problem patron in the academic library," *The Reference Librarian* 75/76 (2002): 155.
2. Joseph Gibaldi. *MLA Style Manual and Guide to Scholarly Publishing* (New York: The Modern Language Association of America, 1998): 151.

3. Thomas Mallon. *Stolen Words* (San Diego: Harcourt, 2001): xi.

4. Mallon, xiii.

5. Elizabeth M. Nuss. "Academic integrity: Comparing faculty and student attitudes," *Improving College and University Teaching*, Summer 1984, 140-144.

6. Gibaldi, *MLA Style Manual*.

7. Sue Carter Simmons. "Compelling notions of authorship: A historical look at students and textbooks on plagiarism and cheating," in *Perspectives on Plagiarism and Intellectual Property in a Postmodern World*, eds. Lise Buranen and Alice M. Roy, (Albany: State University of New York Press, 1999).

8. Judy Anderson. *Plagiarism, Copyright Violation, and Other Thefts of Intellectual Property: An Annotated Bibliography with a Lengthy Introduction* (Jefferson, NC: McFarland & Co., 1998).

9. Wilfried Decoo. *Crisis on Campus: Confronting Academic Misconduct* (Cambridge, Massachusetts: The MIT Press, 2002).

10. D. L. McCabe and W. J. Bowers. "Academic honesty among males in college: A 30-year perspective," *Journal of College Student Development* 35 (1994): 5-10.

11. Gail Junion-Metz. "The e-plagiarism plague," *School Library Journal*, September, 2000, 43.

12. Decoo, *Crisis on campus*.

13. Patrick M. Scanlon and David R. Neumann. "Internet plagiarism among college students," *Journal of College Student Development* 43 (2002): 374-385.

14. Ginny McCormick. "Whose idea was that?" *Stanford Magazine*, September/October, 2003, http://www.stanfordalumni.org/news/magazine/2003/sepoct/features/plagiarism.html.

15. Stephen Wilhoit. "Helping students avoid plagiarism," *College Teaching*, Fall 1994, 161-164.

16. Lenora C. Thompson and Portia G. Williams. "But I changed three words! Plagiarism in the ESL classroom," *The Clearing House*, September-October, 1995, 27-29.

17. Sheilah Maramark and Mindi Barth Maline. *Academic Dishonesty among College Students* (Washington, DC: U.S. Dept. of Education, Office of Educational Research and Improvement, Office of Research, 1993).

18. Arlene Franklyn-Stokes and Stephen E. Newstead. "Undergraduate cheating: Who does what and why?" *Studies in Higher Education* 20 (1995): 159-72.

19. D. L. McCabe, L. K. Trevino, and K. D. Butterfield. "Academic integrity in honor code and non-honor code environments: A qualitative investigation," *Journal of Higher Education* 70 (1999): 211-234.

20. D. L. McCabe and L. K. Trevino. "What we know about cheating in college: Longitudinal trends and recent developments," *Change* 28, January-February, 1996, 28-33.

21. Rebecca Moore Howard. "Forget about policing plagiarism. Just teach," *The Chronicle of Higher Education*, November 16, 2001, B.24.

22. Peter Ashworth and Philip Bannister. "Guilty in whose eyes? University students' perceptions of cheating and plagiarism in academic work and assessment," *Studies in Higher Education*, June, 1997, 187.

23. Denise Hamilton. "Plagiarism: Librarians Help Provide New Solutions to an Old Problem," *Searcher*, April, 2003, 26-28.

24. *Turnitin.com*, www.turnitin.com (accessed October 29, 2003).

25. Hamilton, "Plagiarism."

26. Bugeja, Michael. "Busting the new breed of plagiarist," *The Writer's Chronicle*, September, 2000, 1-7.

27. Bugeja, 4.

28. John Royce. "Has Turnitin.com got it all wrapped up?" *Teacher Librarian*, April, 2003, 26-30.

29. Bugeja, 5.

30. Scott Stebelman. "Cybercheating: Dishonesty goes digital," *American Libraries* 29 (September 1998): 48-50.

31. Brian Hansen. "Combating plagiarism," *The CQ Researcher* 13 (2003): 773-96.

32. Center for Academic Integrity, "About Us," http://www.academicintegrity.org/ (accessed November 3, 2003).

33. D. Scott Brandt. "Copyright's (not so) little cousin, plagiarism," *Computers in Libraries*, May, 2002, 41.

34. Lisa Hinchliffe, "Cut-and-Paste Plagiarism: Preventing, Detecting and Tracking Online Plagiarism." (May 1998) http://alexia.lis.uiuc.edu/~janicke/plagiary.htm (accessed October 26, 2003).

35. C. Brian Smith, "Fighting Cyberplagiarism," *Library Journal*, Summer, 2003, 22.

36. Gregory L. Anderson. "Cyberplagiarism: A Look at the Web term paper sites," *College & Research Libraries News*, May, 1999, 373.

Structures and Choices
for Ready Reference Web Sites

Steven W. Sowards

SUMMARY. The structure of ready reference Web sites in American public and academic libraries reflects answers to consistently encountered design questions. A survey of 100 Web sites shows widespread agreement about naming these resources, using subject categories, and relying on free unlicensed Web sources for content. Opinions are divided about the optimum number of listed sources and the best ways to organize hot links. Guides and explanations rarely are provided for users. Librarians have not built these sites around commercial products, although advanced search features could make the purchase of ready reference tools more appealing. Further study of user behavior would help librarians meet the needs of their clientele. *[Article copies available for a fee from The Haworth Document Delivery Service: 1-800-HAWORTH. E-mail address: <docdelivery@haworthpress.com> Website: <http://www.HaworthPress.com> © 2005 by The Haworth Press, Inc. All rights reserved.]*

KEYWORDS. Ready reference, Web page design

Steven W. Sowards is Head of Main Library Reference, Michigan State University Libraries, 100 Library, East Lansing, MI 48824 (E-mail: sowards@msu.edu).

[Haworth co-indexing entry note]: "Structures and Choices for Ready Reference Web Sites." Sowards, Steven W. Co-published simultaneously in *The Reference Librarian* (The Haworth Information Press, an imprint of The Haworth Press, Inc.) No. 91/92, 2005, pp. 117-138; and: *The Reference Collection: From the Shelf to the Web* (ed: William J. Frost) The Haworth Information Press, an imprint of The Haworth Press, Inc., 2005, pp. 117-138. Single or multiple copies of this article are available for a fee from The Haworth Document Delivery Service [1-800-HAWORTH, 9:00 a.m. - 5:00 p.m. (EST). E-mail address: docdelivery@haworthpress.com].

doi:10.1300/J120v44n91_09

INTRODUCTION

Librarians fell in love with online "ready reference" tools as soon as they discovered the Internet. When the World Wide Web made access to such resources even easier, ready reference Web pages became a common feature of library Web sites. Lists of specific high-quality sources, advice about the design of Web pages to present them, and comments about the use of such tools by library staff and patrons have appeared regularly in library and information science publications. On the basis of past experience with print sources, librarians easily recognized a role for these non-print resources. The novel challenge has been the organization and online presentation of these tools.

William Katz has defined "ready reference" questions as "data queries that require only a single, usually uncomplicated, straightforward answer . . . normally found without difficulty in standard reference works . . . "[1] Simply put, a typical ready reference question can be answered quickly with a fact. "Ready reference sources" are works primarily intended to supply those facts as directly as possible. While factual content appears in many kinds of publications, the typical ready reference tool is a dictionary, encyclopedia, directory, or almanac. Many ready reference sources have become available on the World Wide Web in the last ten years, either as online versions of existing print tools or as new creations.

"Ready reference Web sites" use single or multiple Web pages to direct users to selected online ready reference sources. Hot links to specific online ready reference tools appear in organized lists. The number of links can range from under a dozen to nearly a thousand. Various organizing schemes are possible, especially to handle large numbers of links. There is no mandatory set of Web tools that defines a ready reference site, but ZIP Code and telephone directories, language dictionaries, currency converters, universal calendars, and statistical handbooks are characteristic. Freely available Web sites dominate. Licensed resources can be included, but their employment of logins works against "uncomplicated, straightforward" use of a library's ready reference Web pages.

Libraries have institutional home pages that serve purposes beyond those of ready reference, and their ready reference Web sites are presented in that context. Links to ready reference Web tools may appear in combination with links to other Web sites. When the proportion of ready reference Web sources in such a combination becomes so small that the ready reference tools are lost in the crowd, it is better to think of the presentation as an Internet directory that includes entries for ready reference tools, not as a true ready reference Web site.

The arrangement of elements on ready reference Web sites varies widely, thanks to the flexibility of HTML. Those Web pages are made up of content elements (labeled hot links to actual resources running on distant servers outside the local library) and design elements. The design elements commonly include a title for the main page, lists of categories if sub-sections are used (on separate pages if the site has a hierarchical arrangement), and sometimes supporting features intended to guide readers. Library Web site designers have similar goals in mind, and choose from a shared set of online tools and HTML options. Differences between sites reflect local preferences about selection criteria, navigation options, supporting features, and aesthetics, rather than different purposes.

Numerous publications describe or recommend specific sources found on the Web. For example, the Machine-Assisted Reference Section (MARS) of the Reference and User Services Association (RUSA) of the American Library Association publishes a list of "best" online reference tools annually in the Fall issue of *Reference and User Services Quarterly*.[2] As is often the case, the MARS/RUSA list also suggests criteria for identifying valuable or well-prepared Web-based tools. Such discussions of criteria have been taking place since the mid to late 1990s.[3]

Another set of articles considers the organization and structure of Web pages that present ready reference resources to users. These publications overlap with articles about research "pathfinders" prepared by librarians, and the migration of such subject guides from paper to online versions.[4]

SURVEY OF WEB SITE DESIGNS

Based on the literature and on workplace familiarity with ready reference Web sites, the author identified key alternatives and decisions in their design. To measure the extent to which particular elements actually are found in the ready reference Web sites of American libraries, he prepared twenty questions (see the Appendix for the questions and a table of results). Answers to those questions were tabulated for 100 ready reference Web pages selected from library Web sites listed in *LibDex*: one public library and one academic library from each of the fifty states.[5] The survey results indicate general agreement among librarians about many structure and design choices, but divided approaches to others. Also, some innovative and potentially useful features that have been touted in publications rarely appear on actual Web pages.

If library patrons, Web surfers and researchers are going to find facts (or at least tools offering facts) using library ready reference Web sites, several things must take place. First, patrons must recognize these resource pages when they encounter them. Second, patrons must understand how to make relevant selections among available choices. The design of the site's first screen is therefore crucial.

Question 1: Does the word "reference" appear on the ready reference Web site?

Researchers using the Web are often in a hurry: an informative name for a Web page is important because users must rapidly recognize its purpose. If we assume that library patrons begin on a library Web site (rather than a general search engine like *Google*), then the visible name matters even more than the formal "Title" identified by HTML tags. In their pursuit of clarity, do Web page designers use the word "reference"?

Librarians realize that the word "reference" means nothing to some library users, but continue to use it for lack of a better term. Web page designers have followed this trend. When University of Virginia librarians set up their first "Internet Reference Resources" Web page in 1997, "one of the first tricky issues the Advisory Group had to resolve was what to name the page"–and they decided to include the word "reference."[6] When Kristine Stacy-Bates surveyed Web sites of large academic libraries in 1999, she examined "the title at the top of the ready-reference main page" and found "a pattern of page titles for ready-reference pages, with 109 of 126 (86.5%) containing the word 'Reference.'"[7]

The examples used for the present study were drawn from the state-by-state alphabetical lists of American libraries maintained by *LibDex*. For each state, one academic library and one public library were selected: 50 libraries of each type and two libraries from each state. The resulting pool included a wide range of institutions, from large libraries serving major cities and research universities, to smaller ones found in towns, colleges, and community colleges. The survey questions and a tabular summary of the results appear in the Appendix.

When these 100 sites were surveyed for the present study, "reference" was the word most frequently encountered identifying ready reference Web sites, appearing in 75 percent of sites in the sample. It often was combined with other words to form titles such as "Reference Resources" or "Virtual Reference Desk." Public libraries were more likely than academic libraries to use titles without the word "reference," such as "Selected Internet Sites" or "Helpful Links." Presumably the intent is to help viewers for whom the term "reference" is unfamiliar.

Librarians use a specialized vocabulary because the exact use of key terms contributes precision in a complex and technical profession. For many users, however, the result is confusing jargon. A usability study of Web-based subject guides and pathfinders conducted by Charles Dean in 1998 showed that "terminology common to librarians and experienced researchers (such as 'reference' or 'collections') and other general terms (i.e., 'source,' 'research,' and 'tools') often were misinterpreted."[8] Writing about ready reference sites in 2002, Theresa Mudrock agreed that "readability studies show that wording/language is especially important for user understanding. Library jargon, acronyms, and vendor names can cause confusion for users."[9]

The issue of library jargon is tied to a wider issue that will be addressed later: the tension between designs that reflect staff members' needs and expertise, and designs that cater to users' needs and limitations.

Question 2: Is the ready reference site part of a larger Web page?

The placement of ready reference Web pages within a larger library Web site falls outside the scope of this study. However, three ways in which this is handled are worth mentioning, because of their influence on decisions about the structure of ready reference Web pages.

First, the library may highlight the ready reference Web page as a top-level choice on the home page or Reference Department page. This solution provides a very direct path to ready reference tools. Second, the library may include ready reference tools as part of a large-scale Internet resource directory with links to many kinds of Web sites. If that directory involves multiple separate pages, the "Ready Reference" page will appear as one among many. Users must notice and select that page, but having done so, have direct access to ready reference tools. Third, the library may present ready reference content as only one part of a Web page that fulfills many purposes. That page could be a large-scale Internet resource directory: if this appears as a single very long HTML document, much scrolling may be needed to find the ready reference section of that page. Alternatively, ready reference links may appear on a page that is also devoted to information such as building hours or announcements: if so, users may not notice that ready reference resources have been included. These conditions make it harder to attach a clear name or heading to the ready reference component. In the sample, about one library out of five (21 percent) inserted ready reference content into a larger page. The other 79 percent of sites opted for separate ready reference pages.

Question 3: Are licensed tools included among the ready reference tools?

Librarians have limited incentive to go beyond "free" sites when picking items for ready reference Web sites because so many Web-based reference tools are available without licensing, login authentication, fees, or registration. Libraries pay for many licensed databases, but the same advanced features that make those commercial databases valuable also give them a character that is out of step with the "uncomplicated, straightforward" nature of ready reference activity. In the sample, 70 percent of sites excluded all licensed, for-fee tools. Another 28 percent offered a few. Only two percent included many licensed sources in their ready reference lists.

Question 4: Is a commercial product the main resource?

Some libraries in the sample supplemented their lists of free ready reference sites with links to leased or purchased compilations such as *xrefer* or *Oxford Reference Online*.[10] In theory, products of this kind could replace free ready reference tools completely, but no libraries in the sample adopted that approach. Several small public libraries used the *YouSeeMore* commercial Web page service[11] as a customizable platform for ready reference links. Others relied on consortia for shared ready reference pages. In either case, the tools offered through the platform tended to be free unlicensed Web sites.

Some libraries, including large academic libraries with access to a large number of commercial databases such as indexing and abstracting services, offered lists of links that included only licensed materials. While these lists sometimes included ready reference resources, this arrangement tended to disperse the ready reference items within the longer list to such an extent that no specific part of the site was devoted to ready reference resources alone.

Question 5: How many categories appear in the initial list?

On the first screen of a ready reference Web page, the second feature that must be recognized by viewers is the list of available choices. When more than a few items are offered, they usually are grouped in categories. Users must understand the use of those categories in order to find specific tools.

In the sample, 21 percent of sites had no category structure: that is, all resources were listed together under the name of the page, a sensible decision when the number of links is small and requires no organization except perhaps alphabetizing. Put another way, these sites had one category, and that category was "ready reference."

In the remaining 79 cases, the online connections to actual tools were grouped into as few as three or as many as 48 categories. The median number of categories was nine if all 100 sites are considered, even those with only one category ("ready reference"). The median was 11 if only the 79 more elaborate sites are considered. The 20 sites with the fewest categories among this group of 79 had from three to seven categories. Twenty more had between 7 and 11 categories. Another 20 had from 12 to 20 categories. The remaining 19 sites (the largest) had from 21 to 48 categories.

Question 6: How are categories organized on the page?

Of the 79 sites with multiple categories, 52 (68 percent) arranged those categories in alphabetical order. The display of categories in the other 27 sites had no apparent order. The remaining 21 sites in the full sample had no categories except the main heading of "ready reference" (by whatever name).

Alphabetical order is an attractive way to organize categories because it is easily recognized. If the alphabetical list is very long, users still may have to scan much of the list to find a category corresponding to their area of interest. This problem is mitigated by widespread use of a relatively small number of category names. When users become familiar with ready reference Web sites, they can anticipate likely headings and look for them directly in alphabetical order on the list.

In the sample, the five most common categories for ready reference sources were:

- Directories, including telephone and ZIP Code directories;
- Dictionaries, including thesauri;

- Government or politics;
- Education, colleges and universities, and financial aid/grants; and
- Newspapers.

It is worth noting that even the most frequently used categories appeared on no more than half of the Web sites in the sample. The second most frequently encountered five categories covered:

- Atlases, maps, or geography;
- Encyclopedias;
- Health or medicine;
- Business; and
- Statistics.

The third most commonly seen five categories were:

- Biographies;
- Jobs, careers, or employment;
- Style sheets, writing, or citation guides;
- Quotations; and
- Almanacs.

No authority establishes 'official' category names or the correct heading to which any one source should be assigned. The use of natural language terms instead of controlled vocabularies like Library of Congress Subject Headings risks ambiguity, but users are likely to understand these names. The limited size of ready reference resource lists (compared to full-scale library catalogues) reduces the potential for confusion and frustration.

The categories used by ready reference Web sites refer to subjects (such as medicine) or classes of tools (such as dictionaries) almost without exception. These groupings have become so familiar, that we take them for granted. It is easy to forget that in the recent past, other approaches were possible and sometimes necessary. Librarians may have adopted subject-based organization because it was logical and familiar, but its prevalence across the Web also reflects conditions in the wider online world.

Before general use of the World Wide Web for sharing Internet materials, knowing the online location of a resource was crucial to its use, along with mastery of various protocols, including ftp, gopher, and WAIS. When members of the early online community traded information about new resources, they shared not only the names and purposes of sites, but also the identities of sponsoring authors or agencies, detailed addresses for computer hosts, and exact protocols and login commands. Early lists of ready reference Internet resources reflect these realities. "Scott Yanoff's List," a frequently updated "Special Internet Connections" list from the early 1990s, is characteristic.[12] This lengthy guide to online tools was organized not only under subject headings and by the titles of specific resources, but also by named associations and other Internet publishers, by login protocols, and by the library and university sites that hosted useful projects. Today's search engines make it unnecessary to know the location of resources to use them, and protocols beyond http are rarely in evidence: only subject and title organization now command our interest.

The impact of HTML and the Web on this development can be traced in accounts of early library Web pages. Explaining the superiority of HTML, http, and hypertext over existing gopher systems in 1994, James Powell outlined plans for a "basic library information system" that would include "a basic document classifying some diverse information resources by general *subject* classifications."[13] When Scott Mellendorf added "reference desk-type resources for ready reference situations" to a "no-frills 'Work Page'" at Saginaw Valley State University in 1995, he chose to use "a separate page of bookmarks by *subject*."[14] Mudrock has reported the same decision when

> the University of Washington Libraries' Reference Tools page began as a battered address book that sometime in 1995 became a list on the Web, a glorified bookmark for the convenience of reference staff. The page, named the electronic reference shelf, was a hodge-podge of links arranged by *subject* . . .[15]

Scott Silet noted comparable origins for the University of Virginia's Internet Reference Resources Web page, which in 1997

> started out as a series of handy web sites which . . . reference librarians found and bookmarked. . . . many of us created lists of Internet-accessible resources on our library's reference pages. Unfortunately for our users, most were difficult to find and poorly organized. . . . Some used a straight alphabetic listing while others attempted . . . to group items by *subject*. . . . An Advisory Committee . . . was established to coordinate the creation, design and main-

tenance of the IRR . . . starting with establishing a coherent and logical *subject* hierarchy.[16]

In each case, the simplicity of the Web promoted the use of online reference resources, and then allowed their organization through subject categories, after protocols and locations lost their importance. By the time Hal Kirkwood surveyed academic business library Web sites in 1998-99, he found that 58 out of 60 libraries relied on subject groupings.[17]

The use of subject categories is widespread on ready reference Web sites. The number of categories does vary widely, but this is a practical reflection of the wide variation in the number of sources included.

Question 7: How many total links are found on the site?

The number of links to specific tools offered by libraries in the sample ranges from as few as seven, to as many as 800 or more in two cases. That variation reflects contrasting answers to a basic question about ready reference Web site design: "Is the most helpful site for users one that offers the *best* resources, or the *most* resources?"

Efforts that are too ambitious can be self-defeating. Jorge Luis Borges suggested why in a brief fable about an empire in which "the Schools of Cartography sketched a Map of the Empire which was the size of the Empire and coincided at every point with it." However, "the Following Generations comprehended that this dilated Map was Useless . . . " because without selectivity, no useful purpose was achieved.[18]

The impulse to offer the "most" tools to users–that is, to offer longer lists–is understandable but leads to increased complexity. To help users navigate successfully, it may seem necessary to introduce elaborate supporting features. Ironically, the addition of those features in turn presents the user with more choices and more sources of confusion, and demands even more helping features. Pressed to a logical conclusion, sites with the "most" to offer may deliver the least in practical terms, like Borges' map.

Sites that instead offer the "best" resources face hard choices of their own: sources under consideration must satisfy selection criteria and maintain the simplicity of the site as a whole. Smaller sites do avoid the logical tailspin that can ruin larger sites through elaboration.

The actual size of ready reference Web sites in the sample demonstrates competing answers to the question of larger versus smaller resource lists. The number of sources varied by two orders of magnitude, from seven to 70 to over 700. Contrasting assumptions among site planners about the audience for their ready reference Web sites are lurking behind discussions in the library literature about selection criteria, purpose, and mission. Are these sites being established to serve the needs of library users or library staff?

Previously quoted comments about early ready reference Web sites show that initial projects were driven by staff awareness of Internet resources, staff experiments with bookmarking useful online tools, and staff efforts to streamline the resulting lists. Some reports explicitly stated that new online resources were valuable for library staff members. Mellendorf noted that the "no-frills 'Work Page'" at Saginaw Valley State University "provides reference librarians with quick access to the Internet" and "provides all staff with a wealth of keyword-accessible data."[19] Susan Lynn described the Web in 1999 as a challenge for reference staff because the

> potentially unlimited number of ready-reference resources available through the World Wide Web . . . creates a challenge for librarians attempting to locate the most appropriate source for each ready-reference question posed by patrons.[20]

John Matylonek, Carolyn Ottow, and Terry Reese saw potential value for the Oregon State University library in "Reference Desk Manager" software because "the staff is being overwhelmed by a plethora of frequent and urgent information requests." While admitting that the design plans for ready reference resources tended to reflect the needs of staff members, they accepted that approach because "Librarians who have shown the greatest interest build the contents . . ."[21]

Designs of this kind assumed that library staff would use online ready reference tools to help library users by conducting mediated searches and then delivering answers. A competing approach to ready reference Web sites emphasized library patrons. Advocates for users argued that library staff could offer the most helpful online ready reference service by designing user-friendly Web sites on which patrons could find their own information. Thomas Jevec included "feedback and user expectations" in a list of design considerations for library Web site planners as early as 1997.[22] Dean asked in 1998, "Who are the end-users, what do they want to know, and how can they find it?" when preparing similar guidelines, and included students in focus groups evaluating online subject guides.[23] In 2000, Stacy-Bates adopted a user-centric perspective for her survey of ready-reference and e-mail reference services, saying,

"Librarians must carefully plan the site content and design to serve patrons for whom the Web has become a central source of information." She had no doubt about the audience for ready reference Web tools: "Ready-reference Web resources should guide patrons to facts more quickly or accurately than a general Internet search engine would . . ." Library Web pages would "link patrons with sources that contain answers to ready-reference questions." Precisely because "virtual ready-reference resources . . . can be accessed by patrons who lack instruction or orientation, Web page design issues . . . should be given careful attention" by staff.[24] Diane Kovacs applied the same user-centric principle in her criteria for a core Internet reference collection:

> Decide what kind of reference materials your library's clients need. . . . The reference collection is used by librarians and library clients to find quick and easy answers. . . . The subject coverage of these reference tools must be determined by the library client's needs.[25]

In 2002, Mudrock argued in favor of "Revising Ready Reference Sites" precisely because so many existing

> ready reference pages reflect their library-centric origins and exemplify the 'librarians know best syndrome.' We have created and organized our ready reference pages in our own image with little explicit knowledge of the user's needs and wants.[26]

Mudrock expected that server usage statistics, virtual transaction logs, and usability testing would reveal those needs. In the same vein, Carla Dunsmore foresaw improvements in Web-based pathfinders if librarians would "organize the information in a way the user would look for it . . ."[27]

Because extensive, complicated ready reference Web sites challenge users, advocates of user-centric design often opt for smaller sites. Dean cautioned against letting sites grow into "a 'list of lists' or laundry list of URLs . . . " and suggested featuring only "Web sites of demonstrated quality, content, stability, and institutional credibility . . ."[28] In her 1998 survey of 113 Ohio public library Web sites, Susan Mason found that larger libraries were more likely to have ready reference Web sites. She also warned against confusing the role of those local sites with the role already filled by Internet portals and search engines:

Large numbers of links that are not judiciously selected, organized, or presented are readily available through existing search engines and do not necessarily add value to library Web sites.[29]

Laura Cohen and Julie Still compared the number of links on ready reference Web sites in the libraries of Ph.D.-granting institutions with those of two-year colleges in 1998, and found that

the type of school had a dramatic impact on the size and arrangement of the Web site. . . . patrons of the more complex libraries . . . are asked to select from and use a larger number and variety of materials and to navigate their way through a larger maze . . .[30]

About half of the two-year college sites surveyed by Cohen and Still offered 40 links or more, and one in ten offered more than 150 links. Among the research university sites, about half offered 100 links or more, and one in five offered more than 150 links.[31]

Question 8: What depth and search method options are used?

Web site designers employ a variety of devices to manage content and assist users with larger collections of links. Hierarchies of pages are a common solution: from a central page, the array of categories leads to a subsidiary level of secondary pages, or even a tertiary level. The depth of such hierarchies is limited only by the risk of confusing site visitors. In her survey of large academic libraries' ready reference Web sites, Stacy-Bates found as many as four levels, although more than 93 percent of sites had only one or two levels.[32]

Steven Sowards analyzed such hierarchical sites in 1998 using an "Option" typology in which a Roman numeral indicated the depth of the site and a letter indicated the organizing scheme: A for alphabetical, S for subject, and K for keyword.[33] Applying that method to the 100 sites surveyed for the present article, slightly more than half were found to use "Option I-S" in which all resource links appear on a single top-level page, grouped by subjects. Roughly one library in 10 was using "Option I-A" which also relies on a single top-level page, but arranges the sources in alphabetical order. About one third of the sites used "Option II-S" which groups sources by subject and places those groups on separate Web pages in a two-level hierarchy. These three "Options" account for 96 percent of sites in the sample.

Questions 9: Does the page use frames?
Question 10: Does the page use a left-hand tool bar?

Some complex sites rely on frames. Silet notes that the University of Virginia "Internet Reference Resources" Web site adopted a "left-hand frame and category/topic finders. I should add that it was only after some discussion that the Advisory Group accepted frames as the best way to organize the IRR, and we haven't looked back since."[34] He provides no details about that "discussion" but frames can present problems for users with older computers or limited bandwidth. Jevec noted this issue when discussing user-centered design principles and asked, "What does the use of high-end, dynamic, frames based or graphical interfaces bring to the content of the site? Would the site be better suited to a low-end interface given the mission?"[35] Graphics-laden Web pages also create obstacles for sight-impaired readers and others who rely on special software to make the Internet accessible. While not focusing on ready reference pages, Valerie Lewis and Julie Klauber took issue with today's trendy, graphics-heavy Web page designs: "With the increased use of graphics, keyboard commands became beveled buttons. . . . The Web became user-friendly. Unfortunately, this user-friendly Web was not very friendly to me."[36] Library Web sites that truly intend to reflect user needs must take accessibility into account. Ken Cotterill has argued in favor of designing ready reference Web sites that are accessible to a wide range of browsers.[37]

In the survey sample, 14 percent of sites used frames. A more common approach involved the use of a left-side tool bar to provide comparable convenience and clarity without raising the same issues of accessibility. Thirty-seven percent of sites in the sample used a simple tool bar on the left side of the screen as an aid to site navigation. In combination, frame-based and frame-free left-side navigation bars appeared on half of all the sites in the sample.

Question 11: Is there a note about the purpose of the site?
Question 12: Is there a note about the intended audience for the site?
Question 13: Is there a note about selection criteria for the site?
Question 14: Is there a glossary or key to terms for the site?

When Silet's team at the University of Virginia planned their "Internet Reference Resources" site, they recommended several value-adding features to accompany Web pages and explain their function. These features included texts about the purpose or mission of the site, statements about the anticipated audience, and guidelines for collection development.[38] Given librarians' concerns about library jargon, the presence of a glossary or key to crucial terms is another sensible supporting feature.

These helpful ideas are more prominent in the written literature than in practice. Dunsmore looked for statements of "explicit purposes, concepts and principles" in her survey of business-related online pathfinders. While a majority of the Web pages she studied offered some introductory text, only a minority of them had content that she regarded as stating the scope or purpose of the guide.[39] In the present sample, 18 percent of libraries offered comments about the purpose of their ready reference Web sites. Seven percent described the audience for whom the site was intended. Only eight percent included even brief comments about selection criteria, let alone actual collection development statements. None of the sites in the survey offered a glossary. Even though the author gave credit for very minimal statements, these potentially helpful elements cannot be described as frequent elements on ready reference Web sites.

Question 15: Are categories annotated?
Question 16: Are individual items annotated?

Annotations also help users make intelligent use of ready reference Web sites. Dean described "annotative descriptions" for entries as a way to tap "human intelligence and expertise" when presenting Web-based subject guides.[40] The University of Virginia "Internet Reference Resource" site task force called for annotations, not only to guide users but also to "serve as words which are indexed by the IRR's internal search engine" to improve the results of keyword searching.[41] Cohen and Still praised sites that "supply a descriptive or evaluative blurb about the linked-to site. Such an annotation can provide a helpful guide to users as they scan lists of links and choose those sites they wish to visit." They were disappointed to find that a minority of research university and two-year college library sites offered annotations.[42] Kirkwood found that

> Annotations are important because of the inconsistent and often ambiguous names given by the vendors and designers to many

business information databases and resources. . . . such ambiguity requires that libraries provide some guidance and instruction about the content and appropriateness of a given resource for the user's specific need.

Forty-nine out of the 63 academic business library sites in Kirkwood's study (78 percent) provided some kind of annotation.[43]

In the present survey, annotations for individual sources were much more common on ready reference Web sites than annotations for subject categories. Only five percent of the sites in the sample offered annotations describing any of their categories. The brief names of categories apparently were regarded as self-explanatory. The record was better for annotations describing individual online tools. Thirty-one percent of sites in the sample offered at least some annotations, 16 percent had annotations for most entries, and 28 percent supplied annotated descriptions for every entry in the source lists. Only 25 percent of the sites completely lacked item-level annotations.

Question 17: Is there an online tutorial?

Online help, through tutorials or even simple examples, seems likely to improve users' success with ready reference Web tools. This is another good idea that has not yet been widely adopted. Even on the Web sites of academic business libraries, Kirkwood found instructional aids "only in 33% of sites, an astonishingly low number" despite his use of a very broad definition of tutorials.[44] The present survey found even fewer tutorials in the sample of library ready reference Web sites: only eight percent of sites offered even minimal instructional texts.

Question 18: Is there a link to an "Ask A Librarian" service?

Virtual reference services based on e-mail, chat, or instant messaging offer another method to assist users. Jevec has mentioned feedback as a way to determine the needs of users.[45] The literature on virtual reference has little to say about online ready reference Web sites, but their potential value as resources for remote users is obvious. In the present sample, 33 percent of libraries offered a link to some kind of "Ask A Librarian" service on their ready reference Web site. As more libraries adopt virtual reference services, this seems likely to increase.

Question 19: Is there an index/search feature with surface integration?
Question 20: Is there an index/search feature with deep integration?

Library ready reference Web sites rely on simple HTML features, but interactive features such as site indexes could help users find specific tools and bypass potentially confusing hierarchies and lists. Such features would "integrate" the diverse elements on the site.

Dean reported that faculty focus groups looking at a ready reference Web site in 1998 suggested "the capability to search through all the subject guide's pages by keyword or phrase . . ."[46] Kirkwood praised "sites that met the criteria of being successfully integrated [and that] combined the print, electronic, and Web-based resources into a single set of subject specific categories" whether or not those categories could be keyword-searched or still had to be scanned.[47] Mudrock suggested the use of "'see' references . . . to direct users to other possible categories of information" on other parts of the site.[48] All of these ideas integrate content for improved ease of use, although only at a "surface" level. In other words, only words in the name of the resource, the category titles and any annotations are examined by a keyword search. This kind of "surface integration" merely speeds up a process that can be performed manually by any user with the patience to scan every page on a library's Web site. Only one site in the survey sample offered even a basic keyword search of this kind.

Integration at a "deep" level would be far more effective for users, that is, if the keyword search not only scanned the titles and descriptions of sources, but also could check the full text of their contents. None of the sites in the sample had this kind of "deep integration" because it is a fairly new concept, developed and offered by commercial publishers and content owners rather than libraries managing homegrown Web sites.

Adam Hodgkin, the managing director of the *xrefer* commercial ready reference database, has described the potential impact of "deep integration" and its relationship to his product:

> the founders of xrefer took as their mission the creation of reference services which *aggregate* and *integrate* reference works. In the context of reference works aggregation involves bringing diverse works together into a common web site and then providing users with a search engine which executes searches on the complete aggregated library of reference content. Aggregation leads to efficient distribution (users get to know that a collection of refer-

ence works can be found at one source) and it also enables 'power searching' across a range of titles, but integration would ensure that the whole collection of reference material would contain signposts which relate entries found in disparate sources. A compelling integration strategy would lead to improvements in browsing and navigation.[49]

In a review of *xrefer*, Greg Notess described its "cross-linking technology" as "a master index to the entire collection."[50] The kind of deep integration offered by products like *xrefer* or *Oxford Reference Online* might persuade librarians to begin paying for ready reference sources instead of relying on free unlicensed Web tools.

CONCLUSION

A survey of American libraries shows clear interest in offering Web-based ready reference sources to library users. Ready reference Web sites are common features when libraries have a Web presence. At low cost and relying on basic HTML skills, this approach allows libraries to organize selected Internet tools and provide access for their patrons.

It is also clear that librarians can improve their ready reference Web sites. The use of supporting features–such as mission statements, annotations, and help screens–could be increased easily. Potentially greater contributions–such as "deep" integration–are only beginning to be explored.

Studies of user behavior would also identify helpful improvements. Little is known about the specific ready reference questions that library users bring to these sites, or about the specific tools that provide the best answers to those questions. Usability studies could tell us how online researchers look for and find ready reference tools (whether on the World Wide Web at large, or on libraries' home pages), and which Web site designs promote speed and success.

REFERENCES

1. William A. Katz. *Introduction to Reference Work*, 7th edition (New York: McGraw-Hill, 1997). Vol. I, 15-16.

2. RUSA Machine-Assisted Reference Section (MARS). "Best Free Reference Web Sites: Fourth Annual List." *Reference and User Services Quarterly* 42/1 (Fall 2002): 34-40.

3. Scott A. Silet. "Anatomy of the Internet Reference Resources Web Page: A UVA Library Experiment." *Virginia Libraries* 45/3 (July-Aug.-Sept. 1999): 8-9.

4. Charles W. Dean. "The Public Electronic Library: Web-Based Subject Guides." *Library Hi Tech* 16/3-4 (1998): 80-88.

5. For each state, library Web sites were examined in the order listed (alphabetical) at *LibDex: The Library Index* (http://www.libdex.com). Survey questions were answered based on the first two listed libraries (one academic and one public) that had a readily identifiable ready reference Web site. The survey was conducted between March 17 and April 20, 2003. In many cases, the library used in the sample was not the first one in the *LibDex* list: entries were passed over if the link was broken or the site had no apparent ready reference Web site. Some subjective decisions were unavoidable when determining whether elements were present. Some Web pages mixed ready reference tools with other content such as full-text newspapers, or offered links to mega-sites such as *Librarians' Index to the Internet* (http://lii.org/) or *Yahoo!* (http://www.yahoo.com/) instead of locally selected lists.

6. Silet, 7.

7. Kristine K. Stacy-Bates. "Ready-Reference Resources and E-Mail Reference on Academic ARL Web Sites." *Reference and User Services Quarterly* 40/1 (Fall 2000): 63 and 67.

8. Dean, 85.

9. Theresa Mudrock. "Revising Ready Reference Sites: Listening to Users Through Server Statistics and Query Logs." *Reference and User Services Quarterly* 42/2 (Winter 2002): 161.

10. "Free Showcase." *xrefer*. Available: http://www.xrefer.com/search.jsp (viewed 10 March 2003: as of 17 June 2003 this page was no longer available). "Find Out More." *Oxford Reference Online*. Available: http://www.oxfordreference.com/pub/2col/findoutmore_subscribers/Find_Out_More__subscribers.html (1 August 2003).

11. "Your e-library and much more." *YouSeeMore*. Available: http://www.youseemore.com/ (1 August 2003).

12. Scott Yanoff. "Special Internet Connections: Last update 10/1/93" (1993). Available: http://www.mcs.kent.edu/specconnections.html (1 August 2003).

13. James Powell. "Adventures With The World Wide Web: Creating a Hypertext Library Information System." *Database* 17/1 (February 1994): 62. Emphasis added. Available: http://www.geocities.com/james_e_powell/docs/adventures.html (1 August 2003).

14. Scott A. Mellendorf. "Working the Web with a No-frills 'Work Page.'" *Online* 20/1 (January/February 1996): 22. Emphasis added. Available: http://www.infotoday.com/online/JanOL/mellendorf.html (1 August 2003).

15. Mudrock, 156. Emphasis added.

16. Silet, 6-7. Emphasis added.

17. Hal Kirkwood, Jr. "Business Library Web Sites: A Review of the Organization and Structure of Print, Networked, and Internet Resources." *Journal of Business & Finance Librarianship* 5/4 (2000): 31.

18. Jorge Luis Borges and Adolfo Bioy Casares. "On Exactitude in Science." In: *Extraordinary Tales*, edited and translated by Anthony Kerrigan (London: Condor, 1973): 123.

19. Mellendorf, 22-23.

20. Susan Lynn. "A Comparison of Print vs. WWW-Based Ready-Reference Sources." M.S.L.S. thesis, University of North Carolina at Chapel Hill, 1999: 2.

21. John C. Matylonek, Carolyn Ottow, and Terry Reese. "Organizing Ready Reference and Administrative Information with the Reference Desk Manager." *D-Lib*

Magazine 7/11 (November 2001). Available: http://www.dlib.org/dlib/november01/matylonek/11matylonek.html (1 August 2003).

22. Thomas E. Jevec. "Designing and Maintaining Information in the Fast Lane." *First Monday* 2/8 (August 1997). Available: http://www.firstmonday.dk/issues/issue2_8/jevec/index.html (1 August 2003).

23. Dean, 83 and 85.

24. Stacy-Bates, 61-62.

25. Diane K. Kovacs. "Building A Core Internet Reference Collection." *Reference and User Services Quarterly* 39/3 (Spring 2000): 234.

26. Mudrock, 155.

27. Carla Dunsmore. "A Qualitative Study of Web-Mounted Pathfinders Created by Academic Business Libraries." *Libri* 52/3 (September 2002): 146-147.

28. Dean, 83.

29. Susan Gortner Mason. "Using Links to Facilitate Access to Internet Resources: A Content-Analysis of Ohio Public Library Web Sites." M.L.S. thesis, Kent State University, 1998: 19-20.

30. Laura B. Cohen and Julie M. Still. "A Comparison of Research University and Two-Year College Library Web Sites: Content, Functionality, and Form." *College & Research Libraries* 60/3 (May 1999): 285 and 289.

31. Cohen and Still, 281.

32. Stacy-Bates, 67-68.

33. Steven W. Sowards. "A Typology for Ready Reference Web Sites in Libraries." *First Monday* 3/5 (May 1998). Available: http://www.firstmonday.dk/issues/issue3_5/sowards/index.html (1 August 2003).

34. Silet, 8.

35. Jevec, *First Monday*.

36. Valerie Lewis and Julie Klauber. "[Image] [Image] [Image] [Link] [Link] [Link]: Inaccessible Web Design from the Perspective of a Blind Librarian." *Library Hi Tech* 20/2 (2002): 138.

37. Ken Cotterill. "MetaBookmark > Categories > Information." *MetaBookmark* (2003). Available: http://ken.me.com.au/cgi-bin/mbb_gen.cgi?pg=cat_info (1 August 2003).

38. Silet, 8.

39. Dunsmore, 142-144.

40. Dean, 81.

41. Silet, 8.

42. Cohen and Still, 282.

43. Kirkwood, 26-27.

44. Kirkwood, 28.

45. Jevec. *First Monday*.

46. Dean, 87.

47. Kirkwood, 27.

48. Mudrock, 161.

49. Adam Hodgkin. "Reference Books on the Web." *Ariadne* 30 (December 2001). Available: http://www.ariadne.ac.uk/issue30/ref-books/ (1 August 2003).

50. Greg R. Notess. "Ready-Reference Collections: Bartleby and xrefer." *Online* 25/5 (Sept.-Oct. 2001): 67.

APPENDIX. Survey Questions and Results (First Half, Qs 1-8)

Question		50 Academic Libraries		50 Public Libraries		All 100 Libraries	
		Number	Percent	Number	Percent	Number	Percent
1. Is the page called "reference"?		44	88%	31	62%	75	75%
2. Is ready reference part of a larger page?		12	24%	9	18%	21	21%
3. Are licensed tools included?	None	31	62%	39	78%	70	70%
	A few	18	36%	10	20%	28	28%
	Many	1	2%	1	2%	2	2%
4. Is a commercial product the main resource?		0	0%	0	0%	0	0%
5. How many categories appear?	Only 1	10	20%	11	22%	21	21%
	3-7	12	24%	13	26%	25	25%
	8-16	15	30%	12	24%	27	27%
	18-28	9	18%	8	16%	17	17%
	30-48	4	8%	6	12%	10	10%
6. How are the categories arranged?	Moot: only 1 category	10	20%	11	22%	21	21%
	Alpha-betical	25	50%	27	54%	52	52%
	No order	15	30%	12	24%	27	27%
7. How many links are on the site (est.)?	1-25	10	20%	12	24%	22	22%
	28-46	12	24%	10	20%	22	22%
	56-100	15	30%	7	14%	22	22%
	114-200	9	18%	14	28%	23	23%
	209 or more	4	8%	7	14%	11	11%
8. What is the "Option" class (depth, method)?	I-A	5	10%	6	12%	11	11%
	I-S	26	52%	27	54%	53	53%
	II-A	0	0%	1	2%	1	1%
	II-S	18	36%	14	28%	32	32%
	III-A	0	0%	1	2%	1	1%
	III-S	1	2%	1	2%	2	2%

APPENDIX (continued)

Question		50 Academic Libraries		50 Public Libraries		All 100 Libraries	
		Number	Percent	Number	Percent	Number	Percent
9. Does the page use frames?		8	16%	6	12%	14	14%
10. Does the page use a left-side tool bar?		23	46%	14	28%	37	37%
11. Is there a note about purpose?		10	20%	8	16%	18	18%
12. Is there a note about audience?		3	6%	4	8%	7	7%
13. Is there a note about selection criteria?		4	8%	4	8%	8	8%
14. Is there a glossary?		0	0%	0	0%	0	0%
15. Are categories annotated?	None	48	96%	47	94%	95	95%
	Some	2	4%	1	2%	3	3%
	Most	0	0%	2	4%	2	2%
	All	0	0%	0	0%	0	0%
16. Are individual links annotated?	None	14	28%	11	22%	25	25%
	Some	13	26%	18	36%	31	31%
	Most	11	22%	5	10%	16	16%
	All	12	24%	16	32%	28	28%
17. Is there an online tutorial?		4	8%	4	8%	8	8%
18. Is there an "Ask a Librarian" link?		19	38%	14	28%	33	33%
19. Is there an index with surface integration?		1	2%	0	0%	1	1%
20. Is there an index with deep integration?		0	0%	0	0%	0	0%

Federated Search Tools:
The Next Step in the Quest
for One-Stop-Shopping

Stephen C. Boss
Michael L. Nelson

SUMMARY. The emergence of federated search tools for the library market represents a significant step toward the longstanding goal of a common searching interface in the reference environment. These systems aim to provide integrated access to library resources of all types. This article describes and evaluates federated search tools from four vendors. It suggests criteria that may be useful for libraries attempting to compare and contrast this type of access tool. *[Article copies available for a fee from The Haworth Document Delivery Service: 1-800-HAWORTH. E-mail address: <docdelivery@haworthpress.com> Website: <http://www.HaworthPress.com> © 2005 by The Haworth Press, Inc. All rights reserved.]*

Stephen C. Boss is Systems Librarian (E-mail: sboss@uwyo.edu); and Michael L. Nelson is Social Sciences Reference and Collection Development Librarian (E-mail: mnelson@uwyo.edu), both at the University of Wyoming Libraries, Department 3334, 1000 East University, Laramie, WY 82071-3334.

The authors gratefully acknowledge the assistance of the following: Nancy Chaffin, Metadata Librarian at Colorado State University Libraries, in providing information on MetaLib/SFX and hosting a site visit facilitating the authors' access to full functionality and all licensed databases at that site; Beth Forrest Warner, Director, Digital Library Initiatives and John S. Miller, Special Projects Librarian at the University of Kansas, in providing information on and access to their implementation of Endeavor's ENCompass product; Ellen Starkman, Acting Manager of Library Systems at the University of Illinois at Chicago; the State Library of New Jersey and the authors' colleagues at the University of Wyoming Libraries who provided helpful feedback.

[Haworth co-indexing entry note]: "Federated Search Tools: The Next Step in the Quest for One-Stop-Shopping." Boss, Stephen C., and Michael L. Nelson. Co-published simultaneously in *The Reference Librarian* (The Haworth Information Press, an imprint of The Haworth Press, Inc.) No. 91/92, 2005, pp. 139-160; and: *The Reference Collection: From the Shelf to the Web* (ed: William J. Frost) The Haworth Information Press, an imprint of The Haworth Press, Inc., 2005, pp. 139-160. Single or multiple copies of this article are available for a fee from The Haworth Document Delivery Service [1-800-HAWORTH, 9:00 a.m. - 5:00 p.m. (EST). E-mail address: docdelivery@haworthpress.com].

KEYWORDS. Federated search tools, integrated searching, metasearching, library gateways, library portals, OpenURL resolvers, Z39.50

INTRODUCTION

Library reference staffs have always aimed to provide patrons with quality tools to find information and conduct research. Reference librarians participate in designing library Web sites to guide users to the OPAC, reference databases, in-house databases, and other sources. They recommend database purchases and try to offer as many online reference tools as possible to end-users. Yet all too often end-users are found staring at the screen in frustration, unsure where to begin. The problem typically is not a lack of access or resources, but rather the proliferation of choices. The competitive nature of the database market encourages vendors to differentiate themselves by emphasizing their unique features and user interfaces. Unfortunately, this leads to confusingly complex arrays of "information silos"–disparate resources that do not interact and must be separately searched. Simply finding articles and books requires searching in at least two places, and frequently patrons must locate multiple sources that together meet their needs and then master their varying interfaces and data structures. All this can add up to a user interface that does not serve patrons well.[1]

The proliferation of supercenters says much about what consumers want: singular places where they can shop for everything they need. While retailers have responded to meet this desire, the library world is just beginning to address how we can move toward a "one-stop-shopping" environment. Librarians need to take this path if they expect to remain a viable information source for the Web-savvy student or member of the general public who has discovered the power and convenience of the general Internet. The debut of Google Scholar in late 2004, with its focus on library-oriented resources, only intensifies the need to better integrate library searching.

FEDERATED SEARCH TOOLS: A SOLUTION?

Happily, it appears that the next logical step in the continuing quest for a single common interface and truly integrated access to information in all its varied forms has been taken. Federated search tools independently search clusters of databases: the library's OPAC, other library and consortia catalogs, indexing/abstracting databases, full-text, specialized search engines, digital objects, institutional repositories, document delivery services–pretty much anything that libraries own or access via a database. They search a variety of vendors and systems with a single user interface, merge and deduplicate results, and link to any search tools that cannot be included in the common search interface–thereby providing convenient access to the range of resources listed above. One begins to glimpse here a world where information silos are a thing of the past, where library-provided content truly is presented in a unified, integrated fashion, where hypertext linking begins to realize its ultimate potential and users can customize offerings according to their preferences in a true portal environment. Luther provides a helpful overview of the technology's potential and some relevant links.[2]

These tools, whose function is also called "metasearching" or "broadcast searching," are still in a relatively early stage of development. As with any other type of product they differ in capabilities, overall design, and cost. To fulfill their shared responsibility for selecting products that are affordable while offering the best value for the library and its users, reference personnel need to know as much as possible about the options. Common questions to consider would be: What is the purpose in acquiring the product? Is the tool needed? What does the user interface look like and how customizable is it? What type of end-user will it best serve? How does the tool actually work at a technical level? What will be the impact on bibliographic instruction? How would it impact reference staff in day-to-day work?

The pricing models offered by companies producing federated search tools have matured. Federated searching can be completely outsourced to a vendor or managed in-house. Outsourcing avoids the cost of purchasing and maintaining a server. Some vendors offer different tiers of service depending on the number of database connections needed. It is important to carefully review library workflows, staffing resources and database connectivity needs before purchasing a tool. Although prices have dropped due to a more competitive business environment, implementation and maintenance can still be a substantial investment of money and staff time. Research to find the best tool for a given library is essential. One case the authors discovered in the course of contacting institutions about their experiences implementing federated search tools is instructive. A relatively small college purchased a federated tool after hearing several sales presentations. Once it was implemented, reference staff discovered that it conducted keyword searches, not the more sophisticated searches they were accustomed to doing on their OPAC. They also realized that because of the modest number of databases, there were few overlapping databases covering similar subject areas. For example, the typical patron searching business topics had no need to cross-search ERIC with the business databases. Ultimately the integrated search functions of the tool were disabled despite the investment in it.

The newness of these tools presents a major challenge to reference librarians to review and select. As noted, those currently on the market vary greatly in what they include and in overall concept and design. As Roy Tennant cautions in a *Library Journal* article, "The market is still in an early stage of development, with products varying quite a bit in features, stability, and ease of implementation. This means if you're purchasing a system, you should use due diligence in comparing features, talking with current customers, and making sure that the product will deliver on its promises. It also means that implementation may not be a breeze."[3]

Reference staff must be involved in the decision-making process when the library is considering acquiring a federated search system. It is, after all, the reference department as the front-line users and instructors who will be impacted the most once the system is deployed. Hence, the decision should not solely rest with the systems department or library administration. Reference staff needs to understand and contribute to the entire process from selection to implementation and beyond. They can help articulate the reasons why such a tool should be acquired, review how it operates, plan for impacts on workflow including reference desk service and library instruction, and of course try to see it from the end-user's perspective. The MetaLib review below contains in its discussions of the ResourceStore and administration/configuration issues some good examples of what reference librarians can and should contribute. It is our purpose here to alert reference librarians to these issues while highlighting some primary considerations in evaluating potential acquisitions.

This article will review some of these federated search packages. The reader should bear in mind that the authors were not able to test each product in an identical manner. Some have been on the market longer than others. Fully functional versions of some were available for review, while available versions of others were more limited. The quantity of published information on each varies considerably. Therefore, the differing length and level of detail of each review section is not to be taken as an implicit assessment of relative merit.

The following resources will be reviewed:

- MetaLib by Ex Libris
- ENCompass by Endeavor
- AGent by Auto-Graphics
- WebFeat by WebFeat & Thomson ISI

Metalib/SFX

NOTE: The authors were able to visit Colorado State University (CSU), a nearby institution that has implemented MetaLib. Our discussion incorporates some examples of how CSU has chosen to implement and customize various features.

The MetaLib system is marketed by Ex Libris (http://www.exlibris.co.il/), a company that previously was chiefly known for its integrated library system, ALEPH. MetaLib has a significant and growing customer base. Bundled with MetaLib is SFX, an OpenURL linking component. (OpenURL is a developing standard for dynamic, context-sensitive linking of electronic resources; it eliminates problems inherent to static linking by generating on-the-fly links to library-configured resources that are appropriate to the particular institution and user.) Those who implement MetaLib must also purchase SFX.

MetaLib is designed to serve as a portal to all library-provided resources by providing a single entry point to electronic and print collections–abstracting/indexing and other types of reference databases, full-text sources, library catalogs, digital repositories, selected fee or free Web sources, and document delivery services. It is intended to work independently of the institution's ILS/OPAC so it can be used regardless of ILS vendor. This gateway to local and remote resources overlays the ILS and all other separate components of the library's access tools, allowing the user to remain within one common, familiar system regardless of what is accessed. Customizability that allows the user to personalize the system to best fit his/her needs is also an important part of the portal environment and is supported by MetaLib.

Basic Design and Searching Capabilities

There are two basic levels of searching: the Universal Gateway and the Information Gateway. The former supports federated searching of multiple sources such as reference databases and catalogs, along with displaying search results, using the MetaLib common interface.

To be included in this parallel search environment, a given resource must be configured. Successful configuration is a meticulous process and is dependent on external factors such as vendor support for communication protocols and the structure of database records. Most library catalogs currently are Z39.50 compliant and therefore can be configured for MetaLib searching, but not all database vendors or other information providers are. For those, other suitable translation protocols must be employed. The resources that are configured for the Universal Gateway offer a relatively simple search input screen, with two text boxes offering Boolean options. Available fields besides the broad "all fields" option are: subject, title, author, ISSN, ISBN, and year. Search input is translated into the appropriate syntax of each selected search target, sent to the target systems, and processed; the results are then returned and can be viewed within either the MetaLib interface or the native mode of the originating system. At CSU, up to eight databases can be searched simultaneously. The library determines the number that can be searched together, but Ex Libris recommends eight as a maximum in order to keep loads on the system manageable. One can switch to the native search interface of any of the selected databases at any time.

Since MetaLib is intended as the common presentation of all library resources, the Information Gateway provides "link-to" capability for all sources to which the library wishes to provide access but which are not configured for the Universal Gateway. In this way, the user is able to link to any desired source and is placed in that source's native interface for search and retrieval. The link can lead to the home page or to a location within the resource, depending on what the resource itself allows. The Information Gateway thus serves as the resource discovery component, showing the patron what is available and providing linking to all included resources in the same way that the typical library without a federated tool does, but within the unified MetaLib menu system.

Tying together these two access layers is a resource catalog MetaLib calls the ResourceStore. This database comes prepackaged from MetaLib with a large set of existing resources. Each MetaLib installation is responsible for customizing this catalog to reflect the resources provided at that site. Also included in the ResourceStore is an array of broad subject categories intended to facilitate locating databases by subject. The subject arrangement can be customized to fit each library's requirements. Complementing the structured subject access is a resource locator allowing keyword searching or alphabetical browsing of all available databases. The keyword search can include terms from the database names/titles, descriptions, notes, and additional terms added by librarians to facilitate access and discovery. A given resource can be assigned as many categories or keywords as needed. Lists of databases all include an information icon ("i") leading to the associated resource description; this prevents cluttering the screen while providing one-click access to the information.

Many of the screens and their content are customizable by the library. The subject access system obviously has to accommodate a great variety of libraries and collections, so it is designed to be tailored to each institution's range of available resources, collection strengths, and preferred terminology. The screen appearance, including icons, can be customized to some degree. CSU, for example, created a simpler screen presentation. The subject search is presented as a "Pick A Category" drop-down box that displays the library-assigned subjects. Just below, two search boxes enable keyword searching of all databases by name (title only) and keywords (all words in the local ResourceStore record). Last is an "A-Z List" button for browsing all databases. Lists of available databases are displayed at center screen, with an icon for jumping to the native interface; those searchable via MetaLib also have checkboxes for inclusion in a federated search. Selection tabs allow display of "all resources," "search resources" (Universal Gateway), or "link-to resources." Quite a lot of basic information is included without the screen looking unduly cluttered.

Managing Search Results

Since searches via the Information Gateway are conducted in the native interface with the same look, feel, and functionality as if one had entered the resource from outside MetaLib, results are presented with the original formatting, sorting, etc., as well. The primary value that MetaLib adds here is the availability of SFX OpenURL linking services. The Universal Gateway, on the other hand, attempts to integrate results displays as well as searching, although there are limitations to this capability as there are to the search function, given varying formats and record structures. In addition to linking to the sources pointed to by the database records, one can also refine an initial search based on the ensuing result set–either within that result set in order to narrow the retrieval by using cues in the metadata such as subject terms, or by using metadata within records to launch another search to retrieve more records beyond the initial set.

The results from a MetaLib search are subjected to a variety of conversion programs to convert the records from the native format to the unified MetaLib format, for the sake of consistency. Again, one can go straight to the originating database to view record displays in native mode, even before the system has finished compiling the results for all databases included in the search. Once the search is completed, clicking on the Merge button will combine the summary results into one set with the ability to deduplicate the record list. At CSU the maximum size of this set is 150; this limit is customizable by the institution. According to Ex Libris, the user can sort the merged list by author, title, or year, although that option was not obvious to the authors during their test-drive. Several deduping algorithms are made available, with the institution being able to select the one deemed to best meet its needs. Each full-record display shows all databases from which the record came, again with the option to link to the original record. A merged set from a search on "welfare reform" in 6 databases and limited to 2003 returned 52 records that were deduped down to 32.

User Customization

A popular feature of the typical portal is the ability to personalize the resource selection and display in whatever way the user finds most helpful. MetaLib offers a variety of such options. Probably the key one is creation of one's own list of the most-used resources, both databases and individual e-journals. It becomes part of the user's profile and is the default list for searches. Saving queries for re-use, setting display parameters and formats for displaying and saving records, and establishing alerts to run automatically against selected resources at intervals chosen by the user are other handy options. Of particular note is the e-shelf, to which search or automatic alert results can be saved indefinitely. It thus functions as a personal catalog or inventory of useful information sources, to which users can add comments. The links in the records are preserved for later use.

Administration, Configuration, and Maintenance

Any library choosing to acquire MetaLib and SFX can expect to spend a great deal of time on initial configuration and setup. Configuration tables must be set up for each resource that is to be made searchable within MetaLib, and each SFX target must also be configured individually since the whole SFX concept entails targeting only those resources that are available to a given library's patrons or to defined categories thereof. The word used more than once in the literature to characterize the configuration environment is "meticulous." It can take months to do all the setup and configuration work necessary to roll out the system to the public.

Regarding impacts on staff, of the three MetaLib institutions whose configuration and maintenance staffing patterns are known to the authors, all use a team approach–not surprising given the amount of work and varying knowledge required. Typically, they include representatives from library systems/IT, technical services (acquisitions, cataloging/metadata), and public services. This is a good example of the breaking down of traditional boundaries of library work. In the metasearch environment, all functional areas are involved and must work together to ensure the tool meets the needs of that particular library's users and staff.

ENCompass

ENCompass, produced by Endeavor Information Systems (http://encompass.endinfosys.com), vendor of the Voyager integrated library system, is an integrated series of XML-based tools designed to aid libraries in becoming "digital libraries." (XML, Extensible Markup Language, is a meta-language that allows one to build descriptive documentation. XML documents are a series of text and descriptive tags. The tags, called markup, place a tree structure on the document and allow one to describe the content of the document to be displayed. XML is designed to describe and communicate electronic information.) It combines a federated search function ("ENCompass for Resource Access"), a digital asset management system ("ENCompass for Digital Collections") and an OpenURL resolver ("LinkFinder Plus"). All three are sold separately or as a complete package.

The federated search component includes a comprehensive range of resource types: Abstracting/indexing databases, e-journals, e-books, Web sites, and OPACs. Endeavor has recently partnered with the FAST search engine to enhance response time.

To test the federated search side of ENCompass, the authors used the University of Kansas's (KU) implementation. Accordingly, the authors viewed the product in terms of the institution's value-added customization; it may look quite different at another site. It was not feasible to ar-range full access at a variety of sites, but we were able to gain some insights into basic functionality.

Basic Design and Searching Capabilities

The federated search interface and screen layout are almost completely customizable by the library, so we will not address the screen design or compare it to other systems. Suffice it to say that a primary consideration in choosing a federated system is likely to be the ease and extent of customizing the presentation into one that satisfies the library and, by extension, its users. KU's main search screen follows the apparent practice of most libraries with federated tools in presenting databases grouped by library-defined subject areas (Arts and Humanities, Business, Current Events and News, General and Reference, Science and Engineering, Social Sciences, etc.) plus a "Popular Databases" category accessing five general, multidisciplinary databases. An "all Digital Library Databases A-Z" category ("Digital Library" is KU's name for the ENCompass service) enables searching all federated databases at once. Each category has a checkbox which, if selected, causes the search to be run against each database in the category. Alternatively, one can expand a category by clicking a button beside the category checkbox; this displays a list of all databases within that category, each with its own selection box. Multiple categories can be expanded simultaneously. The user must check a separate box in order to include the KU libraries' catalog in a search. Links to descriptions of each individual resource, as well as each subject category, display next to the entries. In keeping with unified resource access, an A-Z list of all the library's electronic resources is at the bottom of the screen with a note indicating not all electronic resources are available in the Digital Library.

There is no technical limit to the number of resources that can be searched together–and KU has not set one–although in a practical sense the number selected can impact response time. If a number of remote databases are being federated, response time can vary widely depending upon the speed of the university's network and the speed/connectivity to the remote server. The number of results to review is an obvious factor. For a highly specific, focused search, however, this is a desirable capability. Even when a broadcast search of all 40 databases at the KU site was conducted, response time was deemed acceptable. While a search is in progress, the screen refreshes every few seconds and a red flashing "searching . . ." indicator is prominently presented, reassuring the user that the system is still responding.

The default search is a simple input box beside a drop-down menu box for selecting the available search fields: free text, global keyword, title keyword, author keyword, and subject keyword. No Boolean combinations are possible in simple search. The advanced search screen provides three boxes with full Boolean capabilities between the boxes; additionally, each box has a drop-down menu beside it with options for "any of these" (OR) which is the default, "all of these" (AND), and "as a phrase," allowing definition of logical relationships between multiple words within each box. The same search fields are available with the exception of "free text." In many resources a phrase search is actually not possible, in which case it reverts to AND logic. The lack of capability for more sophisticated searching is to be expected; it is endemic to searching across disparate sources regardless of the quality of translation protocols and field mapping. Search history, including options to re-run or edit previous searches, is offered. No limiters are available. A quick navigation box lets the user easily jump between search options, existing results displays, and other available actions.

Managing Search Results

The format of search results is customizable. As delivered to the customer, ENCompass incorporates a standard display similar to MetaLib. KU chose to customize displays in ways that preserve the appearance of the native source. After linking to a full record from the initial brief-record display, one can page forward or back through the full records. In both full and brief records is a prominent button linking to the native interface for searching there. KU has implemented Endeavor's Link-Finder Plus as KULink. The link resolver sends the user to a links resolution screen where one can connect to the full-text display. If the article is full-text one can avoid going through the intermediary screen and launch directly to the article via the evoke command.

After a search completes, a "results summary" screen appears that lists the number of records for each database. One can view records grouped by database, or click a "display all results" button to see a merged set. There is no apparent limit to the number of merged records that can be displayed, although a maximum of 50 is retrieved from each individual resource in most cases. It is not clear what criteria are used to determine which 50 items get displayed–relevance ranking is not used. Results sort alphabetically by title, including initial articles. However, this is not all bad since deduping is not possible at this point and the title sort makes duplicates easy to spot. User-defined sorting by date as well as the default title order is available. Records cannot be marked for later use, but this may become possible with future upgrades or when user personalization features are activated.

User Customization

Endeavor offers user login and associated features such as creating a personal resource collection for the search screen, saving searches, and saving individual records for printing, emailing, etc. (see preceding section). The user customization has not been implemented at KU, and it is not clear how many sites have already done so.

Administration, Configuration, and Maintenance

Any library choosing to implement ENCompass for Resource Access or Digital Collections and LinkFinder Plus will be spending a certain amount of time configuring the system. It should be noted that ENCompass as a suite is a vast tool. Both Kansas and Cornell University have teams devoted towards implementing their projects. Cornell was an ENCompass development partner and they state that presumably they received different levels of training than a "typical" customer. The team at Cornell had to work through many issues on their own and describe themselves as "self-taught." They found the learning curve to be "fairly steep and long."[4]

AGent

NOTE: The authors tested a demo database provided by Auto-graphics, using the Toronto Public Library's implementation of AGent entitled "All in One Search" and also JerseyClicks, a statewide gateway.

AGent by Auto-Graphics, Inc. (http://www4.auto-graphics.com/product_agent.html) is best known as a provider of large, federated, statewide library union catalogs. The customer base includes the states of Wisconsin, New Jersey, and the Texas Education Agency's Texas Library Connection. Auto-Graphics does not offer an OpenURL link resolver at this time, but rather works with a number of existing resolvers already on the market.

AGent can be used by a single library or by a consortium to access and make available a locally installed ILS as well as the catalogs of other libraries from one interface. A&I databases as well as selected Web sites can be searched using this interface. Also searchable are proprietary in-house databases and repositories of Word and PDF documents. Auto-Graphics' marketing literature suggests that a library can start out federating other library databases using the Z39.50 protocol and expanding functionalities as budget allows.

Basic Design and Searching Capabilities

AGent's search screen allows databases to be grouped. For example, the catalogs of a library consortium could be a group, and databases on a specific subject such as business could be another group.

The Keyword or Simple Search searches all indexes (Title, Author, Subject, and Notes). Keywords can be entered in any order; multiple words are ANDed. The Advanced Search is used to create "search queries" with full Boolean capability. This can be done with up to three keyword combinations, across multiple search headings. Within each keyword combination is the option to search all headings. End-users also have the opportunity to narrow the search by choosing from other drop-down box options such as searching specific fields. The system also allows searching a variety of standard publication identification numbers including: ISBN, ISSN, LCCN, and a variety of GPO numbers including: SuDoc, Item, Order, Report, Monthly Catalog, and Ship List. The Original Control Number enables the user to search the number located in the MARC 035 field or Publisher Number which are numbers usually assigned to sound recordings, video recordings, printed music, or other music-related materials.

Managing Search Results

Search qualifier options allow the researcher to narrow the search's scope. Search Qualifier is used with the Advanced and Research search options.

Result "sort by" qualifiers can be preset in Advanced Search. These include sorting by newest title first, newest title last, alphabetically by title, and alphabetically by author. Other narrowing qualifiers include year of publication, language, and media. Form qualifiers include limiting the result set to Braille, electronic, large print, or microform. Another qualification option is to search by miscellaneous. This option appeared to allow limiting by item type such as full-text URL, government publications, and thesis. There did not appear to be any ways to save and re-execute a search.

A results summary screen lists the number of records for each database. Databases return results in no particular order. Results can be grouped by discipline such as All Basic Research, All History, All for Students and Homework Help, All Business, etc. The results display can be configured to meet the needs of a specific library audience. In some installations feedback in the form of a traffic light indicates the success or failure of the search against a database. Next to each database is a traffic light showing red, yellow or green. When the databases successfully return the completed set from each specific database the light turns green. If there was an error during the build the light is red and an error message is displayed. Results sets can be viewed as soon as the returned database names appear in the results list. The return of result sets in AGent was very fast. Both the simple and advanced search allow the user to further modify the search, start a new search or start over within the current set of selected databases. Records are grouped by database. There is no option to merge and view result sets. The results display in their native "look and feel." There did not seem to be a limit to the number of search returns results.

User Customization

AGent has a number of personalization features. My Account allows the user to change password or PIN number. Users can change or edit their personal data, such as e-mail address. Within My Account patrons can view My Search History, which stores the last twenty searches in reverse chronological order. The search history shows the type of search performed (keyword, browse or advanced) as well as the search terms entered. Searches can be modified, stored and re-executed on a regular basis.

My Favorite Search source is a MyAccount feature that remembers the databases that the researcher used on previous searches. Favorite frequently used databases are indicated as being "on" by being pre-checked in the list of choices. Changes to the favorites do not take place until the user logs in again for another search. At this time there is not a way to mark, save, print or manipulate result sets.

Lastly, My Preferences allows researchers to customize a number of system options according to their need. A default display language can be selected from the languages menu. Other customization features include defining the way search results are displayed. A few of the many options available include: (1) The number of records returned can be set to 10, 20, 30, 40, 50, or 100; (2) Sorting results by the criteria listed in the preceding section; (3) Default format for full record display (Card, Labeled, or MARC); (4) Number of searches to save in search history–this can range from 0-50; and (5) Default search method including Keyword Search, Browse, or Advanced Search.

Administration, Configuration, and Maintenance

AGent has an easy-to-use Web-based systems administration (sysadmin) module. Colors, banners, and most of the "look and feel" changes can be managed from this module. The end-user search screen is set up using this tool. The system includes group name management allowing the aggregators or resources to be ranked so they show in the order on the screen.[5,6]

WebFeat

NOTE: The University of Illinois at Chicago was an early WebFeat customer and the first library to implement WebFeat 3, the current version as of early 2005. The authors arranged full access to test this version.

WebFeat (http://www.webfeat.org) originally was marketed primarily to large public libraries systems, most of which have multitudes of disparate databases, but was also targeted to corporations. WebFeat partnered with Thomson ISI to provide a federated search tool for their expanding product portfolio. This gave WebFeat an entry into the large academic market. While it is a stand-alone federated search tool, WebFeat is compatible with the major OpenURL link resolvers, so no bundling is involved in a purchase.

WebFeat's Todd Miller believes that federated search engines should be offered to customers as an ongoing service rather than a software product. Unlike most of his competitors, WebFeat offers a try before you buy program. This is a refreshing change from vendors who send in a representative on a sales call who conducts a preplanned canned demo that works flawlessly, and then expects the library to purchase the product without actually being able to test it in their local environment. Libraries purchase a subscription to WebFeat's services, which include building the custom interface used by the public. The company also develops and maintains the numerous custom "translators" that enable federating the various databases. A subscribing library simply develops a list of the resources that it wishes to federate and WebFeat builds the interface, maintains the translators and develops the end-user interface.

Basic Design and Searching Capabilities

The WebFeat interface at the University of Illinois at Chicago (UIC) is called qUICsearch. UIC set up the "look and feel" of their interface to complement that of their library home page. Not only does WebFeat support library branding in this way, it is also highly customizable in every aspect, with a great range of implementation options.

The initial screen displays a list of broad subject categories headed by the "All Resources" option invoking the complete alphabetical list of 117 federated databases, which persistently displays below the category list. Arts & Humanities, Health Sciences, Multidisciplinary Resources, Science & Technology, and Social & Behavioral Sciences are the other available categories, each having a checkbox for selecting the entire category. Each broad category can be expanded by clicking beside the box, which then displays specific disciplines–for example, Criminal Justice, Education, or Sociology under Social & Behavioral Sciences–that can in turn be selected by clicking one or more boxes. The selections automatically check the boxes beside each applicable resource in the A-Z list. The user can also select any desired resource using that list without having to choose a category first.

UIC's main search screen provides three boxes with all Boolean options. Following typical practice, entering multiple terms within a box defaults to AND. Available search fields are labeled as All, Keyword, Title, Author, Abstract or Subject. The default is set to Keyword. Although we could not obtain absolute confirmation, we suspect that Keyword searches Subject, Title, and Abstract fields simultaneously whereas All is indeed all-inclusive. Available limiters are publication date (all available dates or a range of years may be specified) and full-text articles only. WebFeat apparently supports limiting to peer-reviewed articles as well, but UIC does not offer it. Considering the tiny proportion of available databases that actually offer this limit, it would seem to be of little use in any case since peer-reviewed articles from all databases not featuring this limit would be eliminated.

New to the current version is a thesaurus function containing both LC and MeSH headings. Currently the thesaurus cannot be used in an initial search; it is invoked by a link titled "Find related terms" at the top of any search results screen. A simple alphabetical list with the closest match to input terms appears in a pop-up box; only one heading can be selected. LC and MeSH headings cannot be separated. UIC is hoping to be able eventually to separate them, link MeSH only to the Health Sciences category, allow starting a search using the thesaurus, and enable choosing more than one heading. While not well developed at this point, this certainly is a potentially significant enhancement.

WebFeat presents a simple, clean search interface with a less busy appearance than MetaLib or ENCompass. As one would expect, however, there is a price to be paid for simplicity. All the pitfalls presented by using the same search strategy across a disparate set of databases come into play, a problem that is not unique to WebFeat. With the implicit Boolean AND, especially with full-text searches being executed in many databases, one encounters the usual problem of poor precision when the search terms are far apart. Restricting a search to the subject field does not necessarily mitigate this problem; the field-mapping algorithm appears to cause a subject search to default to the entire record, including full-text, when no subject field exists in a given resource. On the plus side, response time is very good. We did several searches against all 117 resources, and none took more than two minutes to complete.

Managing Search Results

The default order of results is by database of origin ("grouped" in WebFeat parlance). They sort in roughly alphabetical order, but the speed with which results are returned also influences the display order. Within each database display, items are sorted in reverse chronological order. All databases selected for the search are listed at the top of result screens, including those with zero hits. Number of hits is shown for each, and the resource description displays on the right. Each resource name is linked to enable jumping to the results for that resource. The sort order can be changed to: (1) Article title (includes initial articles such as "the" in the sort order); (2) Author (of limited use since it sorts by whatever letter occurs first, which can be either first name, last name, or "Anonymous" as well as "by" which sorts with B); (3) Date; (4) De-duped which sorts by normalized title and seems quite reliable; (5) Selections only, if items have been checked; (6) Relevancy ranked (according to search terms' occurrences in titles); and (7) Merged, which sorts in the same order as the "grouped" display but is numbered continuously instead of starting over with each database group.

The default format is brief records. The library sets the maximum number of records displayed per database. When the number of hits exceeds this limit, the next set of records is linked at the end of the list. A link titled "View" leads to the full record, which always opens in a separate window and displays the record in native format. An OpenURL link button also is available. The native interface in the new window also accesses the search engine for that database where additional searches can be executed or linked full-text viewed. Returning to the brief results list is as easy as closing the window. Results can be selected for printing, e-mailing, or saving to a file.

User Customization

The latest version introduces a "My WebFeat" feature supporting personalization by the user. It enables building custom database menus, subject categories, and automatic alerts to capture newly added records matching saved searches, as well as saving and re-executing saved searches whenever desired. Academic sites are expected to begin implementing My WebFeat in mid-2005. Exporting records to bibliographic management packages such as ProCite, EndNote, and Refworks is also possible.

Administration, Configuration, and Maintenance

WebFeat is a completely outsourced service. The company handles all configuration, maintenance, and upkeep of the "translators." The "look and feel" of the search screen interface is customized by WebFeat for the requesting institution based on their input and specifications.

One problem with federated search tools is that library staff must work very hard to set up and maintain the interface's "look and feel," and establish/maintain the connection infrastructure to the external or internal databases that enables them to be searched. In some cases multiuse, bundled tools that are marketed as an integrated interface also depend upon outsourced companies for the maintenance of their connections. At times these outsourced relationships are complex and can result in non-connectivity issues. Development and maintenance of the translators is one of the WebFeat's strengths. WebFeat's staff has developed over 1,200 pre-built aggregated database "translators." For a fee, additional custom "translators" to accommodate localized databases can be built upon request.

In Todd Miller's article "WebFeat: The Boutique Aggregator," he states, "It (WebFeat) assumes a world where the roads have been built and paved but they lead to many different destinations and local customs. Additionally, WebFeat assumes that, in the foreseeable future, it is unlikely that standards are going to be successfully imposed on the locals." [7]

CONCLUSION

Federated search tools are proving to be a useful addition to the reference librarian's toolbox. Since they rely on a limited set of common attributes across disparate databases they also have severe limitations which preclude viewing them as a catchall solution for precision searching. In their current state of development, the authors see them as a starting point for those end-users who are not sure where to begin in seeking research sources. After reviewing their search results they can always go directly to those databases that appear to have the most material of interest and drill down into more detail. Federated searches seem especially good at facilitating this ability.

A fundamental principle to keep in mind is that the more databases a tool can cross-search, the less precise the results are. This is a major downside to all these systems. They are only as precise as the translators they employ. All databases being federated must have some common searching fields; these are defined, translated as needed, and built during implementation. The fewer fields shared in common by all databases, the poorer the search precision. Most federated searches are keyword searches, most often in title, author, or subject fields. Phrase searching is often problematic or simply unavailable. Limit features, such as restricting article searches to scholarly or full-text journals, are seldom fully functional for these reasons. Reference librarians will need to emphasize the limitations as well as benefits to their users, and use judgment as to when users would benefit from a federated search and when they should use a stand-alone database. For an inexperienced user familiar with the large result sets of general search engines, the typically large and imprecise retrievals characteristic of federated searching may look quite focused by comparison. This perception can perhaps be used as a starting point to guide users toward more sophisticated search instruments and a better understanding of how a library can benefit them–what Zimmerman calls the "teaching moment." [8]

At present, federated searching is likely to work well for many undergraduates and members of the general public who need some information. For those at a research or specialist level, it does not begin to emulate the sophisticated capabilities (such as thesauri and limiters) of the native interfaces of specialized databases. Many of these users will, for the time being at least, continue to be best served by "going native" unless they are seeking background information outside their areas of specialization.

It is beyond the scope of this paper to make detailed evaluative comparisons between the systems under review. Each combines functions and resources in its own unique ways. Customizability, one of the strengths of federated tools, presents a challenge to review and compare. Instead of assessing one interface, libraries will likely need to compare several implementations of each system. Focusing on existing installations in institutions similar to those of the potential buyer should help to mitigate this challenge.

In all cases, each library will need to make careful judgments based on solid research. Exactly what one wishes to accomplish with whatever system is adopted is, as always, the driving factor. Representative questions that may be considered include:

- Who is the target audience of the library and ultimately the software? (The general public, undergraduates, graduates, faculty . . .)
- Will it be used only to federate multiple databases, or are additional functions–such as context-sensitive linking via OpenURL, implementing a digital asset management system, or integrating institutional repositories into the package–also desired?
- Will the majority of the target databases be external (i.e., subscribed databases such as those offered by OCLC, EBSCOhost, Gale Group, and ProQuest) or internal, created by the library or its parent institution?
- Is there a plan to use the federated tools in a consortium? (On campus or multiple academic or public sites?)
- How is the tool bundled? If a federated search tool is purchased, does the library also have to purchase an OpenURL resolver as part of the package?
- How will the tool affect library workflow? Is there enough staff to implement and maintain a federated search tool or should the library consider an outsourced tool?
- How much configuration does the library want to do? What impacts will such a tool have on the reference or systems staffs?
- What can the library afford?

More generally, how effective are these tools at accomplishing their stated purpose of simplifying information discovery, search, and retrieval? The intent is to reduce or eliminate barriers to effective library use. At the same time, the hope is that library-provided resources in all their diversity will become more visible to the user and hence better utilized–creating more synergy among the resources and helping libraries to justify the considerable investment they make in physical and virtual collections. But what is the potential for realizing these goals? While some tools are more "mature" than others, all have been on the market for such a brief period that it is too early to draw definitive conclusions.

This review has, however, led to some general impressions of their utility at this time. The resource discovery component is the most advanced in development. The tools reviewed here all do fairly well at bringing together in a unified presentation the institutions' available electronic and print resources. This goes far toward eliminating confusion over where to find desired information by erasing traditional distinctions between discrete categories of library resources. Although a common search-retrieval-display interface is unavailable to those users needing resources that cannot be configured for federated searching, all resources still are more easily located. Different systems and varying local implementations accomplish this to differing degrees depending on interface design, but in principle the concept of a gateway or portal is being realized.

The true unified search and display of disparate resources is much more challenging and hence not fully developed by any means. As we have seen, any tool is limited by the configurability of the target resources, which in turn is highly dependent on their design/structure and the technically complex translation protocols currently needed to achieve an integrated presentation. On the other hand, given that multiple vendors are competing for customers and that data interchange standards continue to evolve rapidly, every indication is that the inherent limitations to federated searching will be gradually ameliorated over time. While comprehensive yet simple one-stop-shopping is probably a long way off, incremental improvements can be expected on a continuous basis. These may accelerate if the Metasearch Initiative is successful. Launched in 2003 and sponsored by the National Information Standards Organization (NISO), it is a working group of library and industry professionals attempting to "identify, develop, and frame the standards and other common understandings that are needed to enable an efficient and robust information environment."[9]

REFERENCES

1. Roy Tennant, "Library Catalogs: The Wrong Solution," Library Journal, February 15, 2003, 28.

2. Judy Luther, "Trumping Google? Metasearching's Promise," Library Journal, October 1, 2003, 36-39.

3. Roy Tennant, "The Right Solution: Federated Search Tools," Library Journal, June 15, 2003, 28-30.

4. Cornell University Library, "FAQ: About Cornell's ENCompass Development Project," http://www.library.cornell.edu/cts/encompass/ENC_FAQ.htm, (accessed July 29, 2003).

5. Agent Powers Jersey Clicks, Library Journal, June 15, 2004, http://www.libraryjournal.com/article/CA423770.html, (accessed May 20, 2005).

6. JerseyClicks: New Jersey's One-Stop Library Gateway to Quality Information, http://www.jerseyclicks.org, (accessed May 21, 2005).

7. Todd Miller, "WebFeat: The Boutique Aggregator," in National Online 2001, 22nd: Proceedings (New York: Information Today, 2001), 249-256.

8. Devin Zimmerman, "Metasearching's Teaching Moments," Library Journal, September 1, 2004, 54.

9. Andrew K. Pace, "Technically Speaking: Much Ado About Metasearch," American Libraries, June/July 2004.

APPENDIX. Comparison Table

	MetaLib	ENCompass	AGent	WebFeat
Digital Asset Management System		X		
Open-URL	X Ex Libris offers SFX	X Endeavor offers LinkFinder Plus	Works with multiple vendors	Works with multiple vendors
Bundling Requirements	X			
Number of Databases That Can Be Searched Simultaneously	No limit* 8	No limit	No limit 5 -10	No limit
Deduplication	X			
Native Search Interface Available	X	X	X	X
End-User Customization	X	X	X	X
Advanced Search		X	X	X
Boolean Search	X	X	X	X
Phrase Search**	X	X	X	
E-Mail Results	X	X		
Search History	X	X	X	

*Vendor recommended limits
**Does not work in all databases

Internet Reference Sources in the Humanities

Dennis Dillon

SUMMARY. Discusses collection development issues involving humanities Internet resources with a particular focus on sustainability, and highlights a few of the major Internet vendors and resources. *[Article copies available for a fee from The Haworth Document Delivery Service: 1-800-HAWORTH. E-mail address: <docdelivery@haworthpress.com> Website: <http://www.HaworthPress.com> © 2005 by The Haworth Press, Inc. All rights reserved.]*

KEYWORDS. Humanities, collection development, electronic information, World Wide Web, Internet

INTRODUCTION

The humanities, broadly defined, are those branches of learning that chronicle what it means to be human. Anyone reflecting upon humanities resources on the Internet can't help but be struck by two thoughts. The first is that many of the surviving artifacts of the last 5,000 years of

Dennis Dillon is Assistant Director for Collections and Information Resources, the General Libraries, The University of Texas at Austin, Austin, TX (E-mail: dillon@mail.utexas.edu).

[Haworth co-indexing entry note]: "Internet Reference Sources in the Humanities." Dillon, Dennis. Co-published simultaneously in *The Reference Librarian* (The Haworth Information Press, an imprint of The Haworth Press, Inc.) No. 91/92, 2005, pp. 161-174; and: *The Reference Collection: From the Shelf to the Web* (ed: William J. Frost) The Haworth Information Press, an imprint of The Haworth Press, Inc., 2005, pp. 161-174. Single or multiple copies of this article are available for a fee from The Haworth Document Delivery Service [1-800-HAWORTH, 9:00 a.m. - 5:00 p.m. (EST). E-mail address: docdelivery@haworthpress.com].

human civilization are candidates for being converted into new Web accessible versions (along with commentary), and the second is that most of the humanities resources that are currently available on the Web are the initial products of easy opportunity–meaning that new and improved products, some of them quite different from today's offerings, are likely to emerge over time.

A brief examination of the Web's humanities resources reveals that they are large in number, increase daily, and that they sometimes change both their content and Web address without warning–which, immediately raises a host of practical questions for anyone attempting to track and evaluate them.

Librarians puzzling over how to come to grips with these and other issues raised by the spread of Internet humanities resources have three primary concerns:

1. How to make sense of this increasing wealth of resources–in other words how to categorize and form a mental model of Internet humanities resources that will be of practical assistance in establishing a library collecting plan,
2. How to sustain access to these resources over time, and
3. How to select these resources so that they form a comprehensive, sustainable collection that meets the needs of the library audience (while appropriately complementing the library's humanities resources in print and other formats).

Librarians have also come to recognize that the new Internet resources bring with them fundamentally new challenges. Many of these challenges are caused by the ubiquity and complexity of the Web environment in which the library operates. The Web has enlarged the boundaries of the library, increased user expectations, and in the words of Wendy Pratt Lougee, it has made the library more diffuse.[1] When the library's newly enlarged and diffuse boundaries are combined with the immediacy of the Web, one of the obvious features that confronts libraries is that the Web provides greater opportunities for outside pressures to play a role in library collection planning. For example, users who would have never bothered to come to the library to look at microfilm of the *New York Times*, now expect to have access to it online.

Not only has the Web increased both the number of library users and the number of potential resources, it has also increased the potential number of stakeholders in the library's collecting activities. Nowadays, it is not unusual for pressures from a library's fellow consortia members to threaten to carry more weight in collection planning than local needs, it is not unusual for influential customers to exert political pressure on the library to purchase inappropriate databases that the customer cannot obtain through any other means, and it is not unusual for library users to view the removal of a favorite library Web resource in a much more personal way than if the library had merely cancelled a print subscription. As the library increases its opportunities to be more deeply integrated into the daily lives of its users, it is also encountering increased expectations from all of its stakeholders.

Meanwhile new Internet resources in all subject areas are stressing already stretched library budgets. Licenses for multi-year terms with "no cancellation" clauses and built-in inflationary increases are consuming ever greater portions of the library budgets, limiting flexibility, and threatening to destabilize the library's collection. This is of special concern in the humanities since they have long been the core of the library, and humanities users have traditionally been among the library's strongest supporters.

Of course, Internet resources do provide the library with a number of options that were not available in the print environment. The library may decide to lease humanities information rather than purchase it, or to join library consortia in order to obtain limited access rights to certain titles, or the library may choose to add "open access" titles that are freely available on the Web. This collecting of diffused information resources to which the library has varying degrees of ownership rights, is quite different from the stand alone physical library of a generation ago, when a library controlled its collection of printed books and periodicals with reasonable certainty, knowing that each item resided safely on the library shelves.

Internet resources in the humanities are extending the library's reach and providing added convenience for library users. They also furnish added value options such as OpenURL linking, customizability, and the possibility of sharing consortially purchased content. However, these increased benefits have been accompanied by an increase in overall costs. For example, an online humanities database will typically cost more than the printed index it replaced. These increased costs affect not only the library, but are also passed on to users who may have to upgrade their Internet connection and computers, in addition to bearing the costs of printing (or downloading to a portable device) information that in the past they would have simply borrowed. Making effective collection judgments in this increasingly complex environment can be helped by a systematic and analytical approach to the library's collecting efforts, in which the overall collection goals in all formats are considered, and weighed against practical considerations such as use, cost, sustainability, and affect on the library's audience.

CATEGORIZING WEB RESOURCES

Among those items of traditional interest to reference librarians, current Web resources in the humanities consist primarily of converted print-based indexes, digitized texts and images, and miscellaneous aggregations of loosely organized resources with a common subject or theme. Tim Jewell's publication, *Selection and Presentation of Commercially Available Electronic Resources*,[2] is helpful in categorizing the various types of current Web resources in ways that can assist librarians in analyzing available humanities resources. Using these categories as a guide can also make it easier to determine how these resources best fit within a library's existing collection framework. Of course, the Internet tends to blur distinctions that were once clear in the offline environment, such as the previously simple distinction between a book and a database. Consequently any practical collection development plan has to consider the implications of changeable formats and the value of added options, such as reference books that have become online databases, and Web-based indexes that have enabled OpenURL linking so that they are suddenly able to become full-text gateways. This is another way of introducing one of the key questions of modern humanities collection development–how can a library build a sustainable and balanced collection of Internet resources when new resources appear every day, and when all of theses resources are competing for the same scarce subscription funding?

SELECTION FOR SUSTAINABLE ACCESS

The Web has significantly altered the collecting strategies of libraries.

1. It has changed the depth and breadth of humanities resources that are available to the average library.
2. It has permanently changed the information environment in which library users, vendors, libraries, and library's parent funding agencies operate.

3. It has forever altered pricing options so that libraries no longer have a simple choice between making a one-time payment for a book or a recurring charge for a journal, but instead must make budget calculations that take into account numerous additional permutations and considerations.
4. It has resulted in complicated budget strategies involving bulk purchasing, annual versus multi-year commitments, pricing based on projected usage, purchase versus lease decisions, the careful weighing of the pricing and stability of various competing consortia and vendor proposals, the multi-variant analysis of a bewildering array of added-value and access options, and the consideration of whether or not to pay for archival rights.
5. It has also resulted in what is essentially a portfolio approach to collection management in which the library attempts to balance both its long and short-term obligations and risks–weighing for example, the advantages and disadvantages of short-term leased access against long-term ownership, and of cross-institutional consortia commitments against the freedom of being able to make a decision based on immediate local institutional needs.

The halcyon days of being able to make a simple selection decision based on a straightforward weighing of the cost of a title versus its value to one's institution, are fading into the past. Many current online humanities resources may be licensed in any of several different ways. They may be purchased outright with one-time funds in the same way that librarians have traditionally purchased monographs or microfilm, or they may be subscribed to much like periodical. Increasingly online resources may also be purchased with one-time funds that also incur annual maintenance fees in order to pay for the vendor's care of the server. In some cases, a library may choose to purchase a portion of an online resource while subscribing (or purchasing) any content that supplements or adds to the original purchase. In still other instances a resource may be established as a pay-per-view account, or licensed through a consortia contract. Archival rights to a resource may involve additional costs, and many humanities databases are often subdivided, with access to different subsets each having their own prices.

Nowadays in order to compare one resource with another, librarians must routinely total up all the associated costs over a multi-year period, in order to insure that true and comparable costs have been part of their decision-making. One commonly used mechanism is to compare all the associated costs of two given resources over a ten-year period, since this tends to even out the effect of one-time sales promotions, as well as any initial cost differences associated with purchase versus lease, or locally loaded data versus data accessed remotely on a vendor's server.

While these factors have complicated collection decision making for all Web resources, humanities resources include additional considerations since they frequently retain or even increase their value over time. A good introduction to some of the issues particular to online humanities resources may be found in the recent publication from the Digital Library Federation and Council on Library and Information Resources entitled, *Scholarly Work in the Humanities and the Evolving Information Environment.*[3] Because of the long useful life span of humanities resources, questions about the sustainability of any humanities resource are critical. Basic questions to be asked of any resource include: how viable is the vendor, can the vendor be trusted to provide a migration path forward if technical changes are necessary, what are the library's recourses if the vendor fails, and how sustainable is the library's funding for the resource given all the currently unforeseen obligations the library will have in the future?

The question of sustainable funding for online humanities resources is one of several critical puzzles for librarianship in the 21st century. How can a library insure long-term sustainable access and funding for any Internet resource, while still maintaining the capability of purchasing the constant flow of new resources? The answer to this question cannot be found in any of our current financial or Internet access models, but future technological advances and new access models may very well make these questions appear naive. No matter what transpires in the years ahead, we know that it is the mission of libraries to respect both the past and the future. It is inherent in the mission of libraries to look for solutions to all of these issues. How well libraries are able to do this in a world of ever increasing electronic resources will be a test of both libraries' relevance and effectiveness.

THE RESOURCES

The resources reviewed in this article were selected by reviewing the online offerings of major research libraries in art, music, literature, history, language and area studies, philosophy, religion, classics, performing arts, and general humanities. A preliminary compilation of commonly held commercially produced Internet humanities resources, produced a list of several hundred titles. Because of the high number of useful resources, especially from the more prolific Internet publishers and distributors–these offerings have been summarized by vendor with only a few selected titles receiving individual notice. Online products that are a result of digitizing an individual serial such as the *New York Times* or *Harper's Weekly* are not included. A surprising number of humanities resources are produced by institutions of higher education, scholarly societies, and by small academic publishers. Wherever possible these harder to find items have been included in the compilation. The major publishers and distributors are listed below with information summarizing their offerings, followed by a highly-selective listing of other humanities resources arranged by subject. All databases are available through paid subscriptions, unless they are specifically noted as being free.

Major Publishers and Distributors of Online Humanities Resources

Alexander Street Press (http://www.alexanderstreetpress.com) is known for massive full-text compilations in history, literature, and the performing arts as well as the use of sophisticated retrieval mechanisms. They market their full-text databases on either a subscription or purchase basis, and sell to both consortia and individual libraries. The company was formed by staff from Chadwyck-Healey after Chadwyck-Healey was purchased by ProQuest. Their databases are widely held among academic libraries, and are not available through other distributors.

Cambridge Scientific Abstracts (http://www.csa.com) has traditionally been a distributor of online science and technology databases, however, in recent years CSA has been branching out into both the Humanities and Social Sciences. Among the humanities reference indexes they currently distribute on a subscription basis are the following databases: ARTBibliographies Modern, ATLA Religion Database, BHI: British Humanities Index, Design and Applied Arts Index, Index Islamicus, Linguistics and Language Behavior Abstracts, and RILM Abstracts of Music Literature.

Chadwyck-Healey's (http://www.umi.com/chadwyck) wealth of humanities resources deserve an article all their own. Widely held and widely respected, their databases are particularly strong in literature, music, the performing arts, and full-text content. The company was purchased by ProQuest (http://www.il.proquest.com/proquest) in 1999, which had a strong reservoir of its own humanities resources based on its many years of assembling microfilm content under the UMI brand name. The combined offerings of these two former competitors mesh well, offering high quality humanities content that are not available elsewhere. The scope and variety of ProQuest's humanities databases insure that almost every library will be interested in one or another of their databases. The combined companies are particularly strong in older content. Some of their digital products are available for one time purchase, in addition to more traditional subscription arrangements.

EBSCO (http://www-us.ebsco.com/home), much like Gale and ProQuest, provides Web access to a large aggregator database of full-text periodicals that is sliced and diced and marketed in different iterations with different subject and audience focuses. In addition they provide access to an ever-growing number of third party humanities indexes and full-text collections.

Gale (http://www.galegroup.com) is particularly strong in full-text information about literary authors, as well as genealogy and general biography. They also publish a wealth of general humanities reference books which are now available online, as well as a line-up of full-text databases that aggregate periodical content.

H. W. Wilson's (http://www.hwwilson.com) well known reference titles are available online from many different distributors. Many of their titles are produced as both indexes and as full-text versions.

OCLC FirstSearch (http://www.oclc.org/firstsearch) is a distributor of a full panoply of both their own and third part humanities indexes and databases.

OVID (http://www.ovid.com) is a longtime distributor of third party databases, purchased one of its perennial competitors, SilverPlatter, in 2001 greatly strengthening OVID's humanities product line. The newly formed company offers a lengthy catalog of humanities indexes and related full text.

RLG (http://www.rlg.org) has been a long time home for a handful of academic humanities databases that are generally not available from other distributors. RLG is particularly strong in foreign databases.

Art

Art and Archaeology Technical Abstracts (http://aata.getty.edu/NPS)– A comprehensive database of more than 100,000 abstracts of literature related to the preservation and conservation of material cultural heritage. Free.

The Bibliographic Database of the Conservation Information Network (BCIN) (http://www.bcin.ca/English/home_english.html)–CIN's

objective is to facilitate the retrieval and exchange of information concerning conservation and restoration of cultural property. Free.

Bridgeman Art Library (http://bal-ms.bridgeman.co.uk)–Provides access to 100,000 images of painting, sculpture, architecture, and the decorative arts from the Bridgeman Art Library.

Grove Dictionary of Art Online (http://www.grovereference.com/TDA)–A fully searchable online copy of the print dictionary, including some but not all of the illustrations and photographs in the print version.

Index of Christian Art (http://ica.princeton.edu)–Provides subject and iconographic access to over 200,000 photographic reproductions of Christian art in the east and west from early apostolic times up to A.D. 1400.

ULAN online (http://www.getty.edu/research/tools/vocabulary/ulan)–The standard thesaurus of artists' names, based upon the several operating programs of the Getty Information Institute. Increasingly used in cataloging art objects, image collections, etc. Free.

Music

All Music Guide (http://www.allmusic.com)–A comprehensive listing of sound recordings currently available in the U.S. Combines the print publications of Schwann Opus and Spectrum to cover an array of musical styles, including classical, jazz, and a full range of popular and commercial music. Free.

Grovemusic (New Grove Dictionary of Music and Musicians, New Grove Dictionary of Opera) (http://www.grovemusic.com/index.html)–The authoritative standard for English-language music dictionaries, covering all aspects of music, including biographies, definitions of terms, musical examples, lists of works, links to sounds, etc.

Music Index (http://www.harmonieparkpress.com)–Provides citations to scholarly and popular music journals and magazines, indexing more than 640 international music periodicals.

RILM (Repertoire International de Litterature Musicale) Abstracts (http://www.rilm.org)–An international bibliography of scholarly writings on music and related disciplines, in 202 languages, classified by topic.

RIPM: International Index to Nineteenth-Century Periodicals (http://www.nisc.com/ripm/default.htm)–Covers music periodicals published from the late 18th to the early 20th-centuries in 15 countries. Complements the printed volumes of the ongoing *Repertoire International de la Presse Musicale.*

RISM International Inventory of Musical Sources after 1600 (http://www.nisc.com/factsheets/rism.htm)–The most comprehensive annotated index to music manuscripts produced after 1600.

History

Accessible Archives (http://www.accessible.com)–Provides a searchable collection of American newspapers from the 18th and 19th Centuries.

America: History and Life (http://serials.abc-clio.com)–Citations and abstracts to social science and humanities literature on all aspects of U.S. and Canadian history, culture, and current affairs from prehistoric times to the present.

Avalon Project (http://www.yale.edu/lawweb/avalon/avalon.htm)–Digital historical documents relevant to the fields of law, economics, politics, diplomacy, and government. Free.

Historical Abstracts (http://sb1.abc-clio.com:81/aboutha.html)–Indexing with abstracts for 2,000+ journals and other materials relating to world history (excluding the U.S. and Canada) from 1450 to the present.

History Universe: Primary Sources in U.S. History (http://cisweb.lexis-nexis.com/histuniv)–An index to numerous microfilm collections of primary documents on U.S. history. Entries identify the collection, reel number, and frame number of each document.

History E-Book Project (http://www.historyebook.org)–Full text of over 500 books on American, European, and Middle Eastern History as well as the History of Technology.

International Medieval Bibliography (http://www.leeds.ac.uk/imi/imb/imb.htm)–Lists articles, notes, etc., in journals, Festschriften, conference proceedings, and collected essays on all aspects of medieval studies from 450 to 1500.

ITER: The Bibliography of Renaissance Europe (http://www.itergateway.org)–An online bibliography of the Renaissance (1300-1700). The bibliography covers relevant secondary material published since 1700 to the current year.

Making of America (http://moa.umdl.umich.edu)–A full-text digital library of primary sources in American social history from the antebellum period through Reconstruction. Currently contains over 1,600 books and 50,000 journal articles on all topics. Free.

Nineteenth Century Masterfile (Poole's Plus) (http://poolesplus.odyssi.com)–Provides subject indexing to American and English periodicals covering a period of 105 years and indexing 479 American and English periodicals from 1802-1906.

Literature

Dictionary of Old English Corpus (http://www.press.umich.edu/titles/ 00277.html)–An online database consisting of at least one copy of every Old English text. It includes over 3,000 different texts representing about three million words of Old English and another two million words of Latin.

Evans Digital Edition (http://www.readex.com/scholarl/eai_digi.html)– Based on the renowned American Bibliography by Charles Evans. Upon completion, Evans Digital will consist of more than 36,000 works and 2,400,000 images covering items published between 1639-1800.

Inter-Play (http://www.lib.pdx.edu/resources/databases/db_descriptions. html#interplay)–An online index to plays in collections, anthologies, and periodicals and in a variety of languages. Free.

Middle English Compendium (http://www.press.umich.edu/titles/ 01299.html)–Access to an electronic version of the Middle English Dictionary, a hyper-bibliography of Middle English prose and verse, and the Corpus of Middle English Prose and Verse.

Old English Corpus (http://ets.umdl.umich.edu/o/oec)–The Old English machine-readable corpus is a complete record of surviving Old English except for some variant manuscripts of individual texts.

Victorian Database Online (http://www.victoriandatabase.com)–An electronically searchable version of the Cumulative Bibliography of Victorian Studies put out by the Literary Information and Retrieval group (LITIR) at the University of Alberta. It contains over 100,000 records from 500 plus journals listing books, articles, and dissertation abstracts published since 1945.

Women Writers Online (http://www.wwp.brown.edu)–Contains over 230 texts by pre-Victorian women.

World Shakespeare Bibliography Online (http://www.worldshakesbib. org)–International in scope with coverage extending to more than 92 languages.

Philosophy/Religion/Classics

L'Annee Philologique (Database of Classical Bibliography) (http:// www.annee-philologique.com/aph)–Includes citations articles in 1,500 journals and 500 collections.

DYABOLA (Dynamically Accumulating Database on Objects and Literature About Antiquity) (http://www.dyabola.de)–Provides citations to books, articles, and essays on classical, early Christian, Byzantine, early Medieval, and ancient Middle Eastern antiquities, art, and archaeology.

Past Masters (http://library.nlx.com)–Full-text, searchable versions of works by major philosophical figures, in both the original language and in English translation.

Perseus Project (http://www.perseus.tufts.edu)–A multimedia database containing interactive sources and studies on Ancient Greece, including primary and visual texts. Free.

Thesaurus Linguae Graecae (TLG): A Digital Library of Greek Literature (http://www.tlg.uci.edu)–A searchable database of all Greek texts from Homer to A.D. 600, and many texts dating to the period between A.D. 600 and the fall of Byzantium in 1453.

Area and Language Studies

ABSEES (The American Bibliography of Slavic and East European Studies) (http://gateway.library.uiuc.edu/absees)–Covers North American scholarship on Eastern Europe, Russia, and the former Soviet Union.

AfricaBib (http://www.africabib.org)–Provides bibliographic access to Africana periodical literature and African Women's literature. Free.

African Studies (http://www.nisc.com/factsheets/qafr.asp)–A combination of 16 databases from three continents providing access to multi-disciplinary information on Africa.

ARTFL (American and French Research on the Treasury of the French Language) (http://humanities.uchicago.edu/orgs/ARTFL)–Full-text access to more than 2,000 French texts, primarily in literature and philosophy.

Bibliography of Asian Studies (http://www.aasianst.org/bassub.htm)–Contains over 410,000 citations to western-language periodical articles and books published on all subjects pertaining to East, Southeast, and South Asia.

China Academic Journals (http://www.eastview.com/chinese_databases.asp#academic)–Contains full-text articles (and full images) of 1,710 Chinese-language journals from 1994-present.

Handbook of Latin American Studies (http://memory.loc.gov/hlas)–A bibliography on Latin America consisting of works selected and annotated by scholars. Free.

Hispanic American Periodicals Index (http://hapi.gseis.ucla.edu)–Provides citations drawn from more than 400 journals, primarily in Spanish or English, which cover Latin America, the Caribbean, and Hispanics in the United States.

Kodansha Encyclopedia of Japan (http://www.macmillanonline.net/socialsciences/kodansha.htm)–Searchable and browsable digital resource based on *Japan: An Illustrated Encyclopedia*, published in 1993.

Quarterly Index to Africana Periodical Literature (http://lcweb2.loc.gov:8081/asian/qsihtml/qsihome.html)–Covers over 300 selected periodicals acquired regularly from 29 African countries. Free.

RAMBI (Index of Articles on Jewish Studies) (http://jnul.huji.ac.il/rambi)–Selective bibliography of articles in the various fields of Jewish studies and in the study of Eretz Israel. Free.

General Humanities

Arts & Humanities Citation Index (http://www.isinet.com/isi/products/citation/ahci)–Indexes the contents of about 6,100 journals, covering about 1,000 fully and about 5,100 selectively.

Black Studies Database (http://www.nisc.com/factsheets/blks.htm)–Provides 170,000 citations from more than 150 publications. An electronic version of the Kaiser Index to Black Periodicals.

IBR Online (Internationale Bibliographie der Rezensionen) (http://www.saur.de/dietrich/ibr.html)–The IBR online cites approximately 740,000 reviews drawn from 5,000 periodicals published from 1985 to the present. Also available through Gale (http://www.galegroup.com).

IBZ Online (Internationale Bibliographie der Zeitschriften-literatur) (http://www.gbv.de)–An international bibliography indexing over 8,700 periodicals in the arts, humanities, and social sciences. Also available through Gale (http://www.galegroup.com).

Index Translationum (http://www.unesco.org/culture/xtrans)–Contains cumulative bibliographical information on books translated and published in about a hundred of UNESCO's Member States since 1979. Free.

Infomine (http://infomine.ucr.edu)–A virtual library of 100,000 Internet resources selected by librarians relevant to faculty, students, and research staff at the university level. Free.

Internet Public Library (http://www.ipl.org)–A collection of freely available Internet resources selected by students in the Michigan School of Information and Library Studies and volunteer librarians. Free.

NetLibrary (http://www.netlibrary.com)–Over 60,000 recent electronic books on all topics.

OAIster (http://oaister.umdl.umich.edu/o/oaister)–Uses the Open Archives Initiative (OAI) protocol to search over 270,000+ records of free, useful, and previously difficult to access wide-ranging digital resources hosted at over 55 institutions. Free.

Oxford English Dictionary (http://www.oed.com)–The most complete and authoritative dictionary of the English language.

Internet Scout Project (http://scout.wisc.edu)–A database of 15,000 critical annotations of carefully selected Internet sites and mailing lists. The browsable collection is organized by Library of Congress subject headings. Free.

Performing Arts

FIAF (International Film Archive Database) (http://www.fiafnet.org)–Combined access to International Index to Film Periodicals, International Index to Television Periodicals, International Directory of Film and TV Documentation Collections, and Treasures from the Film Archives, a bibliography of silent films worldwide.

Internet Movie Database (http://www.imdb.com)–Provides access to information about movies (including those made for television) from across the world, starting with the earliest cinema through the latest releases and titles still in production. Free.

REFERENCES

1. Wendy Pradt Lougee, *Diffuse Libraries: Emergent Roles for the Research Library in the Digital Age.* (Washington, DC: Digital Library Federation and Council on Library and Information Resources, 2002).

2. Timothy D. Jewell, *Selection and presentation of Commercially Available Electronic Resources: Issues and Practices* (Washington, DC: Digital Library Federation and Council on Library and Information Resources, 2001).

3. William Brockman, Laura Neumann, Carole Palmer, and Tonyia Tidline, *Scholarly work in the Humanities and the Evolving Information Environment* (Washington DC: Digital Library Federation and Council on Library and Information Resources, 2001).

Science Reference on the Internet

Lori Bronars

SUMMARY. In the sciences, there is a wide assortment of information in electronic form and accessible to anyone with the computer communications, hardware, and software prerequisites. For those in search of literature citations, numerical values, commonly accepted facts, word-for-word of published text, and even sound reproductions and to some extent still or living images, the Internet-posted formats have much to offer. In this paper, especially useful or interesting Web sites for reference in any of the basic science fields are identified. *[Article copies available for a fee from The Haworth Document Delivery Service: 1-800-HAWORTH. E-mail address: <docdelivery@haworthpress.com> Website: <http://www.HaworthPress.com> © 2005 by The Haworth Press, Inc. All rights reserved.]*

KEYWORDS. Science reference Internet sites, science reference Web sites

INTRODUCTION

The purpose of this article is to review and recommend significant and proven useful Internet sites for science reference information. The emphasis of the sites featured in this paper is on useful and interesting

Lori Bronars is Science Reference Librarian, Database Coordinator, and Biology Selector, Kline Science Library, Yale University, 219 Prospect Street, Box 208111, New Haven, CT 06520-8111 (E-mail: lori.bronars@yale.edu).

[Haworth co-indexing entry note]: "Science Reference on the Internet." Bronars, Lori. Co-published simultaneously in *The Reference Librarian* (The Haworth Information Press, an imprint of The Haworth Press, Inc.) No. 91/92, 2005, pp. 175-196; and: *The Reference Collection: From the Shelf to the Web* (ed: William J. Frost) The Haworth Information Press, an imprint of The Haworth Press, Inc., 2005, pp. 175-196. Single or multiple copies of this article are available for a fee from The Haworth Document Delivery Service [1-800-HAWORTH, 9:00 a.m. - 5:00 p.m. (EST). E-mail address: docdelivery@haworthpress.com].

doi:10.1300/J120v44n91_12

information sources of high quality and established or noteworthy authority for reference questions in science.

A secondary purpose is to gauge and compare the pervasiveness of such Internet representation within the disciplines. The process of selecting source sites was selective not only on the traditional reference source evaluation criteria but also was more favorable towards free sites not requiring user registration or password-free subscription-based sites. A great deal of filtering was required in terms of numbers of sources. For an estimate of the universe drawn on, we could consider the statistics provided by Martha Williams in her analysis and, overlapping by one year, the statistics in *Directory of Online Databases*. For the year 1988, the number of databases at least partly related to science, technology, or engineering is given as 1184 out of a total of 3699. For 2002, Williams shows the science, technology, or engineering-related databases to number 2983, more than double the 1988 total although at the same time a slight decrease in the percentage of the total.[1] Even if all of the figures reported in these two works included CD-ROM titles (which are not included in the present paper), the sites highlighted in this article are a highly selected group.

In this article, somewhat over 100 Internet-accessible sources or sites are presented. These were viewed between July and December of 2003. Unless otherwise noted, the reference sources are subscription based.

GENERAL SCIENCE REFERENCE WEB SITES

Standard Reference Works

AccessScience@McGraw-Hill (The McGraw-Hill Companies, Inc.).
http://books.mcgraw-hill.com/accessscience/about.html

Internet edition based on the print editions of the *McGraw-Hill Encyclopedia of Science and Technology*, the *McGraw-Hill Dictionary of Scientific and Technical Terms*, and the recent few years of its *Yearbook of Science and Technology*; limited free content.

Energy Citations Database (Office of Scientific and Technical Information, U.S. Department of Energy).
http://www.osti.gov/energycitations/

Find references to reports and other publications, including conference papers, journal articles, books, dissertations, and patents, 1948 to present, at this regularly-updated site. Applies to energy and related fields of chemistry, physics, material and environmental science, geology, and math; free.

FirstGov for Science (Office of Scientific and Technical Information, U.S. Department of Energy, United States Geological Survey, and National Technical Information Service).
http://www.science.gov

Noted in a recent article,[2] this site applies to all scientific and technical fields. Cited reports and publications are those prepared by U.S. government agencies. Somewhat on the more basic level; free.

General Science Full Text (H. W. Wilson).
http://www.hwwilson.com/databases/gensci.htm

The better-known science magazines or journals in English for the non-specialist reader are covered in this title beginning with 1984. Content derives from just over 280 journal titles.

Web of Science® (ISI).
http://www.isinet.com/products/citation/wos/

Besides the usual author and keyword approach, the cited author or work search capability has been a hallmark feature enabling users to identify additional related publications or to put into quantifiable measures the influence of a particular person, idea, or article. Citations from major science journals going back to 1945 are found using its cited work searching. The best-known scholarly journals are indexed and abstracted (from 1992).

Data Compilations

International Critical Tables of Numerical Data, Physics, Chemistry and Technology (Knovel).
http://www.knovel.com/knovel2/Toc.jsp?BookID=735

The electronic edition of this classic work was first produced in 2003. Data is searchable and is contained mostly in pdf images plus tables with interactive links.

Science and Engineering Indicators 2000 (National Science
Board/National Science Foundation).
http://www.nsf.gov/sbe/srs/seind00/

Useful for text or statistics on salaries, education, and employment
within the U.S. workforce; free in several formats; free.

Ready-Reference Resources

Journal Citation Reports®–Science Edition (ISI).
http://www.isinet.com/products/evaltools/jcr/jcrweb/

A fine source for identifying the more well-known scholarly journals
and their citedness.

Science Citation Index Expanded List of Journals (ISI).
http://www.isinet.com/cgi-bin/jrnlst/jlresults.cgi?PC=D

Useful in deciphering incomplete citations for well-known scholarly
journals in science; free.

Scirus: for Scientific Information Only (Elsevier Science).
http://www.scirus.com

Scirus provides an alternative to other general science search engines. Casual use didn't suggest obvious bias towards the publisher's
products; free.

Today's Science on File (Facts on File News Services).
http://www.facts.com/online-tsof.htm

The online edition of this service is said to be enhanced with "extensive" material not found in the print edition.

Biographical and Historical Sources

American Men and Women of Science (Information Today).
http://www.netlibrary.com/ebook_info.asp?product_id=73078

Currently over 129,000 entries primarily in the U.S. and Canada.

Biography Resource Center (Gale Research).
http://www.galegroup.com/servlet/ItemDetailServlet?region=9
&imprint=000&titleCode=GAL43&type=4&id=114945

Includes:

Notable Black American Scientists
Notable Scientists: from 1900 to the present
Notable Twentieth-Century Scientists
Who's Who in Science and Engineering

Dictionary of Scientists (Oxford Reference Online).
http://www.oxfordreference.com/pages/Subjects_and_Titles_2D_GS10

Abridged and updated version of the Institute of Physics' *Encyclopedia of Scientists* (1993). There are 1,300 current and retrospective entries.

Hutchinson Dictionary of Scientific Biography (Helicon Publishing Ltd.).
http://www.helicon.co.uk/print/titles/contents/dsb.htm

Includes historical reviews and chronologies, Nobel prizes, and some portraits.

Nobel e-Museum (Nobel Foundation).
http://nobelprize.org/

Information and acceptance speech for those receiving the Nobel Prize in Physics, Chemistry, and Physiology or Medicine; free.

BIOLOGY, BOTANY, ZOOLOGY, AND OTHER LIFE SCIENCES

Standard Reference Works

Agricola (National Agricultural Library, U.S. Department of Agriculture).
http://agricola.nal.usda.gov/

This is the well-known citation database for agriculture, especially as it relates to the U.S.; free.

Algology, Mycology, and Protozoology (*Microbiology C*) (CSA).
http://www.csa.com/factsheets/microbiology-c-set-c.php

Citations to the world's published literature on fungi, lichens, or algae from over 580 journals. Online coverage begins with 1982.

Animal Behavior Abstracts (CSA).
http://csa.tsinghua.edu.cn/csa/factsheets/animal_behavior.shtml

Approximately 230 journals are abstracted, with coverage beginning in 1982.

Aquatic Biology, Aquaculture, and Fisheries Resources (NISC).
http://www.nisc.com/frame/NISC_products-f.htm

A composite database product of citations and some abstracts for all aquatic environments whether marine, freshwater, brackish, or estuarine. Research on fish and marine biology topics are emphasized. Coverage begins with 1971.

Biological and Agricultural Index Plus (H. W. Wilson).
http://www.hwwilson.com/databases/bioag.htm

An index to English-language periodical articles from 1983 with a U.S. focus.

BIOSIS Previews (Thomson BIOSIS).
http://www.biosis.org/products/previews/

Web-accessible counterpart to *Biological Abstracts* and *Biological Abstracts/RRM (Reports, Reviews, Meetings)* in print, 1969 to present. This database is the largest and most renowned for citations on an international scale.

CAB Abstracts (CAB International).
http://www.cabi-publishing.org/AbstractDatabases.asp?SubjectArea=&PID=125

This is a major agriculture-related bibliographic database with world-wide emphasis. Many separate abstracts combine to comprise this resource, among them: *Protozoological Abstracts, Helminthological Abstracts, TREECD, Grasslands and Forage Abstracts, Maize Abstracts, Nematological Abstracts, Plant Breeding Abstracts,* and *Seed Abstracts.*

CSA Neurosciences Abstracts (CSA).
http://www.csa.com/factsheets/neurosciences-set-c.php

This abstract tracks over 260 journals with articles on vertebrate or invertebrate neuroscience from 1982.

Dictionary of Biology (Oxford Reference).
http://www.oxfordreference.com/pages/Subjects_and_Titles_2D_GS02

Contains over 4,700 entries. The text with accompanying diagrams or figures is equivalent between the online and print editions.

Dictionary of Cell and Molecular Biology (University of Glasgow).
http://www.mblab.gla.ac.uk/dictionary/

Corresponds to the 3rd edition in print (Academic Press,1999). A little over 7,000 entries with signed entries; free for occasional use only.

Dictionary of Plant Sciences (Oxford Reference).
http://www.oxfordreference.com/pages/Subjects_and_Titles_2D_GS08

Contains over 5,500 definitions. Text with accompanying diagrams is equivalent between the online and print edition (Oxford University Press. 2nd ed., 1998).

Dictionary of Zoology (Oxford Reference).
http://www.oxfordreference.com/pages/Subjects_and_Titles_2D_GS11

Online this work corresponds to the print book of the same title in its 2nd ed. (Oxford University Press, 1999). Approximately 5,000 entries.

Encyclopedia of Life Sciences (John Wiley & Sons).
http://www.els.net/els/

The most complete biology encyclopedia to be published in recent years.

Encyclopedia of Molecular Biology (Knovel/John Wiley & Sons).
http://www.knovel.com/knovel2/Toc.jsp?BookID=737

This is the online version of the 4-volume print encyclopedia of the same title (1999). (Online text not accessed.)

Entomology Abstracts (CSA).
http://www.csa.com/factsheets/entomology-set-c.php

Over 540 worldwide journals are monitored to some degree for citations. Coverage from 1982 includes existing, newly discovered, and fossilized insect topics.

Index Nominum Genericorum (*Plantarum*) (Smithsonian Institution and the International Association for Plant Taxonomy).
http://ravenel.si.edu/botany/ing/

The ING database is based on the online edition of *Index Nominum Genericorum* (*Plantarum*) and its *Supplentum* published in 1979 and 1986 respectively. Plant genus names from around the world are listed in this resource if included in the *International Code of Botanical Nomenclature*. This is a useful source for plant species names with citations to the naming literature; free.

Microbiology Abstracts Section B: Bacteriology (CSA).
http://www.csa.com/csa/factsheets/bacteriology.shtml

This abstract service of over 500 serial titles features coverage of the world's microbiology and bacteriology literature, with related areas of biochemistry and genetics also included. Citations begin with 1982.

PrimateLit (Wisconsin Primate Research Center, Washington National Primate Research Center, and University of Wisconsin-Madison Libraries).
http://primatelit.library.wisc.edu/

An index to the literature of primatology from 1940 to the present. A subset, *Current Primate References*, covers the most recent 6 months; free.

Zoological Record (Thomson BIOSIS).
http://www.biosis.org/products/zr/

This database is the major periodical index for citations to zoology literature from publications worldwide; 1978 to present.

Data Compilations

Amphibian Species of the World: An online reference (American Museum of Natural History, Dept. of Herpetology).
http://research.amnh.org/herpetology/amphibia/index.html

This resource may be searched by common (English) names of species to provide taxonomy and distribution; free.

BioMed Protocols (Humana Press).
http://biomed.humanapress.com/Index.pasp

A relatively new online service includes information from the print volumes of this publisher's *Methods in Molecular Biology* series. Over 12,000 protocols can be accessed.

BRENDA: The Comprehensive Enzyme Information System; (Institute of Biochemistry at the University of Cologne).
http://www.brenda.uni-koeln.de

The BRENDA database is the Internet-accessible edition of the *Enzyme Handbook*, also known as the *Springer Handbook of Enzymes*, originally published in print in 1969 (3rd edition volumes have begun to appear); free for academic non-profit institutions, registration required; subscription needed for commercial use.

Current Protocols (Wiley InterScience).
http://www3.interscience.wiley.com/aboutus/currentProtocols.html

A range of subjects is covered by the various titles within these serial publications. The advanced search may be limited to *Current Protocols*.

eNature Online Field Guides (eNature.com).
http://www.enature.com/guides/select_group.asp

This site is owned by the National Wildlife Federation and contains field guide information on over 4,800 North American species of amphibians, birds, reptiles, butterflies, fishes, insects, mammals, native plants [from the Lady Bird Johnson Wildlife Center], reptiles, seashells, seashore creatures, spiders, trees, and wildflowers; free.

Mammal Species of the World (Smithsonian Institution).
http://www.nmnh.si.edu/msw

Name, status, literature details for more than 4,600 species. Originally published in the print book of the same title (2nd ed., 1993), entries in the online edition may not completely replicate the print entries and uniquely may include a distribution map; free.

Ready-Reference Resources

Animal Diversity Web (The University of Michigan's Museum of Zoology).
http://animaldiversity.ummz.umich.edu/

This site is both an encyclopedia and an interactive taxonomy that provides partial classification and information for the kingdom animalia; natural history facts, pictures, and a few literature citations are also provided; free.

BIOSIS Serial Sources (Thomson BIOSIS).
http://www.biosis.org/products/bss/

Useful when faced with unknown journal abbreviations for journals in the life sciences in any language.

Statistics (Food and Agriculture Organization of the United Nations).
http://www.fao.org/waicent/portal/statistics_en.asp

A collection of databases and reports on: worldwide agriculture, fisheries, forestry, land resources and use, and water management; free.

Biographical and Historical Sources

Foundations of Classical Genetics (Electronic Scholarly Publishing).
http://www.esp.org/foundations/genetics/classical/browse/

A catalog by author or title of a sizeable collection of books, articles, and essays dating back as far as Aristotle. Documents are in pdf; free.

CHEMISTRY

Standard Reference Works

Analytical WebBase (Royal Society of Chemistry).
http://www.rsc.org/publishing/currentawareness/awb/

This is the online version of the print *Analytical Abstracts* and includes citations back to 1980. Approximately 250 international journal titles are regularly reviewed for content.

Beilstein/Gmelin CrossFire (MDL).
http://www.mdl.com/products/knowledge/crossfire_beilstein/
http://www.mdl.com/products/knowledge/crossfire_gmelin/

Online version of *Beilstein Handbuch der Organischen Chemie* (originally published in German and more recently in English) and for inorganic chemistry, the *Gmelin Handbuch der Anorganischen Chemie*. Content is property data, chemical structure, and literature citations beginning in 1771.

Dictionary of Chemistry (Oxford Reference).
http://www.oxfordreference.com/pages/Subjects_and_Titles_2D_GS03

Online version of the print edition.

Hawley's Condensed Chemical Dictionary (Knovel).
http://www.knovel.com/knovel2/Toc.jsp?BookID=704

Online access to this reference book known by the same title in print.

IUPAC Compendium of Chemical Terminology (Royal Society of Chemistry).
http://www.chemsoc.org/cgi-shell/empower.exe?DB=goldbook

The print edition (2nd ed., 1997) was published by Blackwell Science. This work is said to be known more familiarly as the *IUPAC Gold Book*; free.

Kirk-Othmer Encyclopedia of Chemical Technology (Wiley InterScience).
http://www3.interscience.wiley.com/cgi-bin/mrwhome/104554789/HOME

The expected signed articles with literature references are found in this source for topics of interest or use to the industry and applied side of chemistry. Multiple search types with record field-level precision are possible.

Lange's Handbook of Chemistry (Knovel).
http://www.knovel.com/knovel2/Toc.jsp?SpaceID=10093&BookID=47

Data for organic or inorganic chemicals, atoms, spectroscopic or thermodynamic property data, and more is found in this longstanding reference source.

Periodic Table of Isotopes (Lawrence Berkeley National Laboratory).
http://ie.lbl.gov/education/isotopes.htm

Data includes half-life, spin parity, decay mode(s), or abundance; free.

Sax's Dangerous Properties of Industrial Materials (Knovel).
http://www.knovel.com/knovel2/Toc.jsp?BookID=707

Online edition of the multivolume print title of the same name, now in its 10th edition (2000). Toxicity data, physical properties, literature citations, and handling summaries for materials encountered in the workplace. (Full online text not accessed.)

SciFinder (CAS).
http://www.cas.org/SCIFINDER/scicover2.html

SciFinder Scholar (CAS)
http://www.cas.org/SCIFINDER/SCHOLAR/index.html

Both of the above are online versions of *Chemical Abstracts*, with citations dating from 1907. Some subscriptions to this resource include *Medline* citations. The industry version is *SciFinder*, while *SciFinder Scholar* is intended for academic institutions.

Ullmann's Encyclopedia of Industrial Chemistry (Wiley VCH).
http://www.wiley-vch.de/vch/software/ullmann/

Online version of the multivolume print source of the same title.

Data Compilations

Combined Chemical Dictionary (Chapman & Hall/CRC).
http://www.chemnetbase.com/scripts/ccdweb.exe

Chemical, physical, and biological properties of compounds from the *Dictionary of Organic Compounds, Dictionary of Natural Products, Dictionary of Inorganic and Organometallic Compounds, Dictionary of Drugs*, and *Dictionary of Analytical Reagents*. Literature references from these sources are also present.

CRC Handbook of Chemistry and Physics (CRC Press).
http://www.hbcpnetbase.com

The online version of this standard work includes extensive tables of data and conversion factors.

Ready-Reference Resources

Chemical Elements.com (Yinon Bentor).
http://www.chemicalelements.com/

An online, interactive periodic table of the elements; free.

Merck Index (Merck & Co., Inc.)
http://www.merck.com/pubs/mindex/online.html

   This standard source provides a quick way to look for property or factual data on better-known chemicals. (Online edition not accessed.)

Biographical and Historical Sources

Biographies of Chemists (ChemLin Virtual Chemistry Library).
http://www.chemlin.de/chemistry/chemists.htm

   Entries date from the thirteenth century to the present, and many include a portrait. Not all entries are in English; free.

This Week in the History of Chemistry (Carmen Giunta).
http://webserver.lemoyne.edu/faculty/giunta/week.html

   Information is drawn from several reference sources or journal articles including *Notable Women in the Physical Sciences* (1997) and *Biographical Encyclopedia of Scientists*, 2nd edition (1994); free.

EARTH SCIENCE AND ASTRONOMY

Standard Reference Works

GEOBASE (Elsevier/GEO ABSTRACTS).
http:// www.elsevier.com/inca/publications/store/4/2/2/5/9/7/index.htt

   This database is the online counterpart to *Geographical Abstracts, Physical Geography, Human Geography, Geological Abstracts, Eco-*

logical Abstracts, *International Development Abstracts*, and *Oceano-graphic Literature Review*, and *Geomechanics Abstracts*.

GeoRef (American Geological Institute).
http://www.agiweb.org/georef/about/index.html

Publications from all fields of geology and geophysics are indexed and abstracted in this standard database whose worldwide coverage begins with 1785.

Meteorological and Geoastrophysical Abstracts (CSA).
http://www.csa.com/factsheets/mga-set-c.php

Produced by the American Meteorological Society. Content from slightly over 630 titles beginning with 1974.

Oceanic Abstracts (CSA).
http://md1.csa.com/factsheets/oceanic-set-c.php

This title (formerly *Oceanic Index, Oceanic Index Citation Journal*) abstracts the world's literature on oceanography from 1981. Over 560 journals are monitored for inclusion.

Data Compilations

World Ocean Database (U.S. National Oceanographic Data Center).
http://www.nodc.noaa.gov/OC5/WOD01/data2001.html

Temperature, salinity, dissolved oxygen, inorganic phosphate, and 20 other profiles; free.

Navigator Star Finder (Omar Reis).
http://www.tecepe.com.br/cgi-win/cgiasvis.exe

Generates star, constellation, or celestial objects diagrams for a given day from a given city; free.

Sunrise, Sunset, Moonrise, Moonset Tables (U.S. Naval Observatory).
http://aa.usno.navy.mil/data/docs/RS_OneYear.html

Generates a year's worth of day-level data for locations in the U.S. and elsewhere; free.

Ready-Reference Resources

Dictionary of Astronomy (Oxford Reference).
http://www.oxfordreference.com/pages/Subjects_and_Titles_2D_GS01

Online version of the print title with over 1,500 entries.

Dictionary of Earth Sciences (Oxford Reference).
http://www.oxfordreference.com/pages/Subjects_and_Titles_2D_GS04

The online edition is a revision of the print version and has some 6,000 entries.

An Earth Scientist's Periodic Table of the Elements and Their Ions
(L. Bruce Railsback).
http://www.gly.uga.edu/railsback/PT.html

Published in 2003 (*Geology*) this initial revised table was modified for usefulness to earth scientists; a subsequent revision, stemming from Los Alamos Nat'l Lab, has been announced for access through the Knovel Corp.; free.

Nine Planets: A multimedia tour of the solar system (William A. Arnett).
http://www.seds.org/billa/tnp/

An interactive encyclopedia of this solar system; free.

ENGINEERING AND TECHNOLOGY

Standard Reference Works

Applied Science and Technology Full Text (H. W. Wilson).
http://www.hwwilson.com/databases/applieds.htm

Citations to technical and engineering literature including trade publications. All are published in English.

Compendex (Engineering Village 2).
http://www.engineeringvillage2.org/engresources/tour/tour_databases.html

This title, the online equivalent of *Engineering Index* in print, is the best-known source of citations to engineering literature worldwide; from 1970.

Computer Abstracts International Database (Emerald).
http://hermia.emeraldinsight.com/vl=7749313/cl=14/nw=1/rpsv/abstracts/

This is a rather recent online version of an index to English-language articles from approximately 200 periodicals with coverage of artificial intelligence, computers, and data processing. Entries date from 1987.

Computer Database (Thomson Gale).
http://www.galegroup.com/pdf/facts/compdb.pdf

A periodical index with full-text for computer, telecommunications, and electronics products and industry news. About 150 trade journals, newsletters, or other industry publications, from 1980 to the present, are regularly monitored for inclusion. Part of the *InfoTrac* service.

Inspec (Institution of Electrical Engineers).
http://www.iee.org/Publish/Inspec/About/index.cfm

Covers physics, electrical engineering, electronics, communications, control engineering, computers and computing, and information technology back to 1969.

Wiley Encyclopedia of Electrical and Electronics Engineering (Wiley InterScience).
http://www3.interscience.wiley.com/cgi-bin/mrwhome/104554774/HOME

Topics include: computers, energy conversion, industrial electronics, neural networks, and ocean engineering.

Data Compilations

CRC Materials Science and Engineering Handbook (ENGnetBASE).
http://www.engnetbase.com/ejournals/books/book_summary/summary.asp?id=463

Online version of the same title in print with materials properties and reference data tables.

Perry's Chemical Engineering Handbook (Knovel).
http://www.knovel.com/knovel2/Toc.jsp?BookID=48

Contains 30 sections plus interactive tables and graphs.

Ready-Reference Resources

Dictionary of Computing (Oxford University Press).
http://www.oxfordreference.com/pages/Subjects_and_Titles_2D_C01

Online edition of the print work of the same title. (6,000 entries.)

Dictionary of Pure and Applied Physics (ENGnetBASE).
http://www.engnetbase.com/ejournals/books/book_summary/summary.
asp?id=1026

Online edition of the print title with over 3,000 terms are defined by eminent scientists.

Encyclopedic Dictionary of Named Processes in Chemical Technology (ENGnetBASE).
http://www.engnetbase.com/ejournals/books/book_summary/summary.
asp?id=413

Defines 2,600 terms that are not obvious or self-explanatory.

FOLDOC (Imperial College Department of Computing).
http://foldoc.doc.ic.ac.uk/foldoc/index.html

The Free On-line Dictionary of Computing is an interactive dictionary of computing terms; free.

Handbook of Groundwater Engineering (ENGnetBASE).
http://www.engnetbase.com/ejournals/books/book_summary/summary.
asp?id=429

This handbook covers all engineering aspects of subsurface water including treatment, containment, and transportation.

Biographical and Historical Sources

Greatest Engineering Achievements of the Twentieth Century (National Academy of Engineering).
http://www.greatachievements.org/

Histories and brief chronologies are given for most of the 20 areas of achievement listed; free.

ENVIRONMENTAL SCIENCE AND ECOLOGY

Standard Reference Works

Ecology Abstracts (CSA).
http://www.csa.com/factsheets/ecology-set-c.php

Online coverage begins with 1982.

Encyclopedia of Environmental Microbiology (Wiley InterScience).
http://www3.interscience.wiley.com/cgi-bin/mrwhome/104554776/HOME

Topics include: extreme environments, environmental biotechnology, freshwater, and groundwater. (Online text not accessed.)

Environmental Sciences & Pollution Management (CSA).
http://www.csa.com/factsheets/envclust-set-c.php

Extensive coverage of the environmental sciences citing over 6,000 serials with coverage back to 1967.

Wildlife and Ecology Studies Worldwide (NISC).
http://www.nisc.com/Frame/NISC_catproducts-f.htm

This database is a compilation of citations and abstracts from several sources including *Wildlife Review Abstracts*. Citations go back in some cases as far as 1935 and include more gray literature than is typically found in other bibliographic databases. (Online text not accessed.)

Data Compilations

Our Living Resources: A report to the nation on the distribution, abundance, and health of U.S. plants, animals, and ecosystems (U.S. Department of the Interior, National Biological Service).
http://biology.usgs.gov/s+t/index.htm

Reports on species, ecosystems, ecoregions, and special issues; free.

Ready-Reference Resources

Biodiversity Glossary of Terms (World Resources Institute).
http://pubs.wri.org/pubs_content_text.cfm?ContentID=487

An interactive dictionary with links to related glossaries; free.

Dictionary of Ecology (Oxford Reference).
http://www.oxfordreference.com/pages/Subjects_and_Titles_2D_GS05

Online edition of the print work by the same title with 5,000 entries.

ENN (Environmental News Network, Inc.).
http://www.enn.com/

Claiming to be nonpartisan, ENN archives the most recent five days of wire service news on the environment; free.

IUCN Red List of Threatened Species (International Union for Conservation of Nature and Natural Resources).
http://www.redlist.org

Information is provided through this site on the status and distribution of plant or animal species worldwide. Searches can be limited in a number of ways including by scarcity of a species, geography, or habitat; free.

Species Information (U.S. Fish and Wildlife Service).
http://endangered.fws.gov/wildlife.html#species

Lists and data on endangered and threatened species within the U.S.; free.

Biographical and Historical Sources

Conservation Hall of Fame (National Wildlife Federation).
http://www.nwf.org/halloffame/inductees.html

Information on inductees from many walks of life who are known for a commitment to preservation of wildlife in the U.S.; free.

MATH

Standard Reference Works

MathSciNet: Mathematical Reviews on the Web
(American Mathematical Society).
http://www.ams.org/msnhtml/about_mathsci.html

The online equivalent to the well-known print *Mathematical Reviews* plus *Current Mathematical Publications*. It provides reviews or summaries of articles and books containing contributions to mathematical research from nearly 1,800 titles published throughout the world beginning with 1940.

Data Compilations

Wolfram Functions Site (Wolfram Research).
http://functions.wolfram.com

A well-organized site for those in search of formulas, functions, or their definitions; free.

Ready-Reference Resources

Concise Oxford Dictionary of Mathematics (Oxford Reference).
http://www.oxfordreference.com/pages/Subjects_and_Titles_2D_GS06

Text and formulas correspond with the print edition, although an online search often produces multiple hits in addition to the main definition.

Dictionary of Statistics (Oxford Reference).
http://www.oxfordreference.com/pages/Subjects_and_Titles_2D_GS12

This work corresponds to the print edition and has approximately 1,500 entries.

Biographical and Historical Sources

Mathematicians of the 17th and 18th Centuries (D. R. Wilkins, School of Mathematics, Trinity College, Dublin).
http://www.maths.tcd.ie/pub/HistMath/People/RBallHist.html

Selected biographies from *A Short Account of the History of Mathematics* (1908); free.

PHYSICS

Standard Reference Works

Dictionary of Geophysics, Astrophysics and Astronomy (CRC/ENGnetBASE).
http://www.engnetbase.com/ejournals/books/book_summary/summary.asp?id=1037

This is the online edition of the same title in print published by CRC Press. Over 4,000 definitions are found here.

Oxford Dictionary of Physics (Oxford Reference).
http://www.oxfordreference.com/pages/Subjects_and_Titles_2D_GS07

Contains over 3,500 entries. Text with accompanying diagrams is equivalent in the online and print editions.

SPIN Web (American Institute of Physics).
http://ojps.aip.org/spinweb

In print, the *Searchable Physics Information Notices* is roughly *Current Physics Index*. Pre-publication information is also present.

Data Compilations

Landolt-Börnstein (Springer).
http://www.springeronline.com/sgw/cda/frontpage/0,10735,5-10113-2-95874-0,00.html

This resource in print numbers well over 300 volumes. A wide assortment of physics or chemical data including that for solids, liquids, surfaces, mixtures, metals, and other substances, plus energy data and molecular constants. Data dates back to the 19th century.

Physical Reference Data (National Institute of Standards and Technology).
http://physics.nist.gov/PhysRefData/contents.html

NIST data and bibliographies for a range of topics including atomic, spectroscopic, nuclear, and condensed matter physics; free.

Smithsonian Physical Tables (Knovel).
http://www.knovel.com/knovel2/Toc.jsp?SpaceID=10093&BookID=736

Originally published by the Smithsonian Institution, this source contains 901 tables with a handy glossary and hyperlinked index.

Ready-Reference Resources

Directory of Physics, Astronomy & Geophysics Staff
(American Institute of Physics).
http://scitation.aip.org/spinweb/direct.jsp

A listing, with contact information, for relevant persons or organizations in North America.

Biographical and Historical Sources

Contributions of 20th Century Women to Physics (UCLA Department of Physics and Astronomy).
http://www.physics.ucla.edu/~cwp/dev/exp.1.html

Contributions of 86 women from various countries; free.

REFERENCES

1. Martha E. Williams, "The State of Databases Today: 2003," Introduction to *Gale Directory of Databases*, ed. Alan Hedblad (Farmington Hills: Gale, 2003).
2. Roy Tennant, "Science Portals," *Library Journal*, March 15, 2003, 34.

Medical Reference Sources on the Internet:
An Evolving Information Forum
and Marketplace

Gary A. McMillan

SUMMARY. Some of the best standard medical reference works have migrated to the Internet. Corporations, professional organizations, and the federal government have taken advantage of the distribution and public education capabilities of the Internet to launch free or fee-based resources (or a combination thereof offering limited information as a teaser to encourage purchasing or subscriptions). Core medical/health reference works are identified and briefly described, with an emphasis on sites which are comprehensive, up-to-date, and, most importantly, offer information based on credible, evidence-based, scientific sources. *[Article copies available for a fee from The Haworth Document Delivery Service: 1-800-HAWORTH. E-mail address: <docdelivery@haworthpress.com> Website: <http://www.HaworthPress.com> © 2005 by The Haworth Press, Inc. All rights reserved.]*

KEYWORDS. Medical reference, consumer health information, health statistics

---

Gary A. McMillan is Director, Melvin Sabshin Library & Archives, American Psychiatric Association, 1000 Wilson Boulevard, Suite 1825, Arlington, VA 22209 (E-mail: gmcmillan@psych.org).

[Haworth co-indexing entry note]: "Medical Reference Sources on the Internet: An Evolving Information Forum and Marketplace." McMillan, Gary A. Co-published simultaneously in *The Reference Librarian* (The Haworth Information Press, an imprint of The Haworth Press, Inc.) No. 91/92, 2005, pp. 197-209; and: *The Reference Collection: From the Shelf to the Web* (ed: William J. Frost) The Haworth Information Press, an imprint of The Haworth Press, Inc., 2005, pp. 197-209. Single or multiple copies of this article are available for a fee from The Haworth Document Delivery Service [1-800-HAWORTH, 9:00 a.m. - 5:00 p.m. (EST). E-mail address: docdelivery@haworthpress.com].

INTRODUCTION

Although accuracy and thoroughness are the standard litmus tests for quality of reference service across all subject areas, reference librarians generally have a heightened sense of responsibility when the question is health-related. Finding an authoritative and unbiased source of medical information on the Internet can be a challenge and may be quite unnecessary when an easy to use, standard reference work is on the shelf. How often has a librarian watched a student struggle with using the search and display software of a specialized encyclopedia on CD-ROM when the well-indexed print version yields the information in seconds? Furthermore, while government, nonprofit, and some well-reputed commercial sites are making a wealth of information available electronically, one also has to contend with the anti-medicine, advocacy, and for-profit health Web sites which have either a political agenda or financial interest that may not be readily transparent–which is not to say that federal and medical specialty association Web sites are completely bias-free in their content or their silence on controversial topics.

While business, law, and medicine were at the forefront of the electronic revolution, the availability and accessibility (i.e., cost) of standard medicine/health reference sources is more haphazard than these other fields. With the increased accessibility of the Internet–its democratization–and its growing maturity as a communications and distribution medium, the volume of medical information has grown exponentially, if idiosyncratically. The challenge for reference librarians, especially when building user-focused, medical reference collections in electronic format is to maintain standards of accuracy and comprehensiveness while weighing the relative efficiency and cost-effectiveness of print and electronic sources. This challenge is exacerbated by the fleeting nature of many dot.com sites, even those related to health. Veronin[1] followed 184 health Web sites over a three-year period and found that well over half (59%) of the sites were not found at their original address and were not traceable from the former URL or other means. Of those sites that were located, nearly two-thirds (62%) had added no new content in the intervening years.

This article will highlight basic online resources in medicine and health. Most are electronic versions of well-established print products, but some emerged anew to capitalize on the educational and outreach capabilities of the Internet.

Medical reference sources on the Internet are a mix of established print products now in electronic form (hundreds are now available for online licensing) and new resources that have no print equivalent, but clearly are compiled by health care professionals or organizations with the requisite expertise.

DICTIONARIES

While some favorites, such as *Stedman's Medical Dictionary* (http://www.stedmans.com/), are only available free in abridged form (if at all), two excellent alternatives are the basic *On-line Medical Dictionary* (http://cancerweb.ncl.ac.uk/omd/) and the more comprehensive *MedTerms.com Medical Dictionary*.

The European Commission sponsors a searchable *Multilingual Glossary* (http://allserv.rug.ac.be/~rvdstich/eugloss/welcome.html) of medical terms in nine European Languages. The Medical Library Association's *Medspeak Terms* (http://www.mlanet.org/resources/medspeak/) provides plain language definitions for over 100 commonly heard medical terms.

For further general and specialized glossaries, BioMedWorld maintains a listing of *Online Medical & Science Dictionaries* (http://www.sciencekomm.at/advice/dict.html#part2). To complement the dictionary information, over 3,000 medical images and videos are available through *HONmedia* (http://www.hon.ch/HONmedia/), a service of the Health on the Net Foundation.

DIRECTORIES

The three major medical directories are available to the public online, albeit with limited search capabilities, abridged format, and/or other use restrictions. The first two of these directories provide information on physicians: the American Medical Association's *Directory of Physicians in the U.S.* is available as *AMA Physician Select* (http://www.ama-assn.org/aps/amahg.htm), a database searchable by name or location and medical specialty and provides physician contact information, medical specialty and board certification as well as medical school, year of graduation and residency training, with additional information provided for AMA members and a separate directory for physicians offering online consultation. *The Official ABMS Directory of Board Certified Medical Specialists* (http://www.abms.org/login.asp) is searchable by name or location and specialty/subspecialty following a free registration process; however the only information provided is certifications (with no dates, unfortunately). The third key source, the *American Hospital Directory* (http://www.ahd.com/), provides a wonderful public service (follow the "Free Information" link) which allows users to search by hospital name, city, state, zip code, and/or telephone area code. The *Directory* provides contact information, Web site address, type of organization, number of beds, services provided, and data on inpatient utilization by medical service (the latter from the U.S. Centers for Medicare and Medicaid Services). Each of these three directories is available with expanded content and search capabilities for an online subscription fee. The AMA and ABMS directories are also available on CD-ROM for those who wish to retain a backfile for trend analysis.

The Joint Commission on Accreditation of Healthcare Organizations provides *Quality Check* (http://www.jcaho.org/quality+check/index.htm), a quick way to find contact and Web site information for service providers (in 11 categories including hospitals, ambulatory care, behavioral health, home care, and long term care) by name, location, and accreditation status. MEDLINEplus *Directories* (http://www.nlm.nih.gov/medlineplus/directories.html) has an extensive guide to directories of general and specialist medical professionals and health care organizations, especially long-established, federal government-sponsored directories such as the *CMHS Mental Health Services Locator* (http://www.mentalhealth.org/databases/) which lists mental health and substance abuse treatment facilities and selected statistics by state.

ATLASES: MIND AND BODY

A wealth of medical illustrations is available on the Internet from the classic, Gray's *Anatomy of the Human Body*, 12th edition (http://www.bartleby.com/107/) to the American Medical Association's *Atlas of the Body: Anatomy and Medical Illustrations* (http://www.ama-assn.org/ama/pub/category/7140.html) which provides twenty-five excellent images, many from the AMA's *Current Procedural Terminology* (1998 edition). The University of Washington, Seattle provides nearly one hundred illustrations in *A Musculoskeletal Atlas of the Human Body* (http://eduserv.hscer.washington.edu/hubio553/atlas/index.html).

One major undertaking in mapping the body is the National Library of Medicine's *The Visible Human Project*: "It is the creation of complete, anatomically detailed, three-dimensional representations of the normal male and female human bodies. . . . The long-term goal of *The*

Visible Human Project is to produce a system of knowledge structures that will transparently link visual knowledge forms to symbolic knowledge formats such as the names of body parts" (http://www.nlm.nih. gov/research/visible/visible_human.html). Much of the data is still restricted to research scientists; however, some twenty projects are listed as sources of images and animations utilizing this data (http://www. nlm.nih.gov/research/visible/animations.html).

The Departments of Radiology and Neurology at Brigham and Women's Hospital, Harvard Medical School, the Countway Library of Medicine, and the American Academy of Neurology have joined together to provide *The Whole Brain Atlas* (http://www.med.harvard.edu/AANLIB/). This Web site provides a brief description of various imaging technologies followed by images in five categories: the normal brain, cerebrovascular (stroke) disease, brain tumor, degenerative disease (e.g., Alzheimer's and Huntington's), and inflammatory or infectious disease (e.g., multiple sclerosis and AIDS). Another fascinating source of images is *BrainPlace.com: Brain SPECT Information and Resources* (http://www.brainplace.com/bp/) which offers a wealth of information from Daniel G. Amen's book, *Images into Human Behavior: A Brain SPECT Atlas*, including a history and introduction to the technology and the interpretation of images, images related to disease and mood/behavioral states, and a chapter, "Images of Treatment," which provides fascinating "before" and "after" SPECT images of patients who experienced significant improvement following treatment.

TEXTBOOKS, HANDBOOKS, MANUALS, AND RELATED

One or two-volume "textbooks" on medical specialties and sub-specialties are the backbone of much reference work. Electronic versions of such works are most often marketed as stand-alone CD-ROM products or as a print accompaniment. There are, however, notable exceptions. *University of Iowa's Family Practice Handbook*, 4th edition (http://www.vh.org/adult/provider/familymedicine/FPHandbook/ FPContents.html) provides excellent peer-reviewed articles organized by branch of medicine, including sections on HIV/AIDS, emergency medicine, and an herbal formulary. The *Merck Manual of Diagnosis and Therapy*, 17th edition (http://www.merck.com/pubs/mmanual/) and the *Merck Manual of Medical Information-Second Home Edition* (http://www.merck.com/mmhe/index.html) are comprehensive guides to medical conditions, their etiology, signs, symptoms and diagnosis, and treatment and prognosis targeted to the professional and layperson, respectively. See also the *Merck Manual of Geriatrics* (http://www. merck.com/mrkshared/mmg/home.jsp).

The Internet has fostered some noteworthy sites to complement the traditional sources. *Medem's Medical Library* (http://www.medem.com/) brings together content from its 45 national and state medical society partners as well as federal government agencies and other nonprofit health education materials, so the credibility and usefulness is high. On any topic one is likely to find entries authored by a medical specialty society, the National Institutes of Health, or an article from *JAMA: The Journal of the American Medical Association*. The information is organized by popular topics, life stages, diseases and conditions, and therapies and health strategies. *eMedicine.com* claims that "Nearly 10,000 physician authors and editors contribute to the eMedicine Clinical Knowledge Base, which contains articles on 7,000 diseases and disorders." Currently, 33 specialty areas are covered with notable depth in internal medicine and pediatrics but substantial coverage in all areas. Health professionals may also register for continuing medical education credit on any of the topics. The Mayo Foundation for Medical Education and Research offers the public a virtual encyclopedia on diseases and conditions and wellness topics at *MayoClinic.com*. Finally, the MEDLINEplus *Medical Encyclopedia* (http://www.nlm.nih.gov/ medlineplus/encyclopedia.html), covering over 4,000 entries by expert authors drawing upon standard reference works, is thorough and well-illustrated.

The field of computers in health care is well-represented online by the *Handbook of Medical Informatics* (http://www.mihandbook. stanford.edu/handbook/home.htm) compiled by a team of international experts and addresses the role of information systems in support of patient care, the assessment of the quality of care, research, and management and planning.

Of late there has been a burgeoning interest in the media and in academia regarding forensic sciences. Among the many helpful sites are the National Association of Medical Examiners which offers a library (http://www.thename.org/library_index.htm) of guidelines, position statements, case studies, tutorials, a directory of medical examiners and coroner's offices, articles and links to online forensic journals, and the *Handbook of Forensic Services* (http://www.fbi.gov/hq/lab/handbook/ intro.htm) which provides guidance and procedures for safe and efficient methods of collecting and preserving evidence and describes the forensic examinations performed by the FBI Laboratory.

Other sources of expert information can readily be tapped through the *National Guideline Clearinghouse* (http://www.guideline.gov/) which provides lengthy summaries of the key points from over 1,000 practice guidelines. These summaries are fully searchable by key word and there is a "detailed search" capability with several search limits to better refine and target a key word search. References are provided to the source guidelines, many of which are linked to the online full-text document made available free by the sponsoring organization.

PHARMACOLOGY:
MEDICATIONS AND HOME REMEDIES

A subset of the reference handbooks that bears special attention concerns medications. The *Physician's Desk Reference* (PDR), the Bible for prescription drugs, is available as *PDRhealth* (http://www. gettingwell.com/drug_info/) and also includes information on over-the-counter (OTC) drugs, herbal medications, and nutritional supplements. Generic and brand names are provided as well as uses, side effects and contraindications/special warnings, food and drug interactions, and dosage. Each entry includes images of the medications for identification purposes. The MEDLINEplus *Drug Information* site (http://www.nlm. nih.gov/medlineplus/druginformation.html) brings together product information from *MedMaster*, a service of the American Society of Health-System Pharmacists (with its own *SafeMedication.com* Web site), and the *USP DI Advice for the Patient*, a product of the United States Pharmacopeia (which establishes state-of-the-art standards to ensure the quality of medicines).

Drugs undergoing clinical trial or newly approved for specific uses by the U.S. Food & Drug Administration (FDA) are tracked by *CenterWatch Drug Directories* (http://www.centerwatch.com/patient/ drugs/drugdirectories.html). The primary source documents (FDA approval letters and labeling) are available directly from the FDA (http:// www.fda.gov/cder/approval/index.htm) as is the *Electronic Orange Book* (http://www.fda.gov/cder/ob/default.htm) of approved drugs with therapeutic equivalents, searchable by active ingredient, trade name, and manufacturer.

Additionally, in-depth information on alternative remedies is available from the Alternative Medicine Foundation's *HerbMed.org* site which documents scientific, evidence-based information on the use of herbs for health.

MENTAL HEALTH

BehaveNet (http://www.behavenet.com/) is an ambitious site which brings together a vast storehouse of mental health information. Most notable are the capsule diagnostic criteria for mental illnesses, arranged by category and numerical code, from the *Diagnostic and Statistical Manual of Mental Disorders, Fourth Edition, Text Revision* (DSM-IV-TR, American Psychiatric Publishing, Inc., 2000). Other valuable reference features include dictionaries of acronyms, abbreviations, and eponyms, and specialized glossaries (e.g., drugs/pharmacology, psychotherapies, psychoanalysis, and management/reimbursement). It also has very user-friendly directories to health-related state agencies, legislators and laws–a good complement to *Health Hippo* (http://hippo. findlaw.com/hippomen.html) which serves as a gateway to mental health sections from the *U.S. Code*, *Code of Federal Regulations*, and other federal legislation and testimony. In March of 2005, the American Psychiatric Publishing, Inc. launched a new online subscription service (http://www.psychiatryonline.com) which bundles electronic access to the DSM-IV-TR with key reference works on differential diagnosis, the *Textbook on Clinical Psychiatry*, the APA treatment practice guidelines, selected journals, and a PDA eBook Library. Another excellent site, *PsychiatryMatters.MD* (http://www.psychiatrymatters.md), builds on the *DSM-IV-TR* and the *ICD-10 Classification of Mental and Behavioural Disorders* (World Health Organization, 1992), in its compendium, *Current Psychiatric Diagnosis & Treatment*. For each mental disorder, the profile includes definition, etiology and epidemiology, diagnostic criteria (including differential diagnosis) and diagnostic investigation methods, signs and symptoms, complications, prognosis, treatments, follow-up and management, and a core reference list.

Recent years are notable for the emergence of some of the most noteworthy public policy documents on mental health since the community mental health movement in the 1960s. In 1999, the landmark document, *Mental Health: A Report of the Surgeon General* (http://www. surgeongeneral.gov/library/mentalhealth/summary.html), made a comprehensive examination of mental health and mental illness focusing on scientific advances in diagnosis and treatment and the important issues of stigma, access to treatment, and availability of services. Two equally important documents focused attention on particularly vulnerable populations: *Report of the Surgeon General's Conference on Children's*

Mental Health: A National Action Agenda (http://www.surgeongeneral. gov/topics/cmh/childreport.htm) and *Mental Health: Culture, Race, and Ethnicity A Supplement to Mental Health: A Report of the Surgeon General* (http://www.surgeongeneral.gov/library/mentalhealth/cre/). More recently, the President's New Freedom Commission on Mental Health issued its final report, *Achieving the Promise: Transforming Mental Health Care in America* (http://www.mentalhealthcommission.gov/ reports/FinalReport/toc.html) establishing a blueprint for reform of the mental health care system in the United States.

Another important set of reports, *Cultural Competence Standards in Managed Mental Health Care* (http://www.wiche.edu/MentalHealth/ Cultural_Comp/index.htm), is a product of the U.S. Center for Mental Health Services' Managed Care Workforce Training Initiative of the University of Pennsylvania School of Medicine and prepared under the auspices of the Western Interstate Commission for Higher Mental Health Program. Focusing on populations of African descent, Asian and Pacific Islanders, Latinos, and Native Americans, the reports delineate best practices for prevention, education and access/outreach, styles of communication/linguistic support, triage and assessment, treatment/ care planning, self-help and social support networks, and outcome evaluation. The best source for access to these and other full-text documents is *MIMH-PIE*, the Missouri Institute of Mental Health's Policy Information Exchange (http://mimh200.mimh.edu/mimhweb/pie/).

Finally, the American Psychiatric Association (http://www.psych. org/library) makes available a growing full-text, online library of its policy and practice-related publications, including abstracts from the APA Annual Meeting, treatment practice guidelines, positions statements, resource documents, and code of ethics. Links to subspeciality, international, and other psychiatric associations are also provided (http:// www.psych.org/mem_groups/other_orgs/index.cfm).

STATISTICS

The National Center for Health Statistics' *Data 2010, the Healthy-People 2010 Database* (http://wonder.cdc.gov/DATA2010/focus.htm) provides trend data on 28 health focus areas for the U.S. and the states. Two standard reference works are also available in PDF format: *Health, United States*, 1975 to 2002 editions (http://www.cdc.gov/nchs/hus. htm) with the special topic "chartbooks" (e.g., women's health, aging, adolescence, and urban and rural health) and *Mental Health, United States, 2002* (http://www.mentalhealth.org/samhsa.gov/publications/allpubs/SMA04-3938/default.asp). In addition to morbidity and mortality data, these reports also provide data on service utilization, facilities, health care personnel, and financing. *CDC Wonder* (http://wonder.cdc.gov/) is a gateway to the reports by the Centers for Disease Control and Prevention which enables the user to generate on-demand statistical tables based on the Centers' natality, mortality, morbidity, and surveillance (e.g., AIDS, fatal accidents, cancer, occupational health, sexually transmitted disease, tuberculosis, and youth risk behavior) data series.

COMMERCIAL REFERENCE PRODUCTS

Several medical publishers have rolled out online versions of their print product lines of reference standards with great success and sophistication, e.g., McGraw-Hill, Cochrane, Lippincott, and Taylor & Francis. McGraw-Hill's *AccessMedicine.com* is a gateway to the publisher's classic reference titles–updated daily–including Harrison's *Principles of Internal Medicine*, Hurst's *The HEART, The Metabolic and Molecular Bases of Inherited Disease*, and the complete *AccessLANGE.com* collection. The latter includes Lange's basic science and clinical reference series, each incorporating ten standard textbooks with institutional pricing based on the number of concurrent uses. The basic science series covers biochemistry, medical microbiology, histology, pharmacology, neuroanatomy, epidemiology, pathophysiology of disease, medical physiology, and pathology. The clinical sciences (the familiar *Current Diagnosis and Treatment* titles) covers pediatrics, orthopedics, ophthalmology, endocrinology, urology, cardiology, psychiatry, surgery, obstetrics and gynecology, and the *Clinician's Pocket Reference*.

Lippincott Williams & Wilkins (http://www.lww.com) has an extensive online library of journals and newsletters (including the many *Current Opinion* titles covering a broad range of clinical medicine and allied health topics) as well as an extensive collection of reference works online via *Ovid.com* (currently 133 titles) and a growing number of texts on CD-ROM and for the PDA. Taylor & Francis (http://www.ebookstore.tandf.co.uk) has online and off-line access options to "ebooks" with individual licensing by title and institutional licensing by bundles of titles. Currently, over three hundred titles are available in biosciences and clinical medicine and a similar number in the behavioral sciences. The National Academies Press (http://www.nap.edu)

makes its extensive catalog of medical and public health titles available free online with the option to purchase and download chapters and entire books. The Press is particularly known for publishing leading studies on health care policy, financing, and quality of care.

The *Cochrane Library*, an excellent source of timely, evidence-based clinical results information, is now available on CD-ROM and online via *Wiley InterScience* (http://www3.interscience.wiley.com/cgi-bin/mrwhome/106568753/). Of the several databases which comprise the Cochrane Library, the *Cochrane Database of Systematic Reviews (CDSR)* is probably most frequently consulted. Each comprehensive review attempts to synthesize and assess all of the clinical trials literature regarding the effectiveness of a particular disease intervention. *Wiley InterScience* also has a collection of 78 other online medical atlases, handbooks, textbooks, and other reference works. Packaged as *The Cochrane Collaboration*, selected databases are also included in Ovid's *EBM Reviews* (http://www.ovid.com/site/catalog/DataBase/904.jsp) which incorporates the American College of Physicians' *ACP Journal Club* providing enhanced abstracts of articles selected for their methodological soundness and relevance to clinical practice.

The *PDxMD* series on *Medical Conditions* (14 volumes) and *Differential Diagnosis with Clinical Benchmarks* are included in Elsevier's *FIRSTConsult.com* which mines the medical literature and organizes the "gems" in a way particularly useful for clinicians. For a work-in-progress, it's amassed an impressive editorial board and has built Reference Centers (bioterrorism, contraception, and pregnancy collections had been published as of the writing of this article), surgical *Procedure Files* (34 available at the time this article was written), and patient education resources (some in Spanish) on over 300 topics. *FIRSTConsult* information is also available for PDA applications. Another Elsevier innovation, *MDConsult.com*, has four editions targeted to physicians and other health care professionals: a core edition (focusing on primary care) as well as editions on infectious disease, respiratory and critical care, and pain. In-depth content collections are also available on hematology-oncology, infectious disease, Ob/Gyn, pain medicine, pediatrics, and pulmonary medicine. Again, Elsevier provides current awareness information for the PDA.

Another innovator in the electronic medical reference field is the *Stat!Ref Library* (http://www.statref.com) which packages reference titles for access in several formats (online, CD-ROM, DVD, and PDA). Here you can license the American Psychiatric Association's *Diagnos-*

tic & Statistical Manual of Mental Disorders-IV-TR and *Treatments of Psychiatric Disorders*, selected *Current Diagnosis and Treatment* titles, the *Merck Manual, Mosby's Drug Consult*, the *Red Book on Infectious Diseases, Stedman's Medical Dictionary, Taber's Cyclopedic Medical Dictionary, The Medical Letter on Drugs and Therapeutics, USP DI* (drug information volumes for professionals and patients), and *WebMD Scientific American Medicine.*

The commercial area is growing exponentially as nonprofit and for-profit publishers master the technology and, more importantly, resolve issues of access methods and pricing structures for their intellectual property. Most publishers realize that the profitability of their reference standards is in jeopardy as rivals publish online and as new online services synthesize, analyze, and make accessible (in multiple formats) state-of-the-art, evidence-based research with immediate clinical applications.

The growth of online full-text reference sources is not all sunny from a collection development perspective, however. Not only are there competing titles, but the same reference title may be available for licensing from several vendors, creating a truly confusing and tangled Web when making purchasing decisions for one's library. The emergence of bibliographic databases on CD-ROM led to the same consternation in the early 1990s: how many different software interfaces should library users (and librarians) be expected to successfully navigate and what criteria should be applied to judge the cost-effectiveness of electronic over print materials?

FINDING ADDITIONAL RESOURCES

Search the Internet with a greater degree of confidence by using the search engine offered by the Health on the Net (HON) Foundation. *HONcodeHunt* (http://www.hon.ch/HONcode/HONcode_check.html) searches only Web sites which have been screened for conformity with the *HON Code of Conduct (HONcode) for medical and health Web sites* (http://www.hon.ch/HONcode/Conduct.html). While Crocco and Jadad[2] found only two reported cases in the medical literature of adverse consequences to humans of poor quality health information on the Internet, the standards established by the *HON Code* provide an excellent set of criteria for evaluating health content on the Web.

REFERENCES

1. Michael A. Veronin, "Where Are They Now? A Case Study of Health-Related Web Site Attrition," *Journal of Medical Internet Research* 4 (2002) e10, http://www.jmir.org/2002/2/e10/.

2. Anthony G. Crocco, Miguel Villasis-Keever, and Alejandro R. Jadad. "Analysis of Cases of Harm Associated With Use of Health Information on the Internet." *Journal of the American Medical Association* 287 (2002) 2869-71, http://jama.ama-assn.org/cgi/content/full/287/21/2869.

Web-Based Reference Resources
for the Social Sciences

Brian Quinn

SUMMARY. With the growth of the World Wide Web has come a proliferation of online reference sources. Some of these are electronic
versions of already existing paper sources, while others have no paper
counterpart. Many of the best reference resources found on the Web
are subscription-based, but a surprising number of quality resources
are available free. The vastness of the Web makes it difficult to provide a comprehensive and exhaustive survey of all the resources that
are currently available. This article attempts to identify some of the
most significant resources across the social sciences. It includes six
disciplines: anthropology, communications, history, political science,
psychology, and sociology. *[Article copies available for a fee from The
Haworth Document Delivery Service: 1-800-HAWORTH. E-mail address:
<docdelivery@haworthpress.com> Website: <http://www.HaworthPress.com>
© 2005 by The Haworth Press, Inc. All rights reserved.]*

KEYWORDS. Web, reference, social sciences, psychology, sociology,
anthropology, political science, communications, history

Brian Quinn is Social Sciences Librarian and Coordinator of Collection Development, Texas Tech University Libraries, Lubbock, TX 79409-0002 (E-mail: brian.
quinn@ttu.edu).

[Haworth co-indexing entry note]: "Web-Based Reference Resources for the Social Sciences." Quinn,
Brian. Co-published simultaneously in *The Reference Librarian* (The Haworth Information Press, an imprint
of The Haworth Press, Inc.) No. 91/92, 2005, pp. 211-234; and: *The Reference Collection: From the Shelf to
the Web* (ed: William J. Frost) The Haworth Information Press, an imprint of The Haworth Press, Inc., 2005,
pp. 211-234. Single or multiple copies of this article are available for a fee from The Haworth Document Delivery
Service [1-800-HAWORTH, 9:00 a.m. - 5:00 p.m. (EST). E-mail address: docdelivery@haworthpress.com].

211

INTRODUCTION

As is true for many other fields, the growth in Web-based resources in the social sciences has been extremely rapid. The question arises as to what extent this is true for social sciences reference sources, the kinds of sources typically found in reference collections–indexes, directories, encyclopedias, bibliographies, dictionaries, and similar tools that librarians are accustomed to using in daily reference work. Most librarians might be able to name a couple of the most commonly used online indexes for a field, but beyond that, many librarians are probably wondering, "How much is really out there?"

This study is a broad survey of reference sources in the social sciences. It is an attempt to get a general sense of what is currently available on the Web and to determine how far along the migration from paper to electronic sources has progressed. The article is not intended to be comprehensive or exhaustive and to include every possible resource that might be considered as having some relevance to reference work. It does attempt, however, to identify many of the Web resources that potentially seem most useful within the basic categories of reference works that librarians are familiar with. Six areas of the social sciences are addressed: psychology, sociology, anthropology, political science, communications, and history.

PSYCHOLOGY

Over the past decade, there has been an explosion of Web-based reference sources in the field of psychology; indexing and abstracting resources are a good example. *PsycINFO* (American Psychological Association) is still widely regarded as the single best source for locating psychology research, but another subscription index from EBSCO called the Psychology and Behavioral Sciences Collection is growing in popularity. The latter index cannot compare with *PsycINFO* in terms of the quality and comprehensiveness of its content, but it has the advantage of offering much more full text. More recently, the American Psychological Association has created *PsycARTICLES*, a separate subscription-based full-text database of journals and books published by the APA, the Canadian Psychological Association, and other publishers. It has also created a new database called *PsycEXTRA*, which indexes gray literature in psychology, and one called *PsycBOOKS*, which includes full-text access to APA books. The APA now also makes available *PsycVIDEO*, which features annotations of over 2,000 videos related to psychology. Another recent subscription-based entry into the field is e-psyche, which promises to index more than twice as many publications as *PsycINFO*.

There are two free indexes to psychology serials that offer extensive listings of journal titles. One is called *Electronic Journals and Periodicals in Psychology and Related Fields* (http://psych.hanover.edu/Krantz/journal.html). It provides brief descriptions of many of the major psychology journals along with links to conference proceedings and online bibliographies. Another index called *Psycline* offers a searchable database of approximately 2,000 journals in psychology and the social sciences, along with a separate search form that is intended for searching articles (http://www.psycline.org/journals/psycline.html).

Those seeking a high-quality dictionary on the Web might consider subscribing to the *Dictionary of Psychology*, published by Oxford University Press. It features 10,500 entries and a list of 700 abbreviations and symbols used frequently in the field. A free alternative is the *Psybox Com* dictionary of psychology, which purports to be "the web's biggest dictionary of psychology" (http://www.psybox.com/web_dictionary/dictionaryWebindex.htm). The dictionary is much less comprehensive and authoritative than Oxford's, but does include a helpful list of definitions of symbols used in psychological statistics. A much briefer free general dictionary of approximately 400 terms is available from *All Psych Online*, which advertises itself as "The Virtual Psychology Classroom" (http://allpsych.com/dictionary/index.html). A more specialized psychology dictionary that is available free is *The Nonverbal Dictionary of Gestures, Signs, & Body Language Cues*. Compiled and edited by David B. Givens of the Center for Nonverbal Studies, it features detailed definitions along with illustrations (http://members.aol.com/nonverbal2/diction1.htm).

Two noteworthy encyclopedias of psychology are available online. The Department of Psychology at Jacksonville State University offers a free encyclopedia that covers approximately 40 general areas of psychology, with definitions and links to relevant Web sites (http://www.psychology.org/). MIT also offers its own free psychology encyclopedia online, *The MIT Encyclopedia of the Cognitive Sciences*. It includes almost 500 entries by leading scholars that are searchable by key word. The online version provides abstracts only and users must consult the paper version for the full text of the articles. Institutional site licenses are available for libraries wishing online access to full text (http://cognet.mit.edu/login/institution).

MIT also features a subscription database called CogNet, which was originally created to accompany *The MIT Encyclopedia of the Cognitive Sciences*. The database includes full-text access to books, conference proceedings, news, editorials, discussion lists, and employment listings in the cognitive and brain sciences. A related free database is *CogPrints*. This is an electronic archive for papers in all areas of psychology and fields related to cognition (http://cogprints.org). A much broader-based free archive, not limited to cognition but including all areas of psychology, is *Psychological Documents Online*. It includes many full-text articles along with links to online indexes and journals (http://www.psychologie.uni-bonn.de/online-documents/lit_ww.htm).

Many psychology handbooks as well as other reference tools are available online from OCLC's netLibrary via subscription. Books are searchable by keyword, and can be browsed for short periods of time or checked out to allow exclusive use for longer periods. Several standard psychology reference books are available online. The *Diagnostic and Statistical Manual of Mental Disorders* (DSM-IV) can be accessed via subscription to the *STAT! Ref* database from Teton Data Systems, which is a collection of major medical reference books and texts. It is also possible to access Buros' *Mental Measurements Yearbook* online via subscription or by pay per view, which offers information about approximately 4,000 tests. *MMY* can be obtained from SilverPlatter via WebSPIRS as well. The *Annual Review of Psychology* now offers both individual and institutional subscriptions to the online version of this important paper source. One of the most heavily used reference works in psychology, the *Publication Manual of the American Psychological Association*, is freely available online in summary form at various sites, a good example being the version created by the Purdue University Online Writing Lab (http://owl.english.purdue.edu/workshops/hypertext/APA/index.html).

The full text of some historical and classic works in psychology has been made available free of charge at a site called *The Online Books Page*. There the viewer will find links to works by Munsterberg, Baldwin, Wundt, and James (http://onlinebooks.library.upenn.edu/webbin/book/subjectstart?BF). In addition to books there are numerous online sources of psychology books reviews, and some of the better ones maintain archives that can be searched. A list of these can be obtained online at the *University of Illinois Library Gateway* (http://door.library.uiuc.edu/learn/handouts/bookreviews.html).

SOCIOLOGY

Like psychology, the field of sociology has relied for many years on a single online subscription-based indexing and abstracting source, *Sociological Abstracts*. This database is available from Cambridge Scientific Abstracts, OCLC FirstSearch, and other vendors. *Sociological Abstracts* covers the years 1963 to the present and indexes over 2,600 journals as well as dissertations, conference papers, and books. In the last few years, another electronic subscription-based sociology index has emerged that covers the same subject area as *Sociological Abstracts*, called the Sociological Collection from EBSCO. It is unable to equal Sociological Abstracts in terms of its breadth or scope, because it only indexes between 500-600 journals and only covers material dating back to the 1980s.

More specialized sociology indexes are also available, such as the subscription-based *Family and Society Studies Worldwide*, from National Information Services Corporation. It includes citations and abstracts on human development and family studies along with human ecology and social welfare dating back to 1970. The *National Criminal Justice Reference Service* is a free index to abstracts and full-text publications in the fields of criminology and criminal justice covering the early 1970s to the present (http://www.ncjrs.org/). *Population Index on the Web* makes freely available citations and abstracts of books, articles, and papers on population-related topics from the mid-1980s onward (http://popindex.princeton.edu). Those seeking a free index to numeric data in the social sciences can consult Data on the Net, which features statistics and data catalogs from data archives and libraries around the world (http://odwin.ucsd.edu/idata/).

Biographical information about sociologists is available free from a Web site called *Biographies of Sociologists*, which provides brief biographies and photos of approximately 40 sociologists along with links to relevant sites (http://www.soci.canterbury.ac.nz/biograph/index.shtml). A somewhat larger selection of sociology biographies covering over 100 individuals and providing more detail is freely available at *Famous Sociologists* (http://www2.fmg.uva.nl/sociosite/topics/sociologists.html). Another free biographical index that provides considerable detail on 16 sociologists can be found at *Dead Sociologists' Society* (http://www2.pfeiffer.edu/~lridener/DSS/DEADSOC.HTML). Additional biographical information about selected sociologists dating back to the seventeenth century is available free at *A Sociology Timeline from 1600* (http://www.ac.wwu.edu/~stephan/timeline.html).

Keeping tabs on the whereabouts of current sociologists is possible by using the American Sociological Association's *Directory of Departments of Sociology*. The 1999 version is available free online (http://www.asanet.org/pubs/dod.html). Other lists of departments are freely available from sites like *Socio Log* (http://www.sociolog.com/us_links/index.html) or *WWW Virtual Library* (http://socserv2.mcmaster.ca/w3virtsoclib/institut.htm).

There is no shortage of online dictionaries of sociology, and the best of these is a subscription-based dictionary featuring 2,500 entries published by Oxford University Press called *A Dictionary of Sociology*. Xreferplus, a subscription-based online reference service, makes several well-regarded sociology dictionaries available, among them *The Blackwell Dictionary of Sociology* and *The Penguin Dictionary of Sociology*. Several free dictionaries are available as well, the most comprehensive being the *Online Dictionary of the Social Sciences* which covers not only sociology but also criminology, political science, and women's studies (http://bitbucket.icaap.org/). There are also several free online dictionaries that focus exclusively on sociology, including one from *WebRef.org* (http://www.webref.org/sociology/sociology.htm), a glossary of sociological terms from the U. of Canterbury (http://www.soci.canterbury.ac.nz/resources/glossary/index.shtml) and *Elwell's Glossary of Sociology* (http://campus.murraystate.edu/academic/faculty/frank.elwell/prob3/glossary/socgloss.htm). Two more specialized dictionaries that are available free are the *Glossary of Social Science Computer and Social Science Data Terms* (http://odwin.ucsd.edu/glossary/) and the *Dictionary of Critical Sociology* (http://www.public.iastate.edu/~rmazur/dictionary/a.html).

There are relatively few online encyclopedias available in the field of sociology, a notable exception being the freely available multi-volume work *The International Encyclopedia of Sexuality* (vols. 1-3) (http://www2.rz.hu-berlin.de/sexology/GESUND/ARCHIV/IES/BEGIN.HTM). NetLibrary now makes a number of subscription-based handbooks and sourcebooks available online covering euthanasia, adoption, domestic violence, Alzheimer's disease and similar topics. There are also two freely available online handbooks, the *Sourcebook of Criminal Justice Statistics Online* (http://www.albany.edu/sourcebook/) and *The Merck Manual of Geriatrics* (http://www.merck.com/pubs/mm_geriatrics/).

Book reviews of works in sociology are available online from issues of *Contemporary Sociology* and the *American Sociological Review* via the JSTOR archive, though there is a moving wall which makes the most recent issues unavailable. Book reviews are available from a free online journal called *Reviewing Sociology: A Review Journal* which is jointly published in Britain by the U. of Central England at the U. of Reading (http://www.rdg.ac.uk/RevSoc/home.htm). For current awareness, JSTOR also makes available the *Annual Review of Sociology*, but the 5-year moving wall makes a subscription via *Annual Reviews* a better option. Although the *American Sociological Association Style Guide* is available in print from ASA, a free online outline of it is available from the library at California State University, Los Angeles (http://www.calstatela.edu/library/bi/rsalina/asa.styleguide.html).

ANTHROPOLOGY

Two of the most important indexes in the field of anthropology, *Anthropological Literature* and *Anthropological Index*, have recently been combined into a single online CitaDel database called *Anthropology Plus*. It is available by subscription from the Research Libraries Group. Anthropological Index is also available free on the Web (http://aio.anthropology.org.uk/aio/AIO.html). *eHRAF*, the Electronic Human Relations Area Files Collection of Ethnography is an indexed collection of full-text books, articles, manuscripts, and theses on cultural anthropology dating back to 1994 that is available online to subscribers. Also available via subscription on the Web is the *eHRAF Collection of Archaeology* which provides access to full-text materials on archaeological traditions from 1999 to the present. CSAC, the Centre for Social Anthropology and Computing at the University of Kent in the UK, makes freely available the *CSAC Anthropology Bibliography* which contains citations and some abstracts to nearly 14,000 works (http://lucy.ukc.ac.uk/cgi-bin/uncgi/search_bib2/Makhzan). James Weaver of the University of Florida has put together a free index of bibliographies on anthropology and archaeology that is arranged by topic and features many entries.

More specialized online indexes are available, such as the *CSAC UK Theses Index*, which is a free index to post-1970 English doctorates in cultural anthropology (http://lucy.ukc.ac.uk/cgi-bin/uncgi/search_bib/Theses). Two Danish anthropologists have created a free index called *Anthrobase* which contains full-text field notes, essays, reports, theses, articles and conference papers on social anthropology and related areas (http://www.anthrobase.com/). A German anthropologist named Ulrich Oberdiek has created an index to the books and articles on cultural anthropology published in German in Austria, Germany, and Switzerland called *Anthropological Abstracts* (http://www.anthropology-online.de/ Aga/Abstrcts.html). A free index to archaeological materials called *Bibliographies for Anthropological Research* is available from the *Tennessee Archaeology Net* (http://www.mtsu.edu/~kesmith/TNARCHNET/ Pubs/Res_Bib.html). Marcus Banks of the Institute of Social and Cultural Anthropology at the U. of Oxford maintains a free index to more than 1,500 archival ethnographic films covering the years 1895-1945 (http://www.isca.ox.ac.uk/haddon/HADD_home.html). A related index is the freely available *Ur-List: Web Resources for Visual Anthropology* which provides access to 375 Web sites in this area organized by topic (http://www.usc.edu/dept/elab/urlist/). Another interesting free visual resource though not an index per se, is the *World Atlas of Archaeology* on the Web that includes archaeological sites, university programs, a list of individuals conducting current research, and cultural histories of particular countries (http://archaeology.miningco.com/library/atlas/ blindex.htm).

The most comprehensive online source for biographical material on archaeologists is a free site called *Anthropology Biography Web*, which provides biographies of over 500 important figures in the field of anthropology (http://emuseum.mnsu.edu/information/biography). Those seeking biographical material about archaeologists can find it at a free site based at the U. of Glasgow called *Archaeological Biographies* (http://www.gla.ac.uk/archaeology/resources/theory/biographies.html). Samuel Wilson, a faculty member at UT, offers a free site called *Intellectual Biographies in Archaeology* (http://www.utexas.edu/courses/ wilson/ant304/biography/arybios.html).

Anthropology book reviews are freely available online at a site called *ARD–the Anthropology Review Database*, which allows users to search not only by title, author, or subject but also by medium, by reviewer, or by publisher (http://wings.buffalo.edu/ARD/). An unusual reviewing source that is available free is *Public Anthropology: Anthropology Journal Archive Project*, which includes summaries of articles published in major anthropology journals that have been written by anthropology students (http://www.publicanthropology.org/).

Current awareness sources for anthropology include the subscription-based *Annual Review of Anthropology* which is available from the publisher, *Annual Reviews*, and is also indexed in databases like EBSCO's *Academic Search Premier* with a 12-month embargo and archived in JSTOR. Another source featuring recent stories in the news related to anthropology that is freely available is *Anthropology in the News*. It includes archives categorized by major sub-fields (http://www.

tamu.edu/anthropology/news.html). *Yahoo! News* provides similar free coverage of anthropology topics featured recently in the press (http://news.yahoo.com/fc?tmpl=fc&cid=34&in=science&cat=anthropology_and_archaeology).

There are several anthropology-related dictionaries on the Web. A fairly comprehensive free general anthropology dictionary is available from *WebRef* (http://www.webref.org/anthropology/a.htm). Another very good general dictionary for anthropology that is available free on the Web is the *Anthromorphemics Anthropology Glossary*, maintained by the Anthropology Department at the U. of California, Santa Barbara. Several more specialized anthropology indexes can also be found on-line, such as the *Glossary of Archaeological/Anthropological Terms*, which emphasizes archaeology and is available free (http://www.archaeolink.com/glossary_of_archaeology.htm). *Etnografiskt ABC* is a free site that provides definitions of more than 200 specialized terms in both English and Swedish (http://www.etnografiska.se/smvk/jsp/polopoly.jsp?d=202&a=3982).

Southern Methodist University offers an extensive free glossary of archaeological terms that includes variant spellings (http://www.smu.edu/anthro/collections/glossary2.html). Those with an interest in the anthropology of health and illness may find the free *Glossary of Medical Anthropology* terms useful (http://anthro.palomar.edu/medical/glossary.htm). The Dept. of Anthropology at The University of Alabama makes available a free kinship glossary for students of social organization (http://www.as.ua.edu/ant/Faculty/murphy/436/kinship.htm). Oxford University Press makes the *Dictionary of Superstitions* available on a subscription basis along with several dictionaries of folklore. Those searching specifically for object names of cultural artifacts can take advantage of the freely available mda *Archaeological Objects Thesaurus* (http://www.mda.org.uk/archobj/archcon.htm).

Relatively few directories for the field of anthropology are available online. An exception worth noting is the Worldwide *Email Directory of Anthropologists*, hosted by the Department of Anthropology at the University of Buffalo and available free to users (http://wings.buffalo.edu/WEDA/). Many different encyclopedias are available, however. *netLibrary* makes available to subscribers Alan Bernard and Jonathan Spencer's *Encyclopedia of Social and Cultural Anthropology*, as well as encyclopedias of folklore and Native American healing. The Smithsonian Institution offers free access to *Encyclopedia Smithsonian*, which includes a section on anthropological topics related to the holdings at its museum (http://www.si.edu/resource/faq/start.htm). Another free online encyclopedia that offers over 6,100 entries related to folklore and mythology is *Encyclopedia Mythica* (http://www.pantheon.org/). Linguistic anthropologists may find *Ethnologue*, a free online encyclopedia containing data from the 14th edition of *Ethnologue: Language of the World*, to be of interest (http://www.ethnologue.com/info.asp).

Two free handbooks that have been available online are potentially of interest to anthropology researchers. *Indigenous Knowledge* details ethnographic methods for use in international development projects, including recording techniques and case studies (http://web.idrc.ca/en/ev-9310-201-1-DO_TOPIC.html). The American Anthropological Association has posted the *Handbook on Ethical Issues in Anthropology*, edited by Joan Cassell and Sue-Ellen Jacobs, on its Web site (http://www.aaanet.org/committees/ethics/toc.htm). AAA also makes available its style guide free on its Web site in the form of a pdf file which requires Adobe Acrobat to read (http://www.aaanet.org/pubs/style_guide.htm). The Society for American Archaeology has its own style guide that is freely accessible in pdf format at the SAA Web site (http://www.saa.org/publications/StyleGuide/styframe.html).

POLITICAL SCIENCE

Several key indexes in the field of political science can be found on the Web. *International Political Science Abstracts*, which provides citations and abstracts to articles published in political science, political theory, public administration, and international relations from 1989 onward is available to subscribers via SilverPlatter. Another important index that is available online is *Worldwide Political Science Abstracts*, which contains citations and abstracts to approximately 1,300 political science journals dating back to 1975. It is available to subscribers from Cambridge Scientific Abstracts. OCLC makes the *Public Affairs Information Service* (PAIS) database available to subscribers via FirstSearch on the Web, including citations and abstracts to public policy, public affairs, international relations and world politics. An excellent source of research material on international affairs can be accessed on the Web by subscribing to *Columbia International Affairs Online* (CIAO) which is a joint endeavor of Columbia University Libraries and Columbia University Press.

More specific indexes covering particular governments, countries, and aspects of politics can also be found on the Web. *LexisNexis* makes its Congressional database available to subscribers in need of congressional publications, hearings, bills, laws, and regulations, as well as information about congressional committees and their members, with some material dating back as early as 1789. Information about U.S. legislative documents can be obtained free online from Thomas, the Library of Congress site (http://thomas.loc.gov/). OCLC makes its *GPO Monthly Catalog* available through subscription to FirstSearch so that users can have access to a wide range of U.S. government documents from 1976 to the present. U.S. government-related information is also available free online from the *GPO Access* site (http://www.gpoaccess. gov/). Judicial documents pertaining to the Supreme Court such as court files, oral arguments, opinions, and related material can be accessed freely at the Web site of the Supreme Court (http://www.supremecourtus. gov/). U.S. government politics, parties, and politicians along with the activities of government agencies, state governments, think tanks, and voters can be found at a free site called *National Political Index* (http:// www.politicalindex.com/). *Left Index*, a National Information Services Corporation (NISC) database that is available via subscription, provides citations and abstracts as well as some full text relating to left politics covering the years 1982 to the present.

Information about public policy is readily available from several indexes on the Web. *PolicyFile* is available to subscribers via ProQuest, and includes more than 27,000 abstracts covering a wide range of domestic and international policy issues, including some full text. National Journal Group has a subscription-based site called *Policy Central*, which refers to itself as "The Resource on Politics and Policy for the Academic Community" and includes information about political campaigns, congressional activity, legislation, political advertising, and public opinion surveys. *Policy Library* is a free Web site that provides full-text access to research on social and economic policy and on international issues (http://www.policylibrary.com/US/).

Several online indexes with an international emphasis are available to searchers. The University of Minnesota provides free access to over 14,000 human rights documents through its *Human Rights Library* (http://www1.umn.edu/humanrts/). The *Political Database of the Americas* is a free resource that includes political and judicial reference materials, source documents, and statistics for many countries in the Western Hemisphere (http://georgetown.edu/pdba/history.html). Broader coverage of all 192 countries is offered on a subscription basis by SYBWorld, and includes geopolitical data, biographies of key political figures, and policy information. *Countrywatch* also covers political developments in all 192 countries and provides free access to some material and subscription access to other data (http://www.countrywatch. com/). Extensive information on less well-known countries can be obtained free at the *Country Studies* Web site of the Federal Research Division of the Library of Congress, which includes the full text of area handbooks for 102 countries (http://lcweb2.loc.gov/frd/cs/cshome.html). The *CIA World Factbook* offers detailed information about countries around the world (http://www.cia.gov/cia/publications/factbook/). Elections around the world are covered by *Electionworld.org*, a free site that includes independent countries, states, protectorates, and dependencies with indigenous populations (http://www.electionworld.org/index.html). Extensive United Nations material is freely available from the *UN Documentation Centre* site and includes resolutions, decisions, reports, statements, and press releases (http://www.un.org/documents/). An index called *Women in Politics* offers citations and abstracts to books and articles about the role of women in politics (http://www.ipu.org/bdf-e/ BDFsearch.asp).

Quantitative data can be obtained by subscription to ICPSR, the *Inter-University Consortium for Political and Social Research*, an organization that makes data files available that can be analyzed with statistical software. Numerical data at the state level is also made available free by the journal *State Politics and Policy Quarterly*, and includes access to data sets and a codebook (http://www.unl.edu/SPPQ/datasets. html). Statistics from over 100 agencies of the U.S. federal government are available free at *FedStats*, which allows users to search by state or by agency (http://www.fedstats.gov/). Another interesting index to free data is the *General International Data Page* which includes resources about states, alliances, organizations, treaties, and geographic data (http:// garnet.acns.fsu.edu/~phensel/intldata.html). *PollingReport.Com* offers quantitative data on public opinion in both free and subscription-based forms, and includes polling data on elections, politicians, national security, and issues in the news (http://www.pollingreport.com/).

There are many Web-based sources of biographical material for the field of political science. *POTUS*, a Web site that features free material about presidents of the United States, has election results, personal milestones, cabinet members, and audio/visual material (http://www. ipl.org/div/potus/). The Government Publications Department of the University of Memphis makes available a free site called *Uncle Sam– Who's Who in the Federal Government*, which includes biographies of current members of the executive, legislative, and judicial branches of government as well as administrators of various federal agencies (http:// exlibris.memphis.edu/resource/unclesam/whos.html). There is a biographical database for federal judges entitled *Judges of the United States Courts* that provides free information about District Court, Circuit Court, and Courts of Appeals judges from 1789 onward (http://air.fjc.gov/history/ judges_frm.html). For information about deceased political figures, *The Political Graveyard: A Database of Historic Cemeteries*, offers material on judges and diplomats as well as politicians (http:// politicalgraveyard.com/index.html). Several sites also focus on non-U.S. political figures, such as *World Political Leaders 1945-2003*, which contains free information and photos about leaders of many countries and of international organizations such as NATO, the European Union, and the United Nations (http://www.terra.es/personal2/ monolith/00index.htm). Another useful source of free data on international politicians is a site entitled *Chiefs of State and Cabinet Members of Foreign Governments* (http://www.odci.gov/cia/publications/chiefs/ index.html). International coverage of women politicians is provided free at a Web site called *Women World Leaders* (http://www.terra.es/ personal2/monolith/00women.htm).

A variety of political science dictionaries are available online. Oxford University Press makes available via subscription the *Dictionary of Political Biography* and the *Concise Dictionary of Politics*. netLibrary offers *The Blackwell Dictionary of Political Science* on a subscription basis. A nonpartisan publication called *American Spirit* makes available a free political dictionary that contains some economic and military as well as political terms (http://www.fast-times.com/ dictionarybar.html). *ThisNation.com* features a free glossary that defines words, ideas, and concepts discussed at the site, which claims to be "the most comprehensive guide to American government and politics on the net" (http://www.thisnation.com/glossary.html). *The Glossarist*, which is an online index of glossaries, has a collection of government and politics-related dictionaries that it makes available free (http://www.glossarist.com/glossaries/government-politics-military/). Dr. Paul M. Johnson of Auburn University makes available a free online version of his book *A Glossary of Political Economy Terms* (http://www.auburn.edu/~johnspm/gloss/). Robert A. Hinton, the government documents librarian at Indiana University-Purdue University Indianapolis, provides a free online dictionary of abbreviations and acronyms of the U.S. government at his *Government Information Resources* site (http:// www.ulib.iupui.edu/subjectareas/gov/docs_abbrev. html).

Several directories are available for conducting research on politicians and political bodies. Recent issues of the *Congressional Directory* can be found at the GPO Access site, offering free access to biographies, contact information, and Web addresses (http://www.gpoaccess. gov/cdirectory/index.html). Congressional Quarterly, Inc. also makes available subscription-based access to the current *Congressional Staff Directory*. *A Biographical Directory of the United States Congress* provides information about the lives of House and Senate members dating back to 1774 (http://bioguide.congress.gov/biosearch/biosearch.asp). Kathi Foutain, a political science librarian at California State University, Chico has put together a free directory of political advocacy groups that is a useful resource for identifying lobbyists (http://reinert.creighton. edu/advocacy/). A free directory of political parties, interest groups, and social movements around the world is available at Richard Kimber's *Political Science Resources* (http://www.psr.keele.ac.uk/psr.htm). *Embassy World* features a free searchable directory of consulates and embassies from around the world (http://www.embassyworld.com/). A directory of governments from around the world is available at a site called *Governments on the WWW* (http://www.gksoft.com/govt/en/). There is a directory of Parliaments available at the Web site of the Inter-Parliamentary Union, an international organization made up of Parliaments of sovereign states (http://www.ipu.org/english/whatipu. htm).

Political Science encyclopedias and handbooks can be found on the Web. The *Blackwell Encyclopedia of Political Thought* is available online to subscribers from netLibrary. *World Statesmen*, which includes free information about colonies, governments, religious organizations, and other political entities, also includes maps and country facts (http:// www.worldstatesmen.org/). The official handbook of the U.S. federal government, the *United States Government Manual* contains information about U.S. government agencies and is available free online (http:// www.gpoaccess.gov/gmanual/index.html). Older editions of the manual dating back to 1995 are also available at the same site.

COMMUNICATIONS

One of the most important standard print indexes for the field of communications, *Communication Abstracts*, is now indexed on the Web. It provides international coverage of books and articles from 1996 onward on all major aspects of communication, and is available by subscription from Cambridge Scientific Abstracts. Sage, the publisher of *Communication Abstracts*, also makes available online a Sage Full-Text Collection through Cambridge Scientific Abstracts called *Communication Studies*. It includes the full text of 15 journals published by Sage and by professional societies covering the last 20 years.

EBSCO has recently created a new database called *Communication and Mass Media Complete*. It combines two previous communications databases, *CommSearch* and *Mass Media Articles Index*. In creating this new database, EBSCO has substantially expanded coverage beyond the 26 journals plus 6 National Communication Association journals originally covered by *CommSearch*. It has also added additional material to the 60 research journals as well as encyclopedia and handbook material indexed in *Mass Media Articles Index*. The new database features the full text of more than 200 titles as well as citations to additional titles.

The Communication Institute for Online Scholarship (CIOS) makes available to its members an online index called *ComAbstracts*. It features citations and abstracts to professional journals in the communications field from the 1980s and 1990s. CIOS also provides subscription access to *ComIndex*, an electronic index that covers more than 80 communications journals from 1970 onward. Unlike *ComAbstracts*, the *ComIndex* database is a bibliographic database providing citations only and does not offer abstracts.

Another professional organization that features its own online index is the Association for Education in Journalism and Mass Communication (AEJMC). It produces a free index called *Journalism and Mass Communication Abstracts*, which includes abstracts of theses and dissertations accepted for graduate degrees in journalism and mass communication programs. Over 40 universities are included in the database, dating back to 1996. The index is searchable by author, title, institution, or keyword, and is available at: http://www.aejmc.org/abstracts/index. html.

The Television News Archive at Vanderbilt University makes available a free searchable database of the television news broadcasts, press conferences, campaign coverage, and special events available in its collection. The database, which is called *TV-NewsSearch* contains over 700,000 records and can be accessed at: http://lib14.Library.vanderbilt. edu/diglib/tvn-register.pl?RegType=search. Those interested in researching advertising may wish to consult *Ad*Access*, a free online index to over 7,000 print ads that appeared in magazines and newspapers from 1911 to 1955. The index which is produced by the John W. Hartman Center for Sales, Advertising, and Marketing History at Duke University, can be accessed at: http://scriptorium.lib.duke.edu/adacess/. The

Poynter Institute makes available a free searchable index to journalism-related bibliographies called *Poynteronline* at: http://www.poynter.org/search/.

Several specialized communications-related dictionaries are available online. *The Moving Image Genre-Form Guide* is produced by the Library of Congress and features terminology for the various genres of film and television, freely accessible at: www.loc.gov/rr/mopic/migintro.html. A specialized dictionary for advertising terms that is offered by the Advertising Department at the University of Texas is available at: http://advertising.utexas.edu/research/terms/.

Many directories are available online in the field of communication. Notable among these is the *Gale Database of Publications and Broadcast Media*, which provides subscribers with information about 64,000 newspapers, periodicals, television, cable TV, and radio stations in the United States and Canada. Free listings of over 19,000 television and radio stations are available from *100000 Watts U.S. Radio and TV Directory* at: http://www.100000watts.com/. Information about radio stations is available free from radio-locator, a directory that includes over 10,000 radio station Web pages as well as more than 2,500 audio streams, that can be accessed at: http://www.radio-locator.com/. *Kidon Media Link* offers a free international directory of newspapers and news resources that is searchable by country at: http://www.kidon.com/media-link/index.shtml. Another free online source for international information about newspapers is *NewsLink* which provides information about thousands of newspapers indexed by category, as well as state and province, at: http://newslink.org/news.html. A free directory of outdoor advertising that can be searched by advertiser, location, category, or keyword, the *Out of Home Archive*, is available at: http://advertising.utexas.edu/research/gannettarchive/outdoor.html. Information about film and media is freely available online from *CineMedia*, which claims to be "the Internet's largest film and media directory" at: http://www.cinemedia.org/welcomes/hello.html. Several free directories related to the study of communication itself are available online, including the National Communication Association directory, *Communication Studies in Higher Education*. It provides Web links to communications studies programs around the U.S. at: http://www.natcom.org. NCA also provides a *Directory of Graduate Programs* searchable by concentration, degree, or state at: http://www.natcom.org/ComProg/gpdhtm/graddir.htm. *CommuniQuest Interactive* also makes a free online directory of communication programs in the U.S. and Canada available at: http://www.aca.iupui.edu/cqi/home.html. A directory of scholarly societies in communications and media studies is available free online, courtesy of the *Scholarly Societies Project* at the U. of Waterloo and can be accessed at: http://www.scholarly-societies.org/communmedia_soc.html.

Relatively few encyclopedias and handbooks are available online. *netLibrary* offers subscription-based access to the *Encyclopedia of Television News*. A *Handbook of Rhetorical Devices* is available free from a Web site called *Virtual Salt* at: http://www.virtualsalt.com/rhetoric. htm. Unlike encyclopedias and handbooks, legal works abound on the Web. Subscribers can now obtain access to a Web edition of Pike and Fischer's *Communications Regulation*, which provides information about FCC rules, regulations, cases, statutes, and treaties, at: http://commreg.pf.com/default.asp. The Federal Communications Commission itself makes case information available free from both the FCC and FRC covering the years 1928-2002 at: http://www.fcc.gov/ogc/caselist. html. The National Telecommunications and Information Administration makes information about NTIA regulations, procedures, policies, and legal proceedings freely available at: http://www.ntia.doc.gov/. Free information about many aspects of communications law is available from *FindLaw* at: http://library.lp.findlaw.com/communicationslaw. html. The Legal Information Institute at Cornell provides free information about media law, including federal and state statutes and regulations at: http://www.law.cornell.edu/topics/media.html. International communications law and regulations can be obtained free from *HierosGamos* at: http://www.hg.org/communi.html.

Statistical information about the field of communications is available in the form of free television network ratings from *Zap2It* at: http://www.zap2it.com/index.

HISTORY

Perhaps no other area of the social sciences has as broad a Web presence as the field of history. Two of the most important indexes in the field, *America: History and Life* and *Historical Abstracts*, are both available on the Web to subscribers via ABC-Clio. Paratext makes available a subscription-based online index called *19th Century Masterfile*, which contains more than 6 million citations covering pre-1920 material from sources such as *Poole's Index to Periodical Literature*, *Stead's Index to Periodicals*, *The New York Times*, and *Harper's Magazine*. The Research Libraries Group makes available to subscribers a database called *RLG Archival Resources* which provides finding aids for archival collections, some of which contain links to actual materials. RLG also provides another subscription-based index called *The History of Science, Technology, and Medicine* which provides citations and some abstracts to articles, proceedings, books, reviews, and dissertations.

Several valuable free indexes are available for history. *The World Wide Web Virtual Library* makes available an extensive collection of books categorized by historical period, topic, and geographic area at: http://vlib.iue.it/history/index.html. *Academic Info* provides an indexed collection of history links that are arranged both topically and by region at: http://www.academicinfo.net/hist.html. A free index to 2,500 archival collections held by the International Institute of Social History in the Netherlands is available online at: http://www.iisg.nl/archives/index.html.

In addition to general indexes, more specialized history indexes are available on the Web. Subscribers to the *International Medieval Bibliography* from Brepols Publishers can search 300,000 records of articles, reviews, and other material related to medieval scholarship. Another subscription-based index from the Faculty of Information Studies at the University of Toronto that contains bibliographic information about the Renaissance and Middle Ages is *Iter*, which includes citations to articles, reviews, bibliographies, and monographs. The *American Civil War Research Database*, available from Historic Data Systems, Inc. offers subscribers access to soldier's records, regimental rosters, regimental chronicles, and other information. Researchers seeking free access to information about women in medieval times can utilize *Feminae: Medieval Women and Gender Index*, which indexes books, journals, and dissertations in this area can be found at: http://www.haverford.edu/library/reference/mschaus/mfi/mfi.html.

Cornell University library hosts Making of America, a free index of primary sources in American social history covering the pre-Civil War period through the reconstruction at: http://www.hti.umich.edu/m/moagrp/. A similar free index covering U.S. history from 1660 through 1840 is *History 1700s.com* and includes articles, period documents, and Internet links to relevant sources at: http://www.history1700s.com/. Another specialized index to American history made freely available by the United States Civil War Center at Louisiana State University is the *Index of Civil War Information Available on the Internet* at: http://www.cwc.lsu.edu/civlink.htm.

Women's history is well indexed by the Gerritsen Collection, a subscription-based index covering the years 1543-1945 that provides access to two million pages of primary source material in 15 languages, and is available from Chadwyck-Healey. American military history is indexed at a free site called *America At War*, which features material from the American Revolution through World War I at: http://www. america-at-war.net/. Naval history researchers may find a free site called *Index to Ships in Books* useful, which provides users with information about books or journals that mention specific ships, at: http:// www.shipindex.org/.

Like indexes, directories of historical material abound on the Web. Several directories of historical societies are available free at *Society Hill Directory* (http://daddezio.com/society/). A directory of history dissertations currently being written at 171 academic departments in the U.S. and Canada is available free at: http://www.theaha.org/pubs/ dissertations/. Repositories that make available primary source material can be found in a free directory called *Repositories of Primary Sources* at: http://www.uidaho.edu/special-collections/Other.Repositories.html. Another directory of repositories that is available on a subscription basis is *ArchivesUSA* from UMI ProQuest. An international directory of history departments has been compiled by the Center for History and New Media at George Mason University accessible at: http://chnm.gmu. edu/assets/historydepts/departments.php. Graduate programs around the world in history can be found in a free directory made available by *GradSchools.com* at: http://www.gradschools.com/listings/menus/ history_menu.html. A free directory of scholarly societies in history can be found at the *Scholarly Society Project* at: http://www.scholarly-societies. org/history_soc.html.

Many directories may also be found on the Web that cater to historical subject matter itself. A good example is *Labyrinth: Resources for Medieval Studies*, which is based at Georgetown University and is freely accessible at: http://www.georgetown.edu/labyrinth/labyrinth-home.html. The *dmoz Open Directory* Project makes available an extensive free directory of Web resources for the Middle Ages and other time periods at: http://newhoo.com/society/History/By_Time_Period/Middle_Ages/. Journals and discussion lists for history can be found in directory form at *The History Journals Guide*, a free site located at: http://www.history-journals.de/. Research about particular individuals in history can be helped by using *Find A Grave*, which indexes grave sites around the world at: http://www.findagrave.com/tocs/geographic.html. *HyperHistory Online* indexes over 2,000 files covering three millennia of world history as well as links to related sites available free at: http://www. hyperhistory.com/online_n2/History_n2/a.html. The University of Virginia provides a directory of free history Web resources at: http://www. lib.virginia.edu/subjects/history/. BUBL also offers a directory to Internet history resources that includes annotations of each site at: http://bubl.ac.uk/link/h/historylinks.htm. A free directory that claims to list the "best" history sites on the Web is called *Best of History Web Sites* and arranges sites by historical period at: http://www. besthistorysites.net/. A directory called *History On-Line* contains evaluated sources that can be searched by category of history, geographical region, time period, and type of resource, and is available free at: http://ihr.sas.ac.uk/ihr/Resources/.

A few good general history bibliographies are now available online. Yahoo! makes available a small collection of history bibliographies at: http://dir.yahoo.com/Arts/Humanities/History/Bibliographies/. The Internet Public Library has assembled a useful group of links at: http://www.ipl.org/div/subject/browse/hum30.00.00/. An interesting group of bibliographies for American and British history has been assembled by Tom Glynn of Rutgers University at: http://www.libraries.rutgers. edu/rul/rr_gateway/research_guides/history/reference.shtml.

Many more specialized bibliographies are in evidence on the Web. The International Institute of Social History features *Viva: A Bibliography of Women's History in Historical and Women's Studies Journals* that includes over 7,500 entries covering articles published from 1975 onward, available free at: http://www.iisg.nl/~womhist/vivahome.html. *H-Net* offers a collection of bibliographies about women that is arranged in categories for easy reference at: http://www.h-net.msu.edu/~ women/bibs/. A bibliography of the history of the working class that includes references to books, articles, films, and songs can be found at: http://www.as.ysu.edu/~cwcs/Bibliography.htm. *The World Wide Web Virtual Library* features a collection of bibliographies about Native Americans and their history at: http://www.hanksville.org/NAresources/.

Several bibliographies pertaining to U.S. naval history are available at the Web site of the *Naval Historical Center* located at: http://www.history. navy.mil/nhc5.htm. A bibliography of basic resources for the American Civil War that includes battlefield guides and cemeteries and monuments can be found at: http://book-smith.tripod.com/civ-war-top.html. The Institute of Information and Computing Sciences at the University of Utrecht offers an extensive *U.S. Civil War Reading List* at: http://www.cs.uu.nl/wais/html/na-dir/civil-war-usa/reading-list.html. A lengthy bibliography of the Vietnam War conveniently arranged into topical categories is accessible at: http://hubcap.clemson.edu/~eemoise/bibliography.html.

As with many other types of history resources, biographical sources are numerous on the Web. An online version of *Biography and Genealogy Master Index* is available via subscription from The Gale Group. *Biography Index* is available online to subscribers through OCLC's FirstSearch. Subscribers may also consult *American National Biography on the Web* from Oxford University Press, which provides access to over 1,800 biographies. Heads of state dating back to 1700 can be researched at a free Web site called *Rulers*, which arranges them by country and by territory at: http://rulers.org/. A more limited selection of nobles may be found at *Kings and Queens of England and Scotland*, which is a free site that is available at: http://www.genuki.org.uk/big/royalty/. PBS offers free access to an interactive biographical dictionary of important figures in the American West, part of a site called *New Perspectives on The West*, which can be found at: http://www.pbs.org/weta/thewest/people/.

History-related dictionaries are also in abundance on the Web. Oxford Reference Online makes available several dictionaries on a subscription basis, including *A Dictionary of British History* and *A Dictionary of Twentieth Century World History*. An individual at Texas A&M University has assembled a collection of several hundred free online dictionaries and glossaries arranged by subject that includes many history titles at: http://stommel.tamu.edu/~baum/hyperref.html. A Web site called *The Glossarist* offers free access to a small collection of online history dictionaries at: http://www.glossarist.com/glossaries/humanities-social-sciences/history.asp?Page=1. *The Britannia Lexicon* offers a free dictionary of feudal and medieval terms and plans to add lengthier entries on key events, wars, organizations, and movements at: http://www.britannia.com/history/resource/gloss.html. Those with an interest in medieval urban history will find a free glossary of medieval English towns at: http://historymedren.about.com/gi/dynamic/offsite.htm?site=http%3A%2F%2Fwww.trytel.com%2F%7Etristan%2Ftowns%2Fglossary.html. A free dictionary of castle terminology with hyperlinks that illustrate examples of the terms is available at: http://www.castlewales.com/casterms.html. Additional castle terms may be found at *Castles on the Web*, a free glossary of castle-related terms that emphasizes architectural features and that can be accessed at: http://www.castlesontheweb.com/glossary.html.

A wide variety of history encyclopedias are available on the Web. NodeWorks also features a group of history encyclopedias with brief annotations describing each one, available free at: http://dir.nodeworks.com/Reference/Encyclopedias/Subject_Encyclopedias/History/. *The A-Z*

Encyclopedia of World History, that is searchable by keyword is available free from historytoday.com at: http://www.historytoday.com/dt_dictionary.asp?gid=3575&aid=&tgid=&amid=3575&g3575=x&g30034=x&g21011=x&g19965=x&g19963=x. Those seeking information about the history of Rome will find the free *Encyclopedia Romana* of interest at: http://itsa.ucsf.edu/~snlrc/encyclopaedia_romana/. High quality, peer-reviewed research on medieval history is contained in *ORB: The Online Reference Book for Medieval Studies* available free at: http://www.the-orb.net/. *The Encyclopedia of British History 1500-1950* features numerous links to UK history and can be accessed free at: http://www.spartacus.schoolnet.co.uk/Britain.html. The same site also features a free *Encyclopedia of the First World War* at: http://www.spartacus.schoolnet.co.uk/FWW.htm. Material on the First World War, including some primary sources, photos, and maps, can be freely accessed at: http://www.firstworldwar.com/index.htm. Joan Johnson Lewis's *Encyclopedia of Women's History* offers an extensive index to topics for easy searching and can be accessed free at: http://womenshistory.about.com/library/ency/blwh_index.htm.

A few history handbooks are available online. Paul Halsall at Fordham University has collected a number of these at a site called the *Internet History Sourcebooks Project,* which covers ancient, medieval, and modern history as well as a number of sub-themes in history. Several extensive bibliographies are also available at this site which can be found at: http://www.fordham.edu/halsall/.

There are many history chronologies that can be found on the Web. Yahoo! offers a collection of timelines that is arranged both alphabetically and by popularity and is available free at: http://dir.yahoo.com/Arts/Humanities/History/By_Time_Period/Timelines/. The Open Directory Project, dmoz, also has a free collection of chronologies available at: http://dmoz.org/Society/History/Timelines/. A highly eclectic free list of chronologies that includes timelines of important historical figures and an extensive set of chronologies for sports history has been assembled by Ken Fussichen at: http://users.commkey.net/fussichen/otd$1.htm. *Timelines of History* includes a history of the world that dates back to the big bang and is arranged chronologically by historical period available free at: http://timelines.ws/. *WebChron: The Web Chronology Project,* which is sponsored by the History Department at North Park University, provides a free series of chronologies that are arranged by region and by topic at: http://campus.northpark.edu/history/WebChron/.

More specialized chronologies and collections of chronologies are also available. DMOZ, the Open Directory Project, makes some world history chronologies available at: http://dmoz.org/Society/History/Timelines/. The BBC makes available a series of history timelines for Britain, Ireland, Scotland, and Wales along with timelines for ancient Egypt and British monarchy at: http://www.bbc.co.uk/history/timelines/index.shtml. Dr. Kenneth W. Harl of Tulane University has assembled free chronologies for classical Greece, Rome, and Byzantium that is arranged by time period at: http://www.tulane.edu/~august/allchron.htm. A Romantic chronology that covers selected events from 1792-1851 is available free at: http://english.ucsb.edu:591/rchrono/. Robert Beard at Bucknell University has created a free chronology of Russian history that includes both major and minor events and includes links to related chronologies at: http://www.bucknell.edu/Academics/Colleges_Departments/Academic_Departments/Foreign_Language_Programs/Russian_Studies/Resources/History/Chronology.html. A site called *African History* on the Internet features a number of timelines related to colonialism, witchcraft, and slavery at: http://www-sul.stanford.edu/depts/ssrg/africa/history/hischron.html. A series of timelines that cover Asian history, including country histories as well as key events and individuals is available free from *AsiaSource* at: http://www.asiasource.org/features/timelines.cfm. Significant events in American history can be found at a free timeline called *Important Events in American History* at: http://www.polytechnic.org/faculty/gfeldmeth/chronology.html. Various free chronologies of military history can be found at a site called *Keele Wargames and Boardgames: Military History of the World* at: http://www.keele.ac.uk/socs/ks45/PageHistory/4Area/General/Chronologies.htm.

CONCLUSION

From the preceding study, it can be seen that an extensive number of social sciences reference sources can now be found on the Web. Many of the paper sources commonly found in the reference collections of academic libraries now have Web-based counterparts, and a significant percentage of these are free. Some social sciences disciplines appear to be more digitized than others. History, for example, seems to have a stronger Web presence than other fields. Within particular fields, the development of Web-based reference tools is not uniform. One field may have many directories but few dictionaries; another may have a plethora of encyclopedias but few bibliographies.

Overall, both the quality and quantity of reference sources available online in the social sciences is impressive. In some cases, the Web versions of reference sources are not as authoritative or exhaustive as their paper counterparts. Yet they may also have unique features, such as the ability to conduct keyword searches or to follow hypertext links, which make them more useful than paper reference sources. Many are also available at no cost. It is not easy to predict the future, but if the present trend is any indication, an increasingly Web-based reference collection in the social sciences appears likely.

Briefcases and Databases:
Web-Based Reference Sources
for Business Librarians
and Their Client Communities

Gail M. Golderman
Bruce Connolly

SUMMARY. Drawing upon work done by a select group of business libraries and business library associations as well as their own electronic collection development, reference, and searching experience, the authors identify and assess the content and capabilities of the premiere business reference products available in the current market.

Additionally, they review a secondary group of highly recommended (if more modestly configured) business indexing and abstracting tools, examine subscription-based sources of economic indicators and forecasting information and of financial and company information. A directory of the best of the freely-available academic, government, and commercial business Web sites is appended. *[Article copies available for a fee from The Haworth Document Delivery Service: 1-800-HAWORTH. E-mail address: <docdelivery@haworthpress.com> Website: <http://www.HaworthPress.com> © 2005 by The Haworth Press, Inc. All rights reserved.]*

Gail M. Golderman is Electronic Media Librarian (E-mail: goldermg@union.edu); and Bruce Connolly is Reference Librarian (E-mail: connollb@union.edu), both at Union College, Schenectady, NY 12308.

[Haworth co-indexing entry note]: "Briefcases and Databases: Web-Based Reference Sources for Business Librarians and Their Client Communities." Golderman, Gail M., and Bruce Connolly. Co-published simultaneously in *The Reference Librarian* (The Haworth Information Press, an imprint of The Haworth Press, Inc.) No. 91/92, 2005, pp. 235-261; and: *The Reference Collection: From the Shelf to the Web* (ed: William J. Frost) The Haworth Information Press, an imprint of The Haworth Press, Inc., 2005, pp. 235-261. Single or multiple copies of this article are available for a fee from The Haworth Document Delivery Service [1-800-HAWORTH, 9:00 a.m. - 5:00 p.m. (EST). E-mail address: docdelivery@haworthpress.com].

doi:10.1300/J120v44n91_15

KEYWORDS. Web-based business resources, full-text databases, Internet resources, business library Web sites

INTRODUCTION

Increasingly, the Web has become the vehicle of choice for the publication and delivery of reference materials of all types. Business librarians, in attempting to meet the needs of a client community whose success, even survival, depends in no small measure on easy access to accurate and up-to-date news, information, and data are an extremely receptive audience for the increasingly comprehensive suites of business reference sources that are vying for position in the online marketplace.

The authors attempt to identify and evaluate the content and features of these one-stop resources, and to review a secondary group of highly recommended (if more conventionally configured) business indexing and abstracting tools. The article also examines sources of information on economic indicators, forecasting, and company financial conditions. The contents of some of the chief business-related periodicals portals are described as well.

The open side of the Internet, obviously, remains a key source of information, and consequently, the article includes a listing of those Web sites that emerge as the consensus choices regarding what constitutes the best academic, government, and commercial business Web sites. The "methodology" for making this determination involved visiting a group of highly-regarded library Web sites–the Library of Congress, the New York Public Library's Science, Industry and Business Library, the business libraries at Harvard and Stanford, the Business Reference and Services Section (BRASS) of ALA's Reference and User Services Association, and the Librarians' Index to the Internet for Business, Finance, & Jobs–that all pursue a clear mission of serving the business and business school communities. The resulting directory of authoritative Internet resources for business researchers appears as a sidebar.

BUSINESS REFERENCE SUITES

Increasingly, the publishers of electronic resources are attempting to identify and meet a more comprehensive range of business information needs with multifaceted suites of reference products. Detailed descriptions of these one-stop electronic business libraries–containing the full text on business newspapers, magazines, and journals supplemented by additional resources including company and industry profiles, corporate histories, financial data, reference material, international economic reports, retrospective journal coverage, and local and regional business coverage–appear in this section.

ABI/INFORM
ProQuest Information and Learning
http://www.il.proquest.com

Historically significant as one of the pioneering electronic databases in the fledgling online industry with *no* print legacy, *ABI/INFORM* still stands as the source of choice for international business information in academic and research settings. Why is its status undiminished after more than three decades in the trenches? Content, content, content.

In its fullest stand-alone configuration, *ABI/INFORM Global* includes abstracts of over 1,100 current business and management publications, with roughly 900 of them in some type of full-text format. (Retrospectively, the title list for the database identifies nearly 2,000 sources indexed since 1971, including more than 350 English-language titles from outside the U.S.) Executive profiles, market condition reports, and case studies of global business trends, plus extensive information on more than 60,000 companies augment the journal literature coverage.

Targeting undergraduate and large public libraries, the *ABI/INFORM Research* edition of the database de-emphasizes *Global*'s focus on international titles while providing bibliographic information and abstracts for 700 publications. *ABI/INFORM Select*, the basic configuration intended for smaller institutions, includes some 350 popular sources, with coverage extending back to 1991.

With the database as the centerpiece, *ABI/INFORM* has spawned a variety of add-on products that includes *ABI/INFORM Trade & Industry* with more than 700 full-text titles and *ABI/INFORM Dateline*, containing nearly 150 local and regional business publications, as well as the contents of U.S. and Canadian business newswires.

Recognizing the increasing demand for primary source materials in academic settings, ProQuest has also added access to the *ABI/INFORM Archive*, a database of historical back file content digitized from the microform masters in the *ProQuest Digital Vault*. This free enhancement gives the researcher access to searchable text versions of the articles along with page images with illustrations and advertisements of complete runs of 100 titles back to 1918. ProQuest integrates *Trade & Industry, Dateline, Archive* into the *Global* suite.

ProQuest has further enhanced *ABI/INFORM* with content from an array of internal and external sources including the John Wiley & Sons, Inc. *BoldIdeas Collection* of 40 business journals, the full text of 11 academic journals from Palgrave Macmillan, and 125 business and economics journals from Kluwer Academic Publishers.

Beside the ProQuest interface, *ABI/INFORM* is available via Dialog, OCLC FirstSearch, SilverPlatter, and Ovid Technologies. There is also a CD-ROM version of the resource.

Searchers using *ABI/INFORM* may restrict by date and enhance precision with field searching and the full range of Boolean. (They may also run the search in multiple ProQuest databases to which the library subscribes.) A Topic Guide provides access to the controlled vocabulary for subjects, company names, people, and locations. Results may be limited after the fact to scholarly journals, magazines, trade publications, or newspaper sources, and full text availability is clearly indicated.

Within the full record, authors name, publication title (and issue), subject, and classification codes are all linked and immediately searchable. Marked results may be exported into several citation management software packages, and articles may be e-mailed to the searcher or anyone else. Search activity is captured in ProQuest's My Research Summary, where marked articles, search strategies, and selected publication may be saved as a Web page and revisited later or shared with colleagues and students.

ProQuest has made a concerted effort to upgrade *ABI/INFORM*'s scholarly content, interface, and features, with the result of making an excellent resource even more attractive. The product is highly recommended for public and academic libraries, and its various configurations aim to accommodate a range of budgetary and fiscal situations.

Business & Company Resource Center
RDS Business Reference Suite
Gale Group
http://www.gale.com/

The Gale Group's *Business & Company Resource Center* is a formidable source of international business information with some 4,600 company histories (updated annually), investment reports, financials, rankings, suits and claims, products, and industry reviews. Company profiles (for U.S. and international public and private firms) and industry profiles represent just the starting point, however, in that the database also abstracts roughly 3,650 business periodicals–2,600 of them in full text starting from 1985–providing news and analysis, consumer marketing data, emerging technology reports, and even delayed stock quotes.

Updated daily, the resource is further enhanced with company and industry intelligence for 300,000 companies, the full text of the business sections from 100 newspapers, the Knight-Ridder/Tribune Business News Service, and *Financial Times*. There is also abstracting coverage of the *Wall Street Journal* and the *New York Times*. Gale extracts content from a variety of databases, including *American Wholesalers and Distributors Directory, Brands and Their Companies, Business Rankings Annual Encyclopedia of Associations: International Organizations,* and *Ward's Business Directory of U.S. Private and Public Companies.*

Additionally, Gale offers *Business & Company Resource Center* subscribers an extensive array of specialty modules. *PROMT (Predicast's Overview of Markets and Technology)* features abstracts and full text from international trade and business journals, industry newsletters, and newspapers, and summaries from *Investext* investment firm reports detailing market size and market share information, industry trends, emerging technologies, and competitive opportunities. *Investext Plus*, an investment and financial analysis database covering global companies and industries, delivers reports in their original formats. Research from more than 500 investment banks and nearly 200 trade associations is included, along with data on 10,000 publicly held U.S. companies from *Mergent Online*. In all, more than 700,000 reports are available, with 5,000 added weekly.

Despite these staggering numbers, Gale is relentlessly adding new internal and external resources to its business suite. *First Call Consensus Snapshot* from Thomson Financial, industry overviews from *Gale's Encyclopedia of American Industries, Encyclopedia of Emerging Industries* and *Encyclopedia of Global Industries*, and market share information from Gale's *Market Share Reporter* and *World Market Share Reporter*. Global coverage was upgraded via licensing agreements with such sources as *The Economist*, which provides country intelligence.

Gale's recently upgraded interface–one that tested InfoTrac users would be comfortable with–supports new modes like Quick Start Search and Advanced Search modes and a more extensive array of search options, as well as a more comprehensive set of internal links from search results to related material within the database.

Users can perform searches on subjects, geographic locations, personal and company names, or on ticker symbols and SIC or NAICS codes. Limits include full text only and peer-reviewed publications, date range, and content area.

Hyperlinked SIC/NAICS codes, for example, facilitate comparison of similar companies in various geographic regions, with results ranked by revenue. Articles may be e-mailed and printed individually or in batches, and users may save and re-execute searches.

In *Business & Company Resource Center*, Gale offers an extensive array of detailed, up-to-date company and industry news and information making this an *exceptionally* attractive resource for academic institutions supporting management, finance, marketing, or economics programs and for public libraries serving the serious business researcher.

The Gale Group's *Business & Company Resource Center* (and all its add-on modules) is not the company's only entry in the business reference suite category. Geared specifically to meet the needs of researchers requiring company and industry analysis, Gale's *RDS Business Reference Suite* is a collection of three complementary resources–*Business & Industry*, *Business & Management Practices*, and *TableBase* that, taken together, represent a comprehensive source for news, management practice, and market research information with a distinct international flavor. As a suite, the product contains more than 1,400 business sources, 60% of which are full text.

International in scope, *Business & Industry* is a broad-based source of data on companies, industries, products, and markets covering activities in nearly 200 countries. *B&I* extracts content from over 1,000 trade and industry publications, regional, national and international newspapers, business dailies and newsletters from 1995 to the present. It is also available as a stand-alone subscription.

Business & Management Practices includes material pertinent to the fields of management, planning, production, finance, marketing, information technology, and human resources culled from more than 300 professional and trade journals. Taking the practical approach to management processes and methods, *BaMP* represents a source of advice on real-life applications, case studies, and guidelines for a wide array of everyday business issues. *BaMP* is also available as an individual subscription.

The third piece of the puzzle, *TableBase*, consists primarily of tabular information with, in many cases, textual content that supports the corresponding market share, market size, capacity, production, imports, exports, sales, product and brand rankings, forecasts, healthcare, and demographics data in the tables. Tables are drawn from the 1,000 or so sources incorporated into the *Business & Industry* database as well as from external trade and governmental reports. Gale's practice of indexing the contents of the table, as opposed to the accompanying text, produces exceptionally accurate retrieval results when looking for information on companies and industries that is represented graphically.

PROMPT: Predicast's Overview of Markets and Technology provides comprehensive and global coverage of companies, products, and technologies. The database covers the previous 3 years plus current year and includes summaries and full text from nearly 1,000 business and trade journals, industry newsletters, local, national and international newspapers, market research studies, news releases, and investment and brokerage firm reports. Updated daily except for Sunday. Of approximately 1,000 indexed publications, 700 are full text. Also includes government publications, and abstracts of *Investext* reports. Like the other Gale products, *PROMTP* may be added as a module to the *Business & Company Resource Center* or accessed as a stand-alone subscription.

The *RDS* interface allows databases to be searched individually or simultaneously, which means that the users can retrieve relevant articles, along with supporting statistics, illustrations, and tabular data related to their research needs in one efficient search.

The clean interface–with its search boxes and pull-down menus displaying controlled vocabulary index terms for concepts, industry names, document types, or geographic regions–facilitates easy access of the resource's varied contents.

Academic researchers and anyone else interested in international company and market research data are the target audience for Gale's *RDS Business Reference Suite*, which is available as an integrated package or in any combination of its component databases.

EBSCOhost
http://www.epnet.com/

Comprehensive for all aspects of the business literature from 1965 to the present, EBSCO Publishing's *Business Source Premier* delivers indexing and abstracting coverage of some 3,350 titles to the serious business researcher. Over 80% of these titles are currently available online in full text and a 900+ subset of this number are peer-reviewed, revealing a strong scholarly concentration. Boardroom staples like *Fortune, Forbes,* and *Business Week* are here along with substantive academic journals such as *Harvard Business Review, Administrative Science Quarterly,* and *Journal of Marketing Research.*

It's the extras that really set *Business Source Premier* apart, though. For selected titles, retrospective coverage (in PDF format) extends back as early as the mid-1920s, giving users of the resource a much more intimate look at the past century's economic history than most other business reference suites can hope to offer. In the Company Profiles component of the database, succinct summary entries are linked to an extensive up-to-date PDF version of the complete Datamonitor research report. Additionally, subscribers may supplement coverage of big picture business developments with local and regional business coverage via EBSCO's *Regional Business News* database, which provides the full text of 75 business journals, newspapers, and newswires. Both resources are updated daily.

Sophisticated searchers can take advantage of an extensive array of capabilities to limit search results to full-text articles only, to peer-reviewed journals, to a particular range of dates, or to a specified publication type. Searching by journal title, product name, NAICS/Industry Code, company name, Duns Number, and Ticker Symbol are supported as well.

EBSCO employs permanent links, facilitating the creation of Web-based documents, bibliographies, and reading lists. A local holdings statement enhances hard copy retrieval, full-text availability is clearly indicated at the results list level, and external linking to additional full-text providers further augment document retrieval. *Business Source Premier* even offers translations of its full-text contents into Spanish, French, and German.

EBSCO targets *Business Source Premier*–with its substantial scholarly component–squarely at academe generally and business schools specifically. Irrespective of the library setting, however, business researchers, investors, public policy makers, consumers, and consumer advocates will all find that this is an extraordinarily useful suite of resources.

LexisNexis Academic
http://www.lexisnexis.com/academic

Academic subscribers have full-text access to an extensive range of business information sources, including roughly 1,800 business and financial newspapers and journals, U.S. and international company financial information from government or private sources, market research, industry reports, and SEC filings. Search features are geared to making company-to-company comparisons (on a variety of specific criteria) a simple process for the researcher. News sources include *Accountancy Age, Ad Age Global, American Economic Review, Chain Store Age, IPO Reporter, Mergers and Acquisitions Report*, and more. Financial information sources include *Standard & Poor's Corporate Descriptions, Hoover's Company Reports, Disclosure Reports, IRRC*, international company and stock reports. SEC filings and reports include SEC 10-Q Reports, SEC 10-K Reports, SEC 8-K Reports, SEC 20-F Reports, SEC Annual Reports to Shareholders, Proxy Statements, Prospectuses, Registration, and Williams Act Filings. There is a strong accounting component, and directory-type information sources include *Eventline, The American Marketplace, Federal Business Opportunities, SIC Directory*, and *World Business Opportunities*. Legal Resources, also of tremendous potential value to the corporate world, is the next menu down in *LexisNexis*. Finally, the Reference section, and particularly the biographical entries, is also a useful resource.

STAND-ALONE DATABASES

Additional subscription databases offering indexing and abstracting of business publications and selective full text. Gale–with four distinct products that are available as stand-alone subscriptions or as modules of the more comprehensive *RDS Business Reference Suite*–is also an active player in this category.

ECONbase
http://www.economicsdirect.com

A Web database from Elsevier Science, enables searching in abstracts and full text of articles from 79 professional journals (60,000+ online papers) from economics, finance, and trade. ECONbase enables the user to display a citation of a particular article or the table of contents of an issue of a respective periodical. Full text of articles is available to those users whose library is registered with *ScienceDirect Web editions* (basic electronic access for Elsevier Science print subscribers), or subscribed to *ScienceDirect Digital Collections*, and articles can be purchased for a fee to those without licensed access. The resource utilizes Scirus, a comprehensive science-specific search engine, offering Basic and Advanced search capabilities. Searches can be limited by date range, information type, file format and content source. The results page includes PDF and HTML formats, and allows users to refine searches using a system-produced list of keywords found in the results. Current issues include links to "Articles in press."

EconLit
American Economic Association
http://www.econlit.org

EconLit abstracts more than 750 journals, books, dissertations, and book reviews from *Journal of Economic Literature*, and includes the abstracts of *Working Papers in Economics*. Citations in the database include links to full-text articles in economics journals worldwide where available. Available via Cambridge Scientific Abstracts, Dialog, EBSCO, OCLC's FirstSearch, Elsevier's ScienceDirect, OVID Technologies, and SilverPlatter, its audience is chiefly academic and special libraries.

JSTOR–Business Collection
http://www.jstor.com

One of six major collections within the *JSTOR Database*, the *Business Collection* is comprised of 46 scholarly titles including extensive runs of the *Journal of Accounting Research*, *Journal of Business* (and its previous incarnations), and *Review of Economics and Statistics*.

A full-image database, users can search the entire *Business Collection* discipline, or expand the journal list to limit to specific titles within the "Business," "Finance," or "Economics" category. Advanced search options include field and proximity searching and limiting by publication, date range, file type, and content availability.

ScienceDirect
http://www.ScienceDirect.com/

This product began as a Web database of Elsevier Science journals, and has grown to include technical and medical disciplines from Elsevier and several other participating publishers as well. Totaling more than 1,900 titles, the "Business, Management and Accounting Journals" subject area is comprised of 106 journals with titles such as *Accounting, Organizations and Society, Financial Services Review, International Journal of Research in Marketing*, and *Organizational Dynamics*. Full-text content extends from 1996 forward and some from 1993 forward. A backfile program for this collection is also available for a one-time purchase fee and new titles are added on a regular basis. Currently 59 core titles are available, with coverage from 1960.

Guest Users (those who do not belong to an institution that has a subscription) can view the Tables of Contents, Abstracts, and retrieve full-text articles from individual journal titles on a "pay-per-view" basis. In addition, these users can create journal issue alerts and can save a favorite journal list.

Licensed Users (are automatically recognized as belonging to an institution that has a subscription) can also access desired content via Quick, Basic, and Advanced search modes. These users have additional customizable options for Alerts and CrossRef linking.

Wilson Business Full Text
H. W. Wilson Co.
http://www.hwwilson.com/

The *Wilson Business Full Text* genealogy can be traced from the publication of *Business Periodicals Index* in 1958. On the format side it evolved from printed index into an online service in 1982, a CD-ROM database, and now a Web-based resource, while on the features side it matured through the indexing and abstracting stages with full-text coverage appearing in 1995. Of the 600 or so magazines, trade journals, annual reports, scholarly journals, and business newspapers, more than 350 titles are currently available in full text. Additionally, the WilsonLink feature enables a researcher to link to additional full-text titles in *any* open-URL compliant resource to which the library subscribes. The library holdings feature directs researchers into your library's catalog for journal holdings information. Given that the Wilson approach has always been to reflect core library resources in its bibliographic products, a library holdings check will typically produce a satisfying outcome for the searcher. A built-in fee-based document delivery capability provides back-up when other routes to the desired information fail.

Constantly undergoing refinement and improvement it seems, the WilsonWeb interface opens in Advanced Search mode where "All–Smart Search" attempts to deliver the most highly relevant research material to the searcher thanks to the integrated efforts of Wilson's dedication to precise indexing principles, its hierarchical search rules, and the Verity Relevancy-Ranking Algorithm. "I need a few good articles" takes on new meaning in a Wilson database.

Boolean searches and truncation, however, are casualties within the All–Smart Search text entry boxes, although Basic mode, in turn, does feature some valuable enhancements–natural language searching, support for using double quotation marks for phrase searching. Searchers also have considerable control over how results are sorted and displayed, and output options include print, e-mail, and save.

ECONOMIC INDICATORS AND FORECASTS

A fair number of resources exist for determining current and historical economic data, as well as tracking forecasts, demographic data, consumer trends, and in-depth analysis of national and world economies. In addition to sites available on the Internet as detailed below, several fee-based services are identified.

Euromonitor International
http://www.euromonitor.com/

Produces more than 50 reference products, country reports, and major market profiles, containing global consumer market information, with demographics, trends and developments, market background, market sizes and forecasts, market shares, socio-economic and economic indicators, business information sources, key players, and company profiles. Full-text market research reports for specific products/industries are available for many countries. Many databases are available in hardcopy only, and online titles include *Global Market Share Planner on the Internet*, *Market Research Europe*, *Market Research Monitor*, *Retail Trade International*, and *World Market Overview*. Also available is *Global Market Information Database* (GMID), an integrated Web version of Euromonitor content, covering over 350 markets and organized by world market data and statistics, consumer lifestyle, forecasts, and consumer market size.

EIU Online
http://www.eiu.com

Produced by the Economist Intelligence Unit, this database provides their trademark *Country Forecasts, Country Reports, CountryData*, and *Viewswires* for nearly 200 countries, regions, and organizations, with both current and retrospective information. *Country Forecasts* present five-year macroeconomic projections for 60 of the world's largest economies and provide a forward-looking assessment of their political, policy, and business environments–with free monthly updates. Country Reports provides in-depth analysis of current political, policy, and economic trends with an 18-month outlook. Covering 115 countries, *EIU CountryData* is a comprehensive source of economic indicators and forecasts, with access to 272 economic series–more than 700,000 individual data points–with data going back to 1980 and forecasts to 2006. Annual, quarterly, and monthly data is available. Data may be retrieved in spreadsheet format. *Country Viewswire* is a daily service offering coverage of political, economic, and business analysis by country.

Market Insight
http://umi.compustat.com/

Market Insight is the online source for many of Standard & Poor's publications, including *S&P Industry Surveys, S&P Stock Reports*, and *Trends & Projections*, providing in-depth analysis of industry trends, key ratios, statistics, and more. The database includes fully interactive, customizable price and volume charts on U.S. companies, source documents including an EDGAR interface, and annual and interim reports for close to 30,000 companies. This service also provides online access to the *ExecuComp* database, *DRI-WEFA Risk Reports*, the *CIA World Factbook*, and Asia/Europe commentary.

Mintel
http://www.mintel.com/

Mintel produces market research reports for Europe, the United Kingdom, and the United States. Reports cover a variety of sectors including consumer goods, travel and tourism, financial industry, Internet industry, retail, and food and drink. Reports discuss market drivers, market size and trends, market segmentation, supply structure, advertising and promotion, retail distribution, consumer attitudes, and market forecasts.

World Bank WDI Online
http://devdata.worldbank.org/dataonline/

Statistical data from the World Bank for more than 550 development indicators and time series data from 1960-2000 for over 207 countries and 18 country groups. Data includes social, economic, financial, natural resources, and environmental indicators. The Web site provides a link to *Data Query*, with free access to a sub-set of *WDI Online*. This segment includes 54 time series indicators for 207 countries and 18 groups, spanning 5 years (1996 to 2000).

FINANCIAL AND COMPANY INFORMATION

Specialized services for facilitating in-depth research on a particular company as well as comparing wide ranges of financial data on publicly- and privately-owned companies in the United States and worldwide.

Bloomberg
http://www.bloomberg.com

An online service providing stock quotes and technical analysis on U.S. and international securities, the service also provides company, industry, and market news, as well as U.S. and international economic indicators–both current and historical exchange rates; stock, bond, and index prices; commodity prices; mortgage markets; interest rates; economic indicators; and treasuries. Company information includes financial data, stock histories, brief descriptions, recent news articles, and comparative return analysis.

factiva.com
http://www.factiva.com

The successor to *Dow Jones Interactive* (DJI) *and Reuters Business Briefing* (RBB) databases, *factiva.com* offers users the latest news from these leading business resources, including national and international sources covering business and general information. The continuously updated database affords customers access to nearly 8,000 sources from 118 countries and 22 languages, including more than 270 newswires and 1,000 newspapers–such as *The Wall Street Journal, The New York Times, Financial Times* (London), *Le Monde, The South China Morning Post*, and 29 Knight Ridder papers.

Hoover's Online
http://www.hoovers.com

Depending on the subscription level–there are four–subscribers can access comprehensive company profiles, in-depth financials, full lists of key people and competitors, competitive analysis, advanced searching, downloadable contact information, create customized, printable reports about public and private companies, and more. Basic information (overview, history, news, officers, employees, locations and subsidiaries, products/operations, and competitors) on more than 21,000 public and private U.S. companies and international companies is included.

Investext
http://research.thomsonib.com/

Investext contains indexing and full-text research/analyst reports on companies and industries in addition to the annual statistical reports of many industry trade associations, government and industry sources, and proprietary market studies. It delivers full-text reports in their original published formats, complete with charts, photographs, and graphics. Users can monitor industry trends, track company financials, and research merger and acquisitions data. Investment research reports are prepared by analysts at investment banks, brokerage houses, and consulting firms who closely follow particular companies or industries. *Investext Plus* includes more than 400,000 reports from 1996 onward. The reports, provided in PDF format, come from over 500 investment banks and 190 trade associations and include financial information from Mergent's Investors Service. (Note: Can be added as a module to *Gale's Business & Company Resource Center*.)

Kompass
http://www2.kompass.com/

Directory information for 1.8 million companies in more than 70 countries, with indexes for company products and services, containing

23 million product and service references, and 790,000 trademarks and brand names.

Mergent Online
http://www.fisonline.com/

Formerly Moody's, *Mergent Online* is a modular database with the basic subscription providing U.S. Company Data and/or International Company Data. Company information includes: business description, executives and directory, current pricing data, company history, joint ventures, subsidiaries with geographic breakdown, properties, long term debt, capital stock, recent financial news, SEC filings, earnings estimates, and financials (15 years historic data and 15 years of financial ratios). Historical news and current insider and institutional holdings are available from the "Create Report" section of the database. Includes pre-defined and customized comparison reports. Additional modules are available.

Research Insight
http://www.compustat.com

Research Insight is a corporate and financial information research database. It includes financial, market, and descriptive data on over 7,600 publicly traded companies, 200 industry composites and 3,000 research companies (companies no longer publicly traded). Data is available for U.S. companies as well as international companies traded on U.S. exchanges. Users can perform calculations, create custom and standard reports and transfer data to Excel spreadsheets. Includes GICS (Global Industry Classification Standard) classification, together with integrated access to Standard & Poor's company, industry, commentary, index, and country analysis. Subscriptions can be customized to include additional financial and market databases.

Thompson Research
http://research.thomsonib.com/

This resource provides Web-based access to complete SEC filings and annual reports for U.S. and international public parent companies, with real-time and historical EDGAR filings. The database includes full-text articles and summaries from 1,300 trade presses, newspapers, wire stories, and newsletters worldwide and also more than 3.4 million research reports, with an average of 3,000 new reports added each business day. Additionally, access to Worldscope global financials and accounting results on more than 28,000 active public companies are integrated into the resource as well.

STATISTICAL DATA FILES

Statistical data represents the lifeblood of virtually every business decision, and not surprisingly, there are abundant stand-alone resources to fill this critical need.

CRSP
http://gsbwww.uchicago.edu/research/crsp/

The Center for Research in Security Prices is a financial research center at the University of Chicago Graduate School of Business. *CRSP* creates and maintains premier historical U.S. databases for stock (NASDAQ, AMEX, NYSE), indices, bond, and mutual fund securities. Used for financial, economic, and accounting research. Standard subscription databases include *CRSP US Stock Databases*, *CRSP US Indices Database*, *CRSP/Compustat Merged Database (CCM)*, *CRSP Survivor Bias-Free US Mutual Fund Database*, and *CRSP US Treasury Databases*.

GDF Online
http://publications.worldbank.org/GDF/

Access to statistical data for the 138 countries that report public and publicly guaranteed debt to the World Bank Debtor Reporting System. The database covers external debt stocks and flows, major economic aggregates, and key debt ratios as well as average terms of new commitments, currency composition of long-term debt, debt restructuring, and scheduled debt service projections.

International Financial Statistics
http://www.bis.org/statistics/

Published by the Bank for International Settlements, *IFS* contains approximately 32,000 time series covering more than 200 countries, which summarize every country's balance of payments, with collateral data on its principal components (trade and reserves) and data on the principal cause and effect elements (monetary expansion and contraction, government surpluses and deficits, production, prices and interest rates). The file contains all time series reported on the IFS country pages of the published counterpart; major Fund accounts series; and most of the world, area, and country series from the IFS World Tables. The Country, World, and Commodity Prices Tables, as presented in the monthly printed copy of IFS, are available as selection options.

LexisNexis Statistical
http://www.lexisnexis.com/

LexisNexis Statistical is the most comprehensive tool for identifying and accessing statistical tables and reports emanating from federal and state government agencies, international intergovernmental organizations, professional and trade organizations, commercial publishers, independent research organizations, and university research centers. Several levels of access to *Statistical* are offered by LexisNexis. The Base Edition table collection includes over 30,000 full-text documents representing statistical compilations issued by Federal agencies, the states, and international intergovernmental organizations. The Research Edition adds another 100,000 documents from government and private-sector sources to your PowerTables searches. The Statistical Abstract and Index modules, the full-service offering, consists of the PowerTables plus the online versions of *American Statistics Index* (ASI), *Statistical Reference Index* (SRI), and *Index to International Statistics* (IIS). Many of these additional documents are available directly in full text online or linked to their issuing sites online.

STAT-USA/Internet
http://www.stat-usa.gov/

STAT-USA/Internet is a fee-based service of an agency in the Economics and Statistics Administration, U.S. Department of Commerce. Free access is available through federal depository libraries. Of interest to the U.S. business, economic, and trade community, in providing timely and authoritative economic, business, and international trade information from the Federal government.

USA Trade Online
http://www.usatradeonline.gov/

USA Trade Online, a sister Web site to *STAT-USA* by the U.S. Dept. of Commerce, provides U.S. import and export data on over 18,000 commodities. The period of coverage is 1992-2 months ago. Useful for researching existing and emerging export markets, determining market share of export markets for specific products, and monitoring trends in specific products, markets, and countries.

APPENDIX

DIRECTORY OF FREELY-AVAILABLE INTERNET RESOURCES IN BUSINESS

A consensus "Best of the Web" directory derived from sources identified by business library organizations and major business libraries.

PROFESSIONAL RESOURCES FOR BUSINESS LIBRARIANS

BRASS
Reference and User Services Association, Business Reference and Services Section (American Library Association)
http://www.ala.org/ala/rusa/rusaourassoc/rusasections/brass/brass.htm

The Internet Collegiate Reference Collection
Harvey A. Andruss Library
Bloomsburg University
http://icrc.bloomu.edu/icrc/searchlc.php?top=HC&bottom=HJ9999

Internet Public Library: Business & Economics
http://www.ipl.org/div/subject/browse/bus00.00.00/

J. Hugh Jackson Library
Rosenberg Corporate Research Center (Stanford Business School)
http://wesley.stanford.edu/library/

Librarians' Index to the Internet: Business, Finance, & Jobs
http://lii.org/search/file/busfinjobs

APPENDIX (continued)

BUSINESS WEB SITES

General

Economist.com Business Encyclopedia
http://www.economist.com/encyclopedia/

bizjournals.com
http://www.bizjournals.com/search.html

Consumer Action Handbook
U.S. Federal Consumer Information Center
http://www.consumeraction.gov

FINDarticles.COM Business/Finance
http://www.findarticles.com/p/articles/tn_bus

Forbes' Lists
http://www.forbes.com/lists/

Fortune Lists
http://www.fortune.com/fortune/alllists

Accounting

Rutgers Accounting Web
http://raw.rutgers.edu

Social Science Research Network: Accounting Research Network
http://www.ssrn.com/arn/index.html

SmartPros
http://accounting.smartpros.com

AuditNet
http://www.auditnet.org/

General Accounting Office
http://www.gao.gov/

American Institute of Certified Public Accountants (AICPA)
http://www.aicpa.org/

Accounting Terminology Guide
New York State Society of CPAs
http://www.nysscpa.org/prof_library/guide.htm

Tax and Accounting Sites Directory
http://www.taxsites.com/

Advertising

AAF: American Advertising Federation
http://www.aaf.org/

Advertising Age
http://www.adage.com/

Advertising World
http://advertising.utexas.edu/world/

Ad*Access
http://scriptorium.lib.duke.edu/adaccess/

adflip
http://www.adflip.com/

Ad-Planner's Glossary
http://www.ad-planners.com/

America's Research Group
http://americasresearchgroup.com/

Emergence of Advertising in America
http://scriptorium.lib.duke.edu/eaa/

Glossary of Marketing terms
http://www.quirks.com/resources/glossary.asp

Retailing Resources
Center for Retailing Studies, Texas A&M University
http://www.crstamu.org/

Banks and Banking

American Banker's Association
http://www.aba.com

Bank Rate Monitor
http://www.bankrate.com

Banking Center
http://www.nytimes.com/partners/banking/index.html

APPENDIX (continued)

Banking on the WWW
http://ifbg.wiwi.uni-goettingen.de/ifbgheim.shtml

Board of Governors, Federal Reserve System
http://www.federalreserve.gov/

Central Bank Websites
http://www.bis.org/cbanks.htm

FDIC Federal Deposit Insurance Corporation
http://www.fdic.gov

FED101: The Federal Reserve Today
http://www.kc.frb.org/fed101/

Global Banking Law Database (GBLD)
http://www.gbld.org/

House Committee on Banking and Financial Services
http://www.house.gov/banking/

International Monetary Fund
http://www.imf.org

National Credit Union Administration
http://ncua.gov/

NIC National Information Center
http://www.ffiec.gov/nic/

The World Bank
http://worldbank.org

Business Ethics

BusinessEthics.ca
http://www.businessethics.ca/

Business Ethics
http://www.web-miner.com/busethics.htm

Co-op America
http://www.coopamerica.org/

CorpWatch: Holding Corporations Accountable
http://www.corpwatch.org/

Stakeholder Alliance
http://www.stakeholderalliance.org/

Transparency International (TI)
http://www.transparency.org/

Finance, Investments, Personal Finance

Annual Reports Library
http://www.zpub.com/sf/arl/index.html

BigCharts
http://bigcharts.marketwatch.com/

Bonds Online
http://www.bondsonline.com/

CNNMONEY
http://money.cnn.com/

Economic Report of the President
U.S. Executive Office of the President
http://www.gpoaccess.gov/eop/

Financial Economics Network
Social Science Research Network
http://www.ssrn.com/

FinWeb.com
http://www.finweb.com/finweb.html

Historical Stock Quotes
BigCharts
http://bigcharts.marketwatch.com/historical/

ICI Mutual Fund Connection
http://www.ici.org

Investopedia.com
http://www.investopedia.com/

Investor Information
http://www.sec.gov/investor.shtml

APPENDIX (continued)

Mutual Fund Investor's Center
Mutual Fund Education Alliance
http://www.mfea.com/

The New York Stock Exchange Glossary of Financial Terms
http://www.nyse.com/

investorguide.com
http://www.investorguide.com/

MarketWatch
http://cbs.marketwatch.com/news/default.asp?siteID=mktw

MoneyCentral
http://moneycentral.msn.com/

Morningstar.com
http://www.morningstar.com/

Personal Finance Terms
Kiplinger
http://www.kiplinger.com/basics/glossary/

SocialFunds.com
http://www.socialfunds.com/

Virtual Finance Library
http://fisher.osu.edu/fin/overview.htm

Wachowicz's Web World: Web Sites for Discerning Finance Students
http://web.utk.edu/~jwachowi/wacho_world.html

10-K Wizard
http://www.10kwizard.com/

International Business

CorporateInformation
http://www.corporateinformation.com/

Deardorff's Glossary of International Economics
http://www-personal.umich.edu/~alandear/glossary/

Europages: The European Business Directory
http://www.europages.com/home-en.html

Foreign Trade Statistics
U.S. Census Bureau
http://www.census.gov/foreign-trade/www/

GlobalEDGE
Michigan State University's Center for International Business Education and Research (CIBER)
http://globaledge.msu.edu/ibrd/ibrd.asp

International Business & Technology: World Level
http://www.brint.com/international.htm

International Chamber of Commerce
http://www.iccwbo.org

International Trade Administration
http://www.ita.doc.gov/

International Trade Web Resources
Federation of International Trade Associations
http://www.fita.org/webindex/

MSU-CIBER Center for International Business Education and Research
http://ciber.msu.edu/

OECD Online
http://www.oecd.org

SICE–Foreign Trade Information System
Sistema de Información al Comercio Exterior
http://www.sice.oas.org/

U.S. International Trade Commission
http://www.usitc.gov/

VIBES: Virtual International Business and Economic Sources
University of North Carolina Charlotte
http://libweb.uncc.edu/ref-bus/vibehome.htm

World Bank
http://www.worldbank.org

World Trade Organization
http://www.wto.org

APPENDIX (continued)

Small Business and Entrepreneurship

BizMove.com: The Small Business Knowledge Base
http://www.bizmove.com/

Business.gov
http://www.business.gov/

BusinessWeek Online: Small Busishess
http://www.businessweek.com/smallbiz/index.html

CCH Business Owner's Toolkit
http://www.toolkit.cch.com/

Entrepreneur.Com: The Online Small Business Authority
Entrepreneur Magazine
http://www.entrepreneurmag.com

Edward Lowe Foundation
http://edwardlowe.org

Entrepreneurs' Help Page
http://www.tannedfeet.com/

Entrepreneur's Reference Guide to Small Business Information
Library of Congress, Business Reference Services' Science, Technology,
and Business Division
http://www.loc.gov/rr/business/guide/guide2/

ENTERWeb: Enterprise Development
http://www.enterweb.org/

EntreWorld
Kauffman Center for Entrepreneurial Leadership
http://www.entreworld.com

FindLaw for Business
http://smallbusiness.findlaw.com/

Idea Cafe: The Small Business Channel
http://www.businessownersideacafe.com

Internal Revenue Service: Small Business/Self-Employed
http://www.irs.gov/businesses/small/

Research Institute for Small & Emerging Business
http://www.rise.org

SCORE (Service Corps of Retired Executives)
http://www.score.org

Startup journal: Wall Street Journal Center for Entrepreneurs
http://www.startupjournal.com/

U.S. Small Business Administration
http://www.sba.gov

Small Business Development Center
National SBDC National Information Clearinghouse
http://sbdcnet.utsa.edu/

Women's Business Center
http://www.sba.gov/financing/special/women.html

Internet Reference Sources in Education

Linda C. Weber

SUMMARY. With so many Internet sites devoted to education for educators, administrators, and librarians, it can be a daunting experience trying to find needed resources. There are special sites devoted to teachers, children, and parents. The government provides free access to database searching, statistics, and full-text publications. State and local levels of government also host valuable data and reports. More and more journals are appearing online in full-text format escalating user expectation to assume all journals will be available via the Internet. Tapping into higher education and academic library sites connects to content rich links. While this is not an exhaustive listing of educational Web sites, it leads to a myriad of valuable resources. *[Article copies available for a fee from The Haworth Document Delivery Service: 1-800-HAWORTH. E-mail address: <docdelivery@haworthpress.com> Website: <http://www.HaworthPress.com> © 2005 by The Haworth Press, Inc. All rights reserved.]*

KEYWORDS. Education, education resources, higher education, Internet resources, reference, Web sites

---

Linda C. Weber is Social Sciences Team Leader, University of Southern California, Von KleinSmid Center, Applied Social Sciences Library B40-B, Los Angeles, CA 90089-0048 (E-mail: lindaweb@usc.edu).

[Haworth co-indexing entry note]: "Internet Reference Sources in Education." Weber, Linda C. Co-published simultaneously in *The Reference Librarian* (The Haworth Information Press, an imprint of The Haworth Press, Inc.) No. 91/92, 2005, pp. 263-277; and: *The Reference Collection: From the Shelf to the Web* (ed: William J. Frost) The Haworth Information Press, an imprint of The Haworth Press, Inc., 2005, pp. 263-277. Single or multiple copies of this article are available for a fee from The Haworth Document Delivery Service [1-800-HAWORTH, 9:00 a.m. - 5:00 p.m. (EST). E-mail address: docdelivery@haworthpress.com].

doi:10.1300/J120v44n91_16

INTRODUCTION

Today's World Wide Web provides a wealth of educational reference resources for educators, administrators, and librarians. Many of these sites have been available for several years, are highly reliable, and regularly updated, making them valuable tools for information and research. Most are maintained by dedicated education specialists in K-12 schools, colleges and universities, and in various levels of government. Some sites provide additional services by answering questions and/or inviting viewers to suggest additional Web sites.

Education reference resources are available in three different formats–print, microform, and online. The field of education has been slower than many disciplines to convert print and microform publications to Internet-based access, but each year is bringing more and more success with electronic formats. According to Webster[1] "the movement from paper library reference works to electronic products is picking up speed." Researchers shy away from using microfiche or microfilm, and institutions prefer online subscriptions to handling microform collections. Basic education reference tools such as subject specific dictionaries, encyclopedias, and handbooks are primarily available in print. The two most common thesauri, *Thesaurus of ERIC (Educational Resources Information Center) Descriptors* for the ERIC database and *Thesaurus of Psychological Index Terms* for the American Psychological Association PsycINFO database, are available in print and have online versions. The ERIC thesaurus is provided free of charge on the Internet. The PscyINFO thesaurus is available online from some vendors but only by subscription as a part of the PscyINFO and PsychARTICLES databases.

Today education journal articles come in many formats. Some are only available in print, but many offer print and electronic versions. Newer journals may only be available online either for free or by subscription. Some online journals offer free journal article summaries, but only provide the full text for subscribers. In discussing electronic and print journals, King et al.[2] makes the observation that there is a "steady shift to electronic collections" and that "Electronic journals will continue to grow in acceptance and strength." Many libraries have banded together to provide their academic communities with access to electronic journals through various projects, two being JSTOR (http://www.jstor.org/) and Project MUSE (http://muse.jhu.edu/). Both of these projects offer online scholarly journals and include some education titles. Electronic journals offer the researcher convenience and flexibility, which has heightened their anticipation, by expecting everything they need to be available online.

The criteria for compiling this set of Web sites focuses on sites that would enhance reference service. These sites are maintained by reputable authors or organizations, and provide quality content with appropriate links to other sites. They offer quick and easy access, search capability and are updated regularly. Simple questions such as "What credentials do I need to be a teacher in Montana?" or "How many K-12 students are there in Virginia?" can be answered along with in-depth research topics that require searching the ERIC database using multiple keywords to retrieve scholarly journal articles.

INDEX AND ABSTRACT SERVICES

Several online index and abstract services provide access to scholarly education-related literature. ERIC and PsycINFO dominate as the two leading abstract databases librarians and researchers consult most often. The ERIC database, produced by the U.S. Department of Education, is the most comprehensive index with abstracts for the field of education. ERIC indexes journal articles and educational documents including research reports, conference papers, speeches, program descriptions, essays, teaching guides, and books. The government provides free access to ERIC on the Internet, plus it is also available by subscription. Subscriptions can be purchased in two formats. The Dialog Corporation and the National Information Services Corporation (NISC) offer ERIC online and on CD-ROM. Cambridge Scientific Abstracts, EBSCO Publishing, Online Computer Library Center (OCLC), and OVID Technologies provide online versions of ERIC. ERIC Processing and Reference Facility and SilverPlatter Information, Inc. also offer ERIC on CD-ROM. To search ERIC, individuals can visit any of the more than 1,000 libraries worldwide that provide free access to ERIC or purchase a CD-ROM for personal use.

The vendors providing the ERIC database have the same data, but package it with different formats and options. In comparing the free government version of ERIC to a paid subscription, it is puzzling to run the same search and receive different retrieval results. In comparing the free government version of ERIC to the OCLC FirstSearch, a few differences are noticeable. The free version lists results in no apparent order, which is frustrating if you are looking for the most current citations, as they will be buried in the search results. Subscription versions of

ERIC usually provide the newest citations first and may even allow sorting by other parameters.

While ERIC and PsycINFO are most frequently consulted, librarians and researchers should not overlook Education Abstracts, and International ERIC comprised of two educational research databases: the Australian Education Index (AEI), and the British Education Index (BEI). Available free online is a database of edcational studies in Chinese communities called the Chinese Educational Resources Information Centre Project (Chinese ERIC) indexing English and Chinese articles in journals from Hong Kong, the Chinese Mainland, and Taiwan with access at: (http://www.fed.cuhk.edu.hk/ceric/). There are a number of interdisciplinary index providers whose scope encompasses many fields including education, such as EBSCOhost, ISI Current Contents Connect, ProQuest Direct, and Wilson Select Plus. A search will yield citations and many times full text, but the search results may be small in number or not as relevant as searching the education specific indexes and abstracts.

EDUCATION WEB SITES

The following Web sites have been organized into six categories. The general education reference section includes ready reference information such as an educational dictionary, book reviews and testing indexes, followed by education specific search engines. The next section is government information provided at the federal level with statistics and a link to state departments of education. The following section is electronic journal directories with two of the four sites providing full-text journal articles free of charge. The last two sections are higher education and a select listing of academic education libraries that provide links to Web resources.

General Education Reference Sites

Buros Institute of Mental Measurements–Test Reviews Online
http://www.unl.edu/buros/

Buros Institute publishes *Mental Measurements Yearbook (MMY)* and provides access to test information. The online record does not provide the actual test, but lists which volume of *MMY* to consult for a review and evaluation of the tests. Searching is available by keyword, an alphabetical list of tests, or a listing of broad categories.

Dictionary of Education PLUS
http://dictionary.soe.umich.edu/plus/

Editors Fred Goodwin and John Miller from the School of Education at the University of Michigan have created the Pedagogical Language Usage Server (PLUS). It is a usage-based dictionary of vocabulary terms "used by educational researchers in journals affiliated with the American Educational Research Association (AERA)." This dictionary was based on three years worth of AERA affiliated journals from 1993-1995, thus common terms may not appear. When a word is located, it produces the text of the article defining the term, and a citation to the article.

Education Book Reviews
http://www.lib.msu.edu/corby/reviews/index.htm

Kate Corby, Reference Librarian, and Education and Psychology Bibliographer at Michigan State University Libraries, provides book reviews of newly published books in the field of education. She indexes the reviews by date (newest reviews), title, author, subject, and publisher. There is also a link to *Education Review: A Journal of Book Reviews*.

Education-Related News Groups
http://learninfreedom.org/ed-newsgroups.html

Karl M. Bunday has compiled an impressive list of education-related newsgroups. There is a short description of each newsgroup to help identify them. He includes a site search which searches not just the newsgroups, but his entire site which focuses on homeschooling.

Educational Testing Service (ETS) TestLink
http://www.ets.org/testcoll/

This test collection index contains over 20,000 tests and research instruments from the 1900s to the present. Searching is available by title, author, or descriptor. The citation includes an abstract and availability.

Educator's Reference Desk
http://www.eduref.org

This site is a project of the Information Institute of Syracuse (IIS) and is responsible for many successful digital education information services. The Educator's Reference Desk provides access to educational resources, a lesson plan collection, a question-and-answer archive, and the ERIC database.

Research in Education, Rand Corporation
http://www.rand.org/research_areas/education

The Rand Corporation is a nonprofit organization conducting research on the problems and challenges facing the world today. One of its focus areas is education. The topics they research are currently in the news or are highly relevant to current public policy debate. Many of their publications are available full text.

Teacher Certification Requirements
http://www.uky.edu/Education/TEP/usacert.html

The University of Kentucky College of Education maintains this site of teacher certification requirements from all 50 states. For those seeking employment in K-12 teaching there is a link called "position announcements" which lists current job openings, also by state.

United Nations Educational, Scientific and Cultural Organization (UNESCO)–Education
http://www.unesco.org/education/index.shtml

For international information, the United Nations Educational, Scientific and Cultural Organization (UNESCO) Education Web site has many topics listed plus a link to the UNESCO Institute for Statistics under Quicklinks. The Institute for Statistics has core themes of education and literacy, which leads to a global offering of statistics.

Search Engines and Directories

Navigating the Web via subject lists or search engines can be frustrating given the overwhelming results which usually appear. Most searchers are familiar with Google (http://directory.google.com/Top/Reference/Education/) and Yahoo (http://d4.dir.scd.yahoo.com/Education/)

which have education as a major category. The following Web pages explore other education-based directories for a valuable overview of the rich offerings that are available.

Digital Librarian: A librarian's choice of the best of the Web
http://www.digital-librarian.com/education.html

This site, maintained by librarian Margaret Vail Anderson, is an alphabetical listing of Web pages. Especially useful are the "see also" links which include children's literature, colleges and universities, K-12 school directories, and languages.

Education Virtual Library
http://www.csu.edu.au/education/library.html

Charles Sturt University in Australia provides links by education level, resource subjects, types of sites, and by country for those interested in international education. Don't miss visiting their top 50 educational sites.

Education World
http://www.education-world.com/

Education World's primary focus is the K-12 audience but at the bottom of the page there is a specialties heading with higher education listed. Librarians will want to visit the "Reference Library" with online tools linking to basic reference resources.

Librarian's Index to the Internet (lii.org)–Education Topics
http://lii.org/search/file/education

The Librarian's Index to the Internet is sponsored by the Library of California and built by librarians trained in indexing and organizing Internet sites. The scope includes California, the United States, and a global perspective with subjects ranging from early childhood to universities and colleges.

Michigan Electronic Library (MEL) Education Collection
http://mel.org/viewtopic.jsp?id=10

The Michigan Electronic Library (MEL) has an education section maintained by Mary de Wolf. The site is primarily for the pre K-12 community with useful sections for parents and other educators. There is a link to copyright information, higher education, and hot topics in education.

Government Information

U.S. Department of Education
http://www.ed.gov/

The U.S. Department of Education has a target audience of serving the education needs of all Americans. The information on their Web site is divided into four key sections: students, parents, teachers, and administrators. There are links to headline news, grants and contracts, financial aid, policy, research and statistics, and programs. The links cover pre-K through adult education and lifelong learning with a search engine, an A-Z index, publications (many full text), budget allocations, and job openings.

Educational Resources Information Center–ERIC
http://www.eric.ed.gov/

The U.S. Department of Education's Institute of Education Sciences provides free access to education literature and resources through the ERIC database. The database goes back to 1966 and includes abstracts to journal articles and many full-text non-journal documents. In January 2004, the department of Education began a reengineering plan for ERIC (http://ericae.net/eric_notice.htm). Many URLs were discontinued after years of success. The popular Clearinghouse services closed in December 2003. For more information, go to Kate Corby's detailed site (http://www.lib.msu.edu/corby/education/doe.htm).

ERIC Digests, from 1980-1992, are included full text in this free version of the ERIC database, and provide introductions to topics in education. They give an excellent overview on a specific subject, plus provide a list of references for further study. To search the Digests in full text, go to the Advanced Search screen and select them in the Publication Type box.

The link to the ERIC Thesaurus shows the controlled vocabulary called descriptors that the ERIC database uses for indexing. The thesaurus allows one to tailor and refine searches for better search results using these descriptors. There is also a browse capability allowing one to see all the descriptors from A to Z.

National Center for Education Statistics (NCES)
http://nces.ed.gov/

National Center for Education Statistics collects, analyzes, and distributes educational data for the public. They provide an electronic catalog to assist in finding publications and data tools. One may search for schools, colleges, and libraries. There is a students' classroom with games and activities for kids and adults.

Education Statistics at a Glance
http://nces.ed.gov/edstats/

The following three publications are available full text: *The Condition of Education*, *The Digest of Education Statistics*, and *Projections of Education Statistics*. Searching is available through the table of contents, by subject area and title word searches. The text includes all tables and figures.

National Library of Education
http://www.ed.gov/NLE/

The National Library of Education (NLE) is one of four National Libraries in the United States. It provides links to its programs, services, and resources. Of special note is GEM, the Gateway to Educational Materials, an excellent source for finding lesson plans by topic and grade level. VRD, the Virtual Reference Desk, provides resources and links to Internet-based reference services. AskA+ Locator gives a listing of AskA services by subject that are available. ED Pubs provides Department of Education Publications free of charge.

State Departments of Education
http://www.teacher.com/sdoe.htm

A map of the United States and a click on a state takes one to that state's Department of Education or similar organization. Many states provide statistics, news items, teacher licensing, and state regulations.

E-Journal Directories

Australian Journals Online
http://www.nla.gov.au/ajol/

The National Library of Australia's electronic journals database is a catalog of journals, newspapers, magazines, webzines, newsletters, and e-mail fanzines. Over 2,000 Australian-related titles can be searched or browsed by title or subject.

Education Journals: An annotated database for K-12 and teacher educators
http://webcat.library.wisc.edu:3102/

The University of Wisconsin-Madison Center for Instructional Materials and Computing provides an annotated listing of print and electronic journals. The journals can be searched or browsed by subject and title. There is a link to the journal, a brief description of the coverage, publisher, language, frequency, type, and subject headings.

Internet Public Library: Online Serials
http://ipl.org.ar/reading/serials/

The Internet Public Library has over 3,000 titles that can be searched by subject. In education, four categories worth viewing are education news, higher education, K-12, and teachers and administrators.

Open Acess Journals in the Field of Education
http://aera-cr.ed.asu.edu/links.html

The American Educational Research Association (AERA) Special Interest Group on Communication of Research has compiled a list of full-text e-journals from around the world that are scholarly, and peer-reviewed. The site is maintained by Webmaster, Tirupalavanam G. Ganish.

Higher Education

2005 Almanac of Higher Education, National Education Association (NEA)
http://www.nea.org/he/almanac.html

The NEA has ten editions of the Almanac of Higher Education going back to 1996 available full text. The almanacs highlight key issues affecting higher education such as faculty salaries, diversity and employment, the federal role, and finances and technology.

American Universities
http://www.clas.ufl.edu/CLAS/american-universities.html

Mike Conlon, Assistant Vice President for Information Systems and Support, and Chief Information Officer, at the University of Florida

Health Science Center maintains an alphabetical listing of American universities with links to international universities, Canadian universities, and community colleges. His Frequently Asked Questions (FAQ) page explains the purpose of the site and the criteria used to include an institution.

Assignment Calculator
http://www.lib.umn.edu/help/calculator/

The University of Minnesota has developed an Assignment Calculator to assist students working on research papers. By providing the starting date, due date, and subject area, the Assignment Calculator produces a timetable for working on the paper with Web link assistance along the way. The e-mail reminder function is limited to the University of Minnesota campus community.

Center for Higher Education Policy Analysis (CHEPA)
http://www.usc.edu/dept/chepa/

The Center for Higher Education Policy Analysis (CHEPA) is housed at the University of Southern California and strives to improve urban higher education through strengthening school-university relationships and focusing on international higher education, specifically Latin America and the Pacific Rim. Links include current events with a newsletter, projects, papers, and cultural literacy resources.

The Chronicle of Higher Education
http://chronicle.com

This online version of The Chronicle of Higher Education provides news and information to the academic world. To access all the links, a subscription is required. Free access is provided to a few sections including the Career Network, listing job openings in higher education.

College and University Rankings
http://door.library.uiuc.edu/edx/rankings.htm

The University of Illinois' Education and Social Science Library has compiled a comprehensive collection of ranking services evaluating colleges and universities. There is a cautionary note explaining that rankings can be difficult to measure and controversial.

College Source Online
http://www.collegesource.org/home.asp

The Career Guidance Foundation provides 25,925 college catalogs from 2-year, 4-year, graduate, professional, and international schools. The resources link includes assessment testing and preparation, career resources, college guides and planning, and financial aid resources.

Higher Education Resource Hub
http://www.higher-ed.org/

James JF Forest, Assistant Dean for Academic Assessment and Assistant Professor of Political Science at the United States Military Academy, West Point has compiled a comprehensive Web directory including assessment, course syllabi, job opportunities, associations, publications, research centers, and more.

Measuring Up 2002: The State-by-State Report Card for Higher Education
http://measuringup.highereducation.org/2002/reporthome.htm

The National Center for Public Policy and Higher Education provides comprehensive state-level higher education data and information. Each state has a report card with grades and performance summaries so it is easy to compare any state with the best performing states.

National Center for Postsecondary Improvement (NCPI)
http://www.stanford.edu/group/ncpi/

This research center sponsored by Stanford University, the University of Pennsylvania, and the University of Michigan, strives to analyze, recommend, and provide conceptual tools for policymakers, employers, faculty, students, parents, and administrators to improve postsecondary education. Their site links to information on state and federal higher education policies, research reports, and publications.

Reinventing Undergraduate Education: A Blueprint for America's Research Universities
http://naples.cc.sunysb.edu/Pres/boyer.nsf

This report from the Boyer Commission on Educating Undergraduates in the Research University focuses on undergraduate education and proposes a new model with ten major recommendations.

World Lecture Hall
http://web.austin.utexas.edu/wlh/

The University of Texas at Austin, Center for Instructional Technologies provides global online course materials for courses offered at accredited colleges and universities around the world. Many courses provide a syllabus and class notes, while others include audio, video, and assignments.

Education Library Web Sites

For several years academic education librarians have played an important role in designing quality Web sites, many with Web links accessible to the public. Below are just a few of the top education institutions providing this service. Keep in mind, these sites generally support the curriculum and research areas of their schools and faculty, thus focusing on specific areas of study. A more comprehensive listing of education libraries is provided by the George B. Brain Education Library at Washington State University Libraries (http://www.wsulibs.wsu.edu/educ/guide/librarian/).

Harvard University, Monroe C. Gutman Library
http://www.gse.harvard.edu/~library/collections/weblinks.html

Indiana University, Education Library
http://www.indiana.iub.edu/index.php?pageId=1294

The Pennsylvania State University, Online Reference Shelf, Education & Funding
http://www.libraries.psu.edu/gateway/referenceshelf/educ.htm

Stanford University, Cubberley Education Library
http://www-sul.stanford.edu/depts/cubberley/research_help/online_res/internet.html

University of California, Berkeley, Education-Psychology Library
http://www.lib.berkeley.edu/EDP/education.html

University of Kentucky Libraries, Education Web Resources Page
http://www.uky.edu/Subject/education.html

University of North Carolina at Charlotte, Curriculum and Instructional Materials Center
http://libweb.uncc.edu/cimc/cimcweb.htm

CONCLUSION

Fifteen years ago education librarians were limited to using only local resources in their libraries. Today librarians have placed an increased reliance on the Internet to access information. While the Internet does provide a rich array of resources not previously available, paper collections are still necessary for research. Tenopir[3] states "Librarians face new challenges in reaching students who only access library resources online and have grown up with the Web." Some frustrations using the Internet include resources not being available, only abstracts or summaries provided, requiring a subscription or login procedure, and search engines that produce an enormous number of sites to sift through. Despite these drawbacks, the Internet has opened up the limited resources we once had and supplemented it with a wealth of information and research materials from around the world.

Visiting these educational Web sites makes one realize the strengths of the Internet. Educational information supplied via the Web ranges from scholarly sites for researchers to fun and entertaining sites for children and adults. It includes, but is not limited to, basic reference information, research database searching, full-text publications, statistics, public policy awareness, and lesson plans. Education librarians and specialists interact through e-mail and chat online answering questions. With such accessibility, the Web has quickly become a vibrant and exciting virtual learning environment.

REFERENCES

1. Peter Webster, "Implications of expanded library electronic reference collections," *Online* 27 (2003): 24-27.

2. Donald W. King, Peter B. Boyce, Carol Hansen Montgomery, and Carol Tenopir, "Library Economic Metrics: Examples of the comparison of electronic and print journal collections and collection services," *Library Trends* 51, (2003): 376-400.

3. Carol Tenopir, "Electronic publishing: Research issues for academic librarians and users," *Library Trends* 51 (2003): 614-635.

OTHER RECOMMENDED READINGS

Ariew, Susan. "Education: A Core List of Web Resources for Researchers and Teachers." *Choice* (2000): 1409-1421.

Freed, Melvyn N., Robert K. Hess and Joseph M. Ryan. *The Educator's Desk Reference (EDR): A Sourcebook of Educational Information and Research.* 2nd. ed. Westport, CT: Praeger, 2002.

Golian, Linda Marie. "Internet Resources for Educational Research." *Journal of Library Administration* 30 (2000): 105-119.

Jobe, Margaret M. "Education Resources." *The Reference Librarian* 57 (1997): 55-62.

Miller, Elizabeth B. *The Internet Resource Directory for K-12 Teachers and Librarians.* Englewood, CO: Libraries Unlimited, 2001.

Morgan, Nancy and Carolyn Sprague. "Internet resources: Question answering, electronic discussion groups, newsgroups." *Teacher Librarian* 28 (2000): 15-17.

Sweet, Ellen A. "The National Library of Education and Government Information." *Legal Reference Services Quarterly* 22 (2003): 3-18.

100 Best Free Reference Web Sites:
A Selected List

Lori Morse

SUMMARY. A listing of 100 free Web sites with brief annotations that are useful for almost all reference librarians, regardless of whether they are in an academic, public, school, or special library setting. *[Article copies available for a fee from The Haworth Document Delivery Service: 1-800-HAWORTH. E-mail address: <docdelivery@haworthpress.com> Website: <http://www.HaworthPress.com> © 2005 by The Haworth Press, Inc. All rights reserved.]*

KEYWORDS. Free Web sites, reference Web sites

INTRODUCTION

Reference Librarianship has been slowly changing over the past decade. More and more, we are turning to our computers to answer the questions that we previously spent hours poring over books, searching for the answer. The use of the Internet has enabled this change. While we all know that the Internet does not have all of the answers (yet), we are coming to rely on many of its resources.

Lori Morse is Reference Librarian, Free Library of Philadelphia, Philadelphia, PA 19103 (E-mail: lmorse@hslc.org).

[Haworth co-indexing entry note]: "100 Best Free Reference Web Sites: A Selected List." Morse, Lori. Co-published simultaneously in *The Reference Librarian* (The Haworth Information Press, an imprint of The Haworth Press, Inc.) No. 91/92, 2005, pp. 279-295; and: *The Reference Collection: From the Shelf to the Web* (ed: William J. Frost) The Haworth Information Press, an imprint of The Haworth Press, Inc., 2005, pp. 279-295. Single or multiple copies of this article are available for a fee from The Haworth Document Delivery Service [1-800-HAWORTH, 9:00 a.m. - 5:00 p.m. (EST). E-mail address: docdelivery@haworthpress.com].

Available online at http://www.haworthpress.com/web/REF
© 2005 by The Haworth Press, Inc. All rights reserved.
doi:10.1300/J120v44n91_17

In 1999, the Machine-Assisted Reference Section (MARS) of RUSA implemented a task force to compile a list of "Best Free Reference Web Sites." This list has been compiled every year since then, with the list available both on the MARS Web page, and in *Reference and User Services Quarterly (RUSQ)*. There are other comparable lists: The Scout Report; LIIWEEK, from the *Librarian's Index to the Internet*; and Gary Price's Resource Shelf, to name a few.

The following list of Web sites, with brief annotations, was compiled primarily from the MARS lists–both sites that are on the final list(s), and those that were nominated. The list is by no means complete or definitive. Since the Web is a changing world, it should be noted that the sites were as listed at the time this list was compiled. (Note: URLs current as of June 1, 2005.)

1. About.Com (http://www.about.com) is an index of evaluated Web sites and articles selected by an "online expert guide."

2. Academic360.com (http://www.academic360.com) contains higher education employment opportunities available on the Internet. This site provides three lead categories related to academia, and academicians working in professional organizations and societies.

3. African American World (http://www.pbs.org/wnet/aaworld/) is a PBS-sponsored guide to African American history and culture. Channels include History, Arts & Culture, Race & Society, and Profiles.

4. All-Music Guide (http://www.allmusic.com) is a comprehensive guide to all forms of popular music and musicians. The site is searchable by artist name, album or song title, music genre, or record label. Detailed biographies, reviews, and links to other Internet resources are offered for most artists.

5. All the Virology on the WWW (http://www.virology.net) contains sections linking to information on jobs, online virology course notes, virology dictionaries, and many other related resources. One of the sections is the Big Picture Book of Viruses. The pictures are categorized by list of virus families, list of individual viruses, by genome type, and in many other ways.

6. AMA Physician Select (http://dbapps.ama-assn.org/aps/amahg. htm). The Physician Select directory on the American Medical Association's Web site contains virtually every licensed physician in the United States. All individual listings include address, medical school

and year of graduation, residency training, primary practice, specialty, and whether or not the physician is an AMA member.

7. Amazon.com (http://www.amazon.com/) is an online bookstore that provides access to several million titles. One feature that is particularly helpful is the indication of whether a title is "permanently out of stock" and, therefore, more difficult to locate. This site also offers book reviews, from the publishers as well as the general public.

8. American Diabetes Association (http://www.diabetes.org). Through this Web site, the ADA provides information for both the lay community and the health care professionals about diabetes research, information, and advocacy.

9. American Family Immigration History Center (http://www.ellisisland.org) contains archival information on over "22 million passengers and members of ships' crews [who] entered the United States through Ellis Island and the Port of New York between 1892 and 1924." These records can be accessed by clicking the "Passenger Search" area on the site's home page and may be searched by name and gender. This site also features a section called "The Immigrant Experience" which chronicles the history of immigration in America.

10. American Memory Historical Collections for the National Digital Library (http://memory.loc.gov/ammem/ammemhome.html). The American Memory Historical Collections is an excellent resource of online digital images, audio, and media clips engulfing all aspects of American history and culture. It is an expansive collection that provides access to over 7 million reproduced, primary sources from over 100 important historical collections within the Library of Congress, as well as from participating museums and institutions. The main page has a site index that allows the user to search by collections or by subject.

11. American Presidents: Life Portraits (http://www.americanpresidents.org) features basic biographical information and "fun facts" about our nation's presidents along with a wide variety of video and sound clips and links to other sites of interest on the Web. Texts of speeches and addresses are included, as well as extensive bibliographies.

12. The Area Decoder (http://www.areadecoder.com/). Area codes can be determined by either the three-digit code, or by entering a location.

13. AskART (http://askart.com/). AskART contains detailed information on nearly 28,000 American artists. Artist entries include a biography, number of museums holding their artwork, a bibliography of books and periodicals about the artist, and an image gallery of the artist's works.

14. Artcyclopedia: The Fine Art Search Engine (http://www.artcyclopedia.com/). The criterion for inclusion in the Artcyclopedia is that the artist must be included in an arts museum collection somewhere in the world. The site's best search is by artist, but the user can also search for artworks, art museums, or browse by movement or medium. An artist search brings up links to online museums, image archives, and articles about the artist.

15. AT&T AnyWho (http://www.anywho.com/index.html) is a comprehensive method for quickly locating listed telephone directory information. The reverse directory function is also very useful.

16. Aviation Accident Database and Synopses (http://www.ntsb.gov/NTSB/query.asp) contains information about aircraft accidents and incidents from 1962 forward investigated by the National Transportation Safety Board. Users may search for accidents by many variables including date or date range, location by city and/or state, airline, aircraft make and/or model, and NTSB accident number. A Monthly Lists section provides a browse option by year and month. Information provided includes a synopsis containing a description of the accident and the probable cause. Many have a link to the full narrative.

17. Bankrate (http://www.bankrate.com/) contains information on mortgages, credit cards, new and used auto loans, money market accounts and CDs, checking and ATM fees, home equity lines and loans, and online banking fees gathered from more than 2,500 financial institutions in 120 markets in 50 states and Puerto Rico. Credit union rates are also included. Six calculators also assist users with mortgages, credit cards, savings, auto leasing, loans, and relocation.

18. Bartleby.com (http://www.bartleby.com) includes works like *Bartlett's Familiar Quotations*, the *King James Bible*, and *Simpson's Contemporary Quotations*. Users may search by keyword across the entire contents of the site or search specific subjects or works. Resources are also listed under the categories "Reference," "Verse," "Fiction," or "Nonfiction." A summary or short note about the origin of the work is given above the search bar for each resource.

19. Baseball-Almanac–The "Official" Baseball History Site (http:// baseball-almanac.com/). This site is a one-stop shopping site for facts and trivia on professional baseball. It is described as an "interactive baseball encyclopedia filled with thousands of pages full of in-depth facts and statistics." Categories include topics such as all-star games, awards, fabulous feats, famous firsts, hall of fame, player stats, record book, and year in review.

20. Best of History Web Sites (http://www.besthistorysites.net/) is intended to be a "portal created for students, history educators, and general history enthusiasts. Here you'll find sites, rated for usefulness and accuracy, that will help you study or teach a wide variety of topics and periods in History." Broad periods such as Prehistory, Medieval, and 20th Century history are listed and each is further subdivided into manageable topics and periods.

21. BBB: Better Business Bureau (http://www.bbb.org/) is a convenient site for linking to local BBB information and for obtaining information on individual companies, as well as on national charities for which the BBB has prepared reports.

22. Big Charts (http://www.bigcharts.com) is an investment charting and research Web site that provides access to stock quotes, industry analysis, market news, and commentary. The Historical Quotes area contains stock price information as far back as 1985.

23. Biographical Dictionary (http://www.s9.com/biography). This dictionary covers more than 28,000 notable men and women from ancient times to the present. The dictionary can be searched by both name and keywords. Only very brief, basic information is given–other sources should be consulted if in-depth information is required.

24. Biography.com (http://www.biography.com) offers over 25,000 biographies for people past and present. The site is searchable, and each biography includes links to related people, places, and organizations, as well as A&E's videos-for-sale section. The site also features "Born on This Day" biographies.

25. Biz Stats (http://www.bizstats.com/) provides access to useful financial ratios, business statistics, and benchmarks. Provides effective and understandable online analysis of businesses and industries.

26. Bureau of Labor Statistics (http://stats.bls.gov) provides past and current statistics for the U.S. economy. Information is arranged under

broad categories such as "Inflation and Spending" and "International Statistics." The latest numbers for the Consumer Price Index, unemployment rate, and the Producer Price Index are readily available.

27. Catholic Online Saints & Angels (http://saints.catholic.org/index.shtml) is a comprehensive index of saints, along with a list of patron saints and a list of feast dates (chronologically through the year). The information on each saint includes background, feast date, and patron saint information.

28. Centers for Disease Control and Prevention (http://www.cdc.gov) is a site for public health and safety information. It includes fact sheets, information, and CDC journal articles on diseases and chronic conditions, and statistics from the National Center for Health Statistics. The full text of several CDC publications, including "Morbidity and Mortality Weekly Report" and "Emerging Infectious Diseases," is also available.

29. CEO Express (http://www.ceoexpress.com/) is a mega-site for all things news and business. The four major headings are: "Daily News & Info" (linking to a long list of news and magazine sites), "Business Research," "Office Tools & Travel," and "Breaktime." The Business Research section is extensive, including many sources for company information, stock market news, and business law and legislation.

30. Citysearch (http://www.citysearch.com) provides information in a subject directory format with topics such as restaurants, hotels, movies, careers, and events. Reviews are provided for restaurants by type of food and neighborhood within the cities. The events calendar gives a day-by-day listing of the happenings for each of the cities. If tickets are required, they may be purchased right from the site. All fifty states are covered and several international cities as well.

31. CNET.com (http://www.cnet.com) contains extensive reviews of new hardware and software products, tech news and tech stock information for investors, free software downloads, Web development tips for beginners and experts, and a help and how-to page.

32. CNN.com (http://www.cnn.com) provides a list of top stories of the day. Users can also go to an index of topical sections to browse current news or may choose to do a keyword search on a particular section or the whole site.

33. Consumer Product Safety Commission (CPSC) (http://www. cpsc.gov). On this Web site, users may search for recently recalled products by product type, company, or product description, or they may search the entire database back to May 1973 by month and year or product description. There is also information about products not under the jurisdiction of the CPSC, including food, drugs, and vehicles with links to the appropriate regulatory agency. The site also offers special sections for children and businesses, as well as an online form to report unsafe or potentially defective or hazardous products.

34. Edmunds.com (http://www.edmunds.com) provides easy access to safety information, road tests, advice, and evaluative information on buying a new or used vehicle.

35. Educator's Reference Desk (http://www.eduref.org/index.shtml) provides resources and service to educators. By the people who created AskERIC, it contains lesson plans and links to online education information.

36. Epinions (http://www.epinions.com/) offers the consumer an opportunity to check out what other users are saying about a particular product, and provide a different perspective.

37. ERIC (Education Resources Information Center) (http://www. eric.ed.gov/) produces the database of journal and non-journal education literature. Citations date back to 1966 on this database, now available on the Web.

38. ESPN.com (http://www.espn.go.com) offers up-to-the-minute scores and statistical and schedule information on all sports. It also provides profiles on professional and college athletes, and job links for those looking for a career in sports and sports nutrition advice. Daily broadcasts of selected ESPN events are available, as well as play-by-play online scores for major sporting events.

39. Fact Monster™ (http://www.factmonster.com/). Intended for children aged 9 to 14, the following 10 subject categories are presented in both text and graphic formats: World & News, U.S., People, Word Wise, Science, Math, Sports, Cool Stuff, Games and Quizzes, and Homework Center. Each category has an Almanac, Special Features, and a Games and Quizzes section which offers appropriate links. An atlas, almanac, dictionary, and an encyclopedia can also be accessed directly from the home page.

40. Farmers Almanac (http://farmersalmanac.com/) is the online version of the popular *Farmers' Almanac*. The site, which provides only a selection of the features contained in the print version, offers astronomical data, gardening information, and cooking and household hints. In addition, the Almanac online also provides a list of links to other useful resources.

41. FedStats (http://www.fedstats.gov/) provides one-stop access to publicly available statistics produced by more than 70 U.S. government agencies, including Agriculture, Census, Education, Health and Human Services, Interior, Justice, Labor, Transportation, and Treasury. It permits several access points to the agency sites, including an A-Z subject index; keyword searching; and searches by state, county, and locality.

42. 50 States and Capitals (http://www.50states.com/) organizes links to a very large array of information on each state, the five U.S. territories, and the District of Columbia. Besides the usual geographic, demographic, political, historical, economic, and tourist information, there are links and images for state birds, flags, songs, flowers, trees, maps, license plates, and symbols, and to whatever live "Web cams" are available online.

43. Findlaw (http://www.findlaw.com) is a comprehensive directory of free legal and governmental resources. It contains a career resource center, a consumer law section, multiple directories of legal organizations and lawyers, links to U.S. cases and legal codes, and a wide array of other governmental resources at the state, national, and international level.

44. FirstGov.gov (http://www.firstgov.gov) is a "private-public partnership" with a vision to connect "the world to all U.S. Government information and services."

45. Food and Drug Administration (http://www.fda.gov/) provides sections aimed at patients, health professionals, state/local officials, business and industry, the press, women, senior citizens, and children. The FDA regulates food, drugs, medical devices, biologics, animal feed and drugs, cosmetics, and radiation-emitting products such as cell phones and microwaves. These sections provide detailed information about the issues and regulations involved in protecting the public's health.

46. Forbes (http://www.forbes.com) contains content from the print publication as well as additional resources. Includes links to lists, such

as the Forbes 500 from 1997-present. Content is free, although there is a premium side which includes more formal reports and lists. Includes daily Reuters Business Headlines and market watch information.

47. Geographic Names Information System (http://geonames.usgs. gov/gnishome.html) "contains information about almost 2 million physical and cultural geographic features in the United States." The GNIS is searchable by name, state or territory, feature type (e.g., cemetery, beach, hospital), county, elevation, and population. Results pages provide longitude and latitude, USGS map names, elevation (if applicable), estimated population of cities and towns, and links to online maps.

48. Getty Thesaurus of Geographic Names Online (http://www. getty.edu/research/tools/vocabulary/tgn/). "A structured vocabulary of more than 1,000,000 geographic names, including vernacular and historical names, coordinates, and place types, focusing on places important for the study of art and architecture." This site traces the history of a particular place (city, province, country, etc.). Short descriptive passages provide brief histories and important aspects of the place over time.

49. GPO Access (http://www.gpoaccess.gov/index.html) provides access to over 2,200 databases of federal information in over 80 applications, many containing full text. These include the Budget of the U.S. Government, numerous congressional resources, the Code of Federal Regulations, Core Documents of U.S. Democracy, Economic Indicators, the Federal Register, the U.S. Code, U.S. Supreme Court decisions, the Weekly Compilation of Presidential Documents and more.

50. Healthfinder® (http://www.healthfinder.gov) leads the user to selected online publications, clearinghouses, databases, Web sites, and support and self-help groups, as well as to government agencies and not-for-profit organizations. The site is clearly arranged by categories: "Hot Topics," "News," "Smart Choices," "More Tools," "Just for You," and "About Us."

51. Hoovers (http://www.hoovers.com/) has information on public and private U.S. companies. Information includes address, number of employees, key people, financial data, news items, links to company Web sites, SEC filings and current stock prices. Part of the site is fee-based, but a large quantity of material is available for free.

52. How Everyday Things Are Made (http://manufacturing.stanford. edu/). "If you've ever wondered how things are made–products like

candy, cars, airplanes, or bottles–or if you've been interested in manu-facturing processes, like forging, casting, or injection molding, then you've come to the right place." AIM has developed an introductory Web site for kids and adults showing how various items are made. It covers over 40 different products and manufacturing processes, and in-cludes almost 4 hours of manufacturing video. It is targeted towards non-engineers and engineers alike.

53. How Much Is That Worth Today? (http://www.eh.net/hmit) an-swers questions of comparative value covering purchasing power, ex-change rates, and other variables between the past and today, such as the purchasing power of money in the United States from any year from 1665 to the present.

54. How to Clean Anything (http://www.howtocleananything.com) is geared towards cleaning problems and challenges in the home, and also gives tips on more common topics.

55. How Stuff Works (http://www.howstuffworks.com/). The arti-cles describe how common "stuff," such as how an appendix, electric-ity, car engines, modems, etc., work. Both fun and informative, the articles contain exceptionally simple and descriptive graphics and nu-merous links to relevant information throughout.

56. HyperHistory Online (http://www.hyperhistory.com/online_n2/History_n2/a.html). The unique construction of the site allows history to be "viewed" rather than read, although the option of browsing and searching brief text biographies is available. The collection of timelines can be viewed by time period, event, and person; names on the timeline are color-coded to indicate area of primary influence (science, arts, reli-gion, politics).

57. Infoplease (http://www.infoplease.com/) is an online source for ready reference with material from the *Information Please Almanac*. The main page is designed for quick access with both a search form and an index of hot links under nine broad topics. Other handy features in-clude: facts behind the news, today in history, and a biography search.

58. The Internet Archive (http://www.archive.org). Using the Internet Archive's "Wayback Machine," users can look at a Web site and track how it has evolved. "Special Wayback Collections" provide a sense of how events such as September 11, 2001, were recorded digitally.

59. Internet Broadway Database (http://www.ibdb.com) is "a comprehensive database of shows produced on Broadway [dating from the 1700s to the present], including all 'title page' [program] information about each production. IBDB also offers historical information about theaters and various statistics and fun facts related to Broadway." Simple search allows you to search by show, people/organization, theatre, and season while advanced search allows many more options including function (director, actor, playwright, etc.), gender, opening and closing dates, character name, and more.

60. The Internet Movie Database (http://www.imdb.com/) is a highly comprehensive and easy to use movie reference tool. The core of the database is the over 2,250,000 filmographies covering some 180,000 movie titles and over 560,000 people. The hyperlinks within the database make cross-referencing the following categories effortless: actors, directors, writers, composers, cinematographers, editors, production designers, costume designers, and producers. Award and biographical information is also readily available.

61. Internet Public Library (http://www.ipl.org) is an excellent jumping off point for anyone doing research on the Internet, the main "Collections" include: "Reference," "Exhibits," "Especially for Librarians," "Magazines and Serials," "Newspapers," "Online Texts," and "Web Searching" as well as extensive "Teen" and "Youth" collections.

62. IRS: Forms and Publications (http://www.irs.ustreas.gov/formspubs/index.html). The IRS site contains a selection of formats available to aid viewing and printing of forms. Links are provided to state tax forms and to federal forms for previous years.

63. JAKE (jointly administered knowledge environment) (http://www.jake-db.org) allows users to search by journal title or ISSN to determine which databases include the journal. Results indicate which databases contain citations, which full text, and, if available, dates of coverage. JAKE can also be used to decipher title abbreviations.

64. Kelley Blue Book (http://www.kbb.com/) is the online version of the printed work, *Kelley Blue Book*. It offers used and new car pricing; values on used motorcycles, dirt bikes, ATVs, scooters, mopeds, and sidecars. New car reviews and a list of the 50 most popular selling cars are also given.

65. Librarians' Index to the Internet (http://www.lii.org) features an extensive directory of 40 clickable subject topics ranging from "arts" to

"women." Users can also locate relevant Web sites by using a detailed subject heading index or by using the keyword search box. A keyword search groups the results into categories; e.g., "Best of . . ." "Directories," "Databases," and "Specific Resources."

66. MapQuest (http://www.mapquest.com/) provides free access to driving directions (door-to-door or city-to-city) between any two points in the U.S. and Canada. It also can provide a map, given an address, in either country. Since the maps can be sized, users can get an overview of an area or city, or specific streets within a city.

67. Martindale's "The Reference Desk" (http://www-martindalecenter.com/) covers a wide range of topics including international business, astronomy, entertainment, and the arts, that are divided into "Information Centers" for easier browsing.

68. Measure 4 Measure (http://www.wolinskyweb.net/measure.htm) is a collection of links to sites that actually perform calculations, doing the work for you. The site is divided into the categories: "Science/Math," "Health," "Finance," and "A Measure of Everything Else." Some examples of the calculators Measure 4 Measure links to include: Area Equivalents, to convert between square units; calorie calculators and loan payment calculators. There are even calendar calculators and converters to translate dates between calendar systems.

69. MEDLINEplus (http://www.nlm.nih.gov/medlineplus/) offers free public searches to MEDLINE, the bibliographic database for medical information, as well as access to a vast amount of other information for the health care consumer.

70. The Merck Manual Home Edition (http://www.merck.com/mmhe/index.html) contains the full-text online version of *The Merck Manual Home Edition* (MMHE) written for the layperson by leading medical experts. Users can select from two formats: the original text-based version and an interactive version. The interactive version contains photos, animations, videos, pronunciations, and illustrations along with a comprehensive search engine to locate specific terms. Both versions, updated frequently, provide an easy-to-use detailed table of contents, comprised of 24 sections plus an appendix, which covers topics ranging from medical fundamentals to accidents and injuries.

71. Monster (http://www.monster.com) is an extensive site that helps workers locate a job or advance within a profession. This site offers ser-

vices such as resume help, salary data, and industry information. To post a personal resume, users create a free account and are allowed up to five resumes and cover letters.

72. NADA Guides (http://www.nada.com) provides new and used car prices and information. Also includes classic cars, motorcycles, boats, RVs, and manufactured homes. Contains new car reviews. Offers car loan, insurance, and extended warranty links.

73. NASA (http://www.nasa.gov/) is an extensive collection of information related to the nation's space program and the cosmos. Access is by audience (educators, children, students, or the media) by resource category (about NASA, News and Events, Multimedia, Missions, Popular Topics), or by a handy search engine on each page that facilitates "Finding it @ NASA."

74. The National Academies (http://www.nas.edu/). The Academy of Sciences includes the National Research Council, the National Academy of Engineering, and the Institute of Medicine. The purpose of the National Academies is to ensure independent advice on matters of science, technology, and medicine for government officials. The results of most of their work is available here for perusal.

75. The New York Times on the Web (http://www.nytimes.com) is the electronic version of the *New York Times*. Updated frequently throughout the day, the *New York Times'* Web site offers comprehensive and detailed coverage on the most important national and international news, business, technology, sports, and the arts. Registration is required; some areas are fee-based.

76. Nobel Foundation (http://www.nobelprize.org) is the official site of the Nobel Foundation, which awards prizes in physics, chemistry, physiology or medicine, literature, and peace. This site includes a list of all winners from 1901 to date (plus a searchable database), biographical information on the awardees, information on the selection process for all six of the Nobel Prize awarding institutions/areas, history behind the prizes, and more.

77. nolo.com–Law for All (http://www.nolo.com/index.html) is a one-stop site for legal information geared toward the consumer and layperson.

78. OandA: The Currency Site (http://www.oanda.com) provides a single access point for the currency conversion needs of consumers and businesses.

79. Occupational Outlook Handbook (http://www.bls.gov/oco/) lists close to 800 occupations and the following characteristics of each: nature of work, working conditions, employment, training, job outlook, earnings, related occupations, and sources of additional information.

80. OneLook Dictionaries (http://www.onelook.com) allows for easy, quick word searches in over 600 online dictionaries, including general, legal, and foreign dictionaries. The search results also contain links to the home page of the indexed dictionaries themselves if the user wants to further explore a particular resource.

81. Online! Citation Styles (http://www.bedfordstmartins.com/online/citex.html) provides citation styles for the total range of online information: World Wide Web site, e-mail message, Web discussion forum posting, listserv message, newsgroup message, real-time communication, etc. Detailed descriptions and examples of each are given for MLA, APA, Chicago, and CBE.

82. Plants Database (http://plants.usda.gov) allows for searching by common name and scientific name with results that include: photographs, distribution by state and county, and complete scientific classification.

83. Project Gutenberg (http://www.promo.net/pg/) has the vision to provide access to books in electronic text format a short time after they enter the public domain. Texts available in Project Gutenberg include light literature (Sir Arthur Conan Doyle, Edgar Rice Burroughs); heavy literature (such as the works of Shakespeare); and reference sources such as almanacs, encyclopedias, and dictionaries. The works may be searched or browsed by author or title and are stored in zip files.

84. Project Vote Smart (http://www.vote-smart.org/) is a product of a national non-partisan, non-profit organization that provides information about elected officials and political candidates on the state and national level. The information offered includes voting records, campaign issue positions, performance evaluations by special interests, campaign contributions, backgrounds, previous experience, and contact information. Levels of government featured on the site include the United States Congress, state governors, and state legislatures.

85. Refdesk.com (http://www.refdesk.com). The Reference Resources and Facts Search sections provide links to a wide array of ready reference sources, from Acronym Finder to Zip+4 Code Lookup. Conveniently located links to *Britannica*, the *Old Farmer's Almanac, Bartlett's Quotations*, and *Roget's Thesaurus* are available, to name just a few. Current News contains an impressive list of electronic journals, newspapers, and news services.

86. RootsWeb.com (http://www.rootsweb.com) is made up of "extensive interactive guides and numerous research tools for tracing family histories." The searcher can type in a name in the search box or follow the link to "The World Connect Project," which contains more than 204 million ancestor names. The RootsWeb Surname List consists of a register of over one million surnames submitted by more than 250,000 genealogists.

87. RxList: The Internet Drug Index (http://rxlist.com/) is a resource for in-depth drug information covering over 4,000 U.S. products. Each drug entry will contain the following information: description, clinical pharmacology, indications, usage, contraindications, warnings, precautions, drug interactions, adverse reactions, drug abuse and dependence, dosage and administration, and animal pharmacology.

88. SICCODE.com–The Worldwide Business Directory (http://www. siccode.com/). Free registration allows visitors to search the database by keyword, SIC–Standard Industry Code, products, or company, and view the resulting company profile(s). Searching is also possible by city, county, state, zip or area code, or by browsing the SIC directory on the home page. Additionally, SICCODE.com provides access to 264 free legal forms, NAICS to SIC comparisons, stock quotes, and weather forecasts.

89. StartSpot Network (http://www.startspot.com) is a family of "Spot" sites, each serving as an in-depth Web portal for its category by guiding users to a wealth of resources, which have been selected by an editorial team. Current spots include BookSpot, CinemaSpot, EmploymentSpot, GovernmentSpot, GenealogySpot, HomeworkSpot, HeadlineSpot, LibrarySpot, MuseumSpot, and TripSpot. Of particular note are LibrarySpot and BookSpot.

90. Telephone Directories on the Web (http://www.infobel.com/ teldir) is an index of online phone books comprising links to Yellow

Pages, White Pages, business directories, e-mail addresses, and fax listings from over 170 countries.

91. U.S. Census Bureau (http://www.census.gov) provides access to U.S. Census information.

92. U.S. Patent and Trademark Office (http://www.uspto.gov/) offers the ability to investigate patents and trademarks on its Web site. The site also provides information about applying for patents, careers with USPTO and in patent law, and intellectual property. A highlight of the USPTO site is the patent full-text and image databases, which contain the full text of over 3,000,000 patents from 1976 to the present and limited bibliographic data for over 4,000,000 earlier patents, along with more than 70,000,000 full-page images of over 7,000,000 patents from 1790 forward.

93. United States Postal Service (http://www.usps.com). The most useful part of the USPS Web site is the zip code directory. By entering a street address, the 9-digit zip code can be located. Likewise, by entering a zip code you can locate the city and state in which it is located or you can enter a city name and see the zip codes associated with it.

94. The Universal Currency Converter (http://www.xe.com/ucc) allows you to perform interactive foreign exchange rate calculations using live, up-to-the-minute currency rates.

95. Weather.Com (http://www.weather.com). Over 1,700 U.S. city forecasts can be retrieved by zip code or city name. The forecast and current conditions page contains the seven-day forecast in graphic form as well as a link to a more detailed forecast issued by the National Weather Service.

96. Weather Underground (http://www.weatherunderground.com/). Users can locate weather information and forecasts for over 60,000 U.S. and international cities and may also search by state, zip code, airport code, or country. In addition, the site includes historical data back to 1994, as well as an astronomy area for sunrise and sun set information and the moon phases.

97. WebElements Periodic Table (http://www.webelements.com) is an online periodic table. Users click on the symbol for any element on the periodic table displayed on the home page. Information given for each element includes the name for the element in several languages, essentials (name, symbol, atomic weight, etc.), description, and isola-

tion. Sidebars provide well-known compounds that contain the element and more detailed information on the element's properties and history.

98. What's that Stuff (http://pubs.acs.org/cen/whatstuff/stuff.html) is a selection of articles on what goes into common products. Useful for health concerns, science projects, and general science discussion.

99. World Factbook (http://www.odci.gov/cia/publications/factbook/). The C.I.A. produces the World Factbook to meet the needs of government officials for background material on economic, geographic, and political conditions in 267 countries around the globe. Locations can be accessed within the "Country Listing" or by "Reference Maps."

100. yourDictionary.com (http://www.yourdictionary.com) serves as a portal for over 1,800 dictionaries and more than 250 languages.

Index

Page numbers followed by n indicate notes.